MW01121274

Criminal Justice
Recent Scholarship

Edited by
Nicholas P. Lovrich

A Series from LFB Scholarly

Estimating Crime Rates from Police Reports and Victim Surveys

Progressive Convergence in Time Series Analyses

Sami Ansari

LFB Scholarly Publishing LLC
El Paso 2013

Library of Congress Cataloging-in-Publication Data

Ansari, Sami, 1966-
Estimating crime rates from police reports and victim surveys : progressive convergence in time series analyses / Sami Ansari.
pages cm. -- (Criminal justice: recent scholarship)
Includes bibliographical references and indexes.
ISBN 978-1-59332-588-6 (hardcover : alk. paper)
1. Victims of crimes. 2. Victims of crimes surveys. 3. Criminal statistics. 4. Police reports. I. Title.
HV6250.25.A57 2013
364.072'7--dc23
2012051272

ISBN 978-1-59332-588-6

Printed on acid-free 250-year-life paper.

Manufactured in the United States of America.

To Rizwana, Fiza, and Nighat

Table of Contents

Acknowledgments

I owe my sincere thanks to all those people, who made possible for me to complete this book. I would like to express my deepest gratitude to Dr. Ni (Phil) He who continuously provided inputs during the research and writing of this book.

I owe a special thanks to Dr. Nicolas Lovrich and Leo Balk and his team for all valuable inputs and their assistance in editing, writing, and formatting of this book. I would like to thank Dr. Glenn Pierce, Dr. Jack McDevitt, and Dr. Kamran M. Dadkhah for their helpful reviews and remarks that helped me in formulating the content and methods of my research. I am especially indebted to Professor Dadkhah who guided me through the complex world of time series analysis.

I am forever indebted to my wife, Rizwana, and my daughters, Fiza and Nighat, who constantly supported me with their patience and endurance throughout this project. Finally, I would like to acknowledge my friends as well as all my colleagues, who assisted, advised, and supported me during the process of writing this book.

CHAPTER 1

Introduction

The official crime statistics provided by the Uniform Crime Reporting (UCR) and National Crime Victimization Survey (NCVS) are a central part of criminal justice research. The vast number of studies addressing the problem of crime and law enforcement use the data provided by these two measures. The use of the data by popular media, law enforcements, policy makers, and researchers establishes their value and relevance. The UCR, which began in 1930, has gone through a significant metamorphosis in recent years. One factor that is considered especially important in bringing about changes in the UCR is the national crime victimization survey, which was initiated in 1973 at the recommendation of a Presidential Commission for the purpose of illuminating dark figures of crime[1] in the UCR. The first report of the national crime victimization survey, entitled the National Crime Survey (NCS), reported more than twice the offenses reported by the official crime statistics of the time (Skogan, 1974). The discrepancies between the two indexes raised several questions. Why are the two measures of crime rates so discrepant when they both purport to measure the same social phenomenon known as *crime*? Which measure is a more valid measure of crime? Will the two measures come together and minimize their divergence over time?

Efforts were made to answer these questions after 1973. The initial focus of researchers was to compare the validity of the two measures of

---

[1] The term *dark figure of crime* is a metaphor for the inability of a crime measure to measure what it is meant to measure. The dark figure of crime, as used in this sense, refers to the fraction of crime not measured by a specific index. No measure, be it the UCR or NCVS, can be perfect in the monitoring of all legal wrongdoing.

crime. Some influential studies, which were published in the late 1970s, compared the validity of the two measures and concluded in favor of one or the other.

Skogan (1974) argued that the UCR was a more valid measure of crime than the victimization survey, while Decker (1977) and O'Brien, Shichor, and Decker (1980) concluded in favor of the NCS and reported considerable doubt concerning the validity of the UCR. Some studies (e.g., Booth, Johnson, & Choldin, 1977) did not report in favor of one measure over the other and suggested that the validity of the measure in question depends on the particular crime being measured. All of these studies used either cross-sectional data of NCS or 26 Cities Survey data. They employed correlational analyses in which correlation coefficients were estimated either between the official crime and victimization data, or between some known correlates of crime and the official crime and victimization data.

Further studies were conducted in the 1980s and 1990s, which focused on explaining the divergence and convergence or correspondence between the UCR and the victimization survey. Most studies reported evidence of considerable correspondence and convergence between the two measures (Biderman, Lynch, & Peterson, 1991; Blumstein, Cohen, & Rosenfeld, 1991; Cohen & Land, 1984; O'Brien, 1990, 1996). It was also predicted that the two indexes of crime would show stronger convergence in the future as the victimization survey matured (Blumstein et al., 1991). The most important facts about these studies are that they accepted the divergence between the two data series as predictable and made efforts to provide explanations for this divergence. They supported the validity of both of the measures and argued that both of them measure the same phenomenon differently and distinctly. An influential book by Biderman et al. (1991) provided comprehensive analyses of divergence between the two measures, and the authors of this book recommended focusing on complementarity rather than on comparability for realizing the full research potential of the two types of crime rate. These studies benefited from the availability of time series data and decreasing discrepancies between the two crime indexes. They used correlational analysis, but also employed detrending of the series before estimating inter-index correlations (Blumstein et al., 1991; O'Brien, 1990, 1996).

Some studies, however, did not find convergence between the two data series (Menard, 1987; Menard & Covey, 1988) and argued that the two series measure somewhat different crime occurrence phenomena. They also questioned the appropriateness and the value of detrending the series before estimating correlations, leading to a long debate on appropriate analytical methodology. More recent studies have focused on explaining the convergence and divergence between the two crime indexes by using time series data and various analytic strategies (Catalano, 2006, 2007; McDowell & Loftin, 2007; Rosenfeld, 2007). The convergence between the two series, at least until 1991, was primarily determined by the increase in UCR rates that was, to some extent, attributed to the increased police productivity that took place because of organizational and technological development in police methods (O'Brien, 1996). The crime rate in the Unites States experienced a turning point in the beginning of 1990s when it started decreasing after having reached the highest level in its history. After the turning point in the early 1990s, the decrease in NCVS rates became a primary reason for decreasing discrepancies. Increased police productivity and some institutional mechanisms such as mandatory arrest policies in domestic violence cases were suggested as possible factors supporting the clear convergence between the two data series (Catalano, 2006, 2007).

PROBLEM STATEMENT

The issue of divergence and convergence between the two measures is important to criminologists (McDowell & Loftin, 2007). The trends in the two indexes in the past, their dynamic and changing relationships, the conflicting results of convergence reported by different studies, and the use of different definitions of *convergence* and different methodologies for testing convergence are some of the critical issues that need to be addressed. This study seeks to contribute to the literature on measuring the occurrences of crime by addressing the following critical issues and known shortcomings of both crime indexes.

First, the UCR and NCVS data are used by criminologists who address a wide variety of policy and theory questions. Because the data are used in addressing theoretical questions, they are important to theoretical discussions in criminology and criminal justice. The UCR and NCVS data, however, typically are not evaluated critically and are used particularly because they are available.. A systematic convergence study provides an opportunity to examine the two crime data series critically and understand their dynamic relationship and comparative validity.

Second, the extent of convergence between the UCR and NCVS was estimated by several studies in the early 1990s, typically using about 15 observation points. No recent study has tested the convergence between the two series because the series are assumed to be converging due to the substantial reduction in their discrepancies in recent years.

The third problem is the disagreement concerning definitions of *convergence* and disagreement regarding the appropriate methodology to use for testing the degree of convergence between the two series. Studies have used at least four different definitions of convergence (McDowell & Loftin, 2007) and employed several methodological tools to test for and explain the processes of convergence. No study has provided comprehensive discussion on methodology and compared the results obtained from different methods of testing the degree of convergence taking place.

The fourth problem is that the evaluative studies done in the past have used different crime categories, with most using violent and serious crime categories for testing for and the processes of convergence. Violent and serious crime categories, such as aggravated assault, robbery, burglary, and motor vehicle theft are more likely to show convergence primarily because the discrepancies between the two series on these offenses are comparatively small. Increased police productivity and institutional changes have affected reporting and recording of serious violent crimes (O, Brien, 1996; Catalano, 2006). In addition, it is not known whether the rates of property offenses are converging because studies have not used the property crime category in their analyses. Studies have excluded larceny theft and the aggregated category of property crime in convergence analysis larceny theft contributed about 60% to the total Part I crime in 2008, and property crime - which includes burglary, motor vehicle theft, and larceny theft - contributed over 88%. That is, when the general population compares the two series for overall crime, the larceny theft category plays the most important role in determining the relationship between the two series and affecting the perception of people.

An overview of the trend lines of the two series in the last 36 years shows that the victimization series remained almost stable between 1973 and 1992 while the UCR kept increasing, leading to the initial convergence between the two series. However, both UCR crime rates and NCVS rates began dropping after 1991 and 1993, coinciding with the methodological changes in the NCVS; consequently, convergence between both of the series after 1992 seems to be substantially affected by the changes in the NCVS. It is not known how much change in the NCVS can be attributed to the general drop in crime after 1991 and how much can be attributed to the methodological changes in the survey. Finding answers to these questions is difficult because the beginning of the drop in the crime rate in 1993 coincided with the methodological changes in the NCVS. However, examination of the convergence pattern does bring considerable understanding to this problem.

PURPOSE OF THE STUDY

The purpose of the present study, therefore, is to address the issue of convergence between the UCR and NCVS. The discussion of this issue, which began after the publication of the first National Crime Survey (NCS) report in 1973, is continuing. The debate among researchers about the findings and the use of various methods (Blumstein et al., 1991; Blumstein, Cohen & Rosenfeld, 1992; Menard, 1991, 1992; O'Brien, 1990, 1991) is still unresolved (McDowell & Loftin, 2007). Continuing discussion on the subject demonstrates the importance of the issue from the policy and research point of view because the data provided by the UCR and the NCVS are probably the primary sources available to policymakers and researchers involved in addressing the problems of crime. The objective of this study is to focus on two major aspects of the topic of convergence.

The first objective of the present research is to understand the reciprocity and dynamics of the relationship between the UCR and the NCVS. The interdependency and dynamic relationship between the two data series can be understood by testing the convergence between the two series through a combination of methods of analysis. The second objective of the research is to provide explanations for the substantial decrease in discrepancies witnessed in recent years. Explanations for the data series' changing relations and potential convergence can be provided by examining the effects of a variety of organizational, methodological, demographic, institutional, attitudinal, and technological factors which played role in changing the estimates of crime and victimization provided by the UCR and NCVS. Finally, this present research should provide meaningful discussion and investigation-based implications for the methodology of testing and explaining the convergence of crime occurrence estimates between the UCR and NCVS using comprehensive time series data.

Data and Method

The data for this research come from multiple sources that provide the time-series-dependent and predictor variables used in the study. The most important sources of the data, however, are the UCR and NCVS, from which the time series of crime and victimization rates are drawn for the period of 1973 to 2008. The UCR is an FBI-administered federal government program of data collection that gathers summary crime data on eight Part I crimes and arrest data on Part II crimes from over 17,000 local, state, county, federal, and special police departments throughout the country. The FBI classifies the data provided to it and publishes crime rates for local and other government jurisdictions annually. The NCVS is a national household survey of crime victimization that collects detailed victimization data on Part I crimes, and then publishes national estimates on crime victimization annually. The detailed descriptions of the two data collection programs and the data reported out are provided in Chapter 4. Many other sources of time series data have been used to determine predictor variables for addressing the second objective of the study, which is another topic addressed in detail in Chapter 4.

The present study uses a combination of methods for testing research hypotheses and addressing the research questions posed. These include graphic, correlational, and time series analysis of cointegration for testing convergence and time series regression modeling for explaining the factors responsible for changing the relationship between the two series in terms of decreasing rate differences between them. Detailed descriptions of the methods appear in Chapter 4.

Contributions to the Literature and Rationale for the Study

The NCVS has been in use for 38 years, and the Bureau of Justice Statistics (BJS) is contemplating making major changes in the design of this survey in the near future (Groves & Cork, 2008; Rand, 2007). The intended changes in the NCVS are likely to be driven by the need for cost reductions, improvement of credibility and validity of the data, and meeting some of the growing challenges in conducting national surveys such as increasing nonresponse among persons selected for interviews (Rand, 2007). The current structure of the survey will change if the bounding process is removed and the reference period is increased from 6 months to one year (Rand, 2007). The proposal to make such changes calls for an examination of the relationship between the nation's two crime data series. Understanding the relationship between the two data series from a historical perspective and in view of current trends will provide important policy and methodological insights to be used in making future changes and improvements in the measurement of the NCVS.

The UCR crimes are a direct reflection of crimes known to police, while in contrast the rate of victimization estimated by the NCVS are based on a national household survey of victims. Both of the measures have limitations in terms of determining the total crimes committed[2]. Researchers do not have the means to know the total crimes committed because the official measures can measure only a fraction of the entire universe of criminal events (Sellin, 1962; Wolfgang, 1963) and are functions of institutional and individual efforts (Biderman & Reiss, 1967). One of the ways to determine the validity of a measure—its

[2] The magnitude of total crimes committed may differ between data series because of different approaches to conceptualizing and defining crime. The total crime statistic as the sum of acts committed against the criminal laws is also problematic. Laws are not absolute, and the official crime statistics primarily reflect political interests of society. The total crime statistic in this context would be the sum of crimes reported by the official crime measures if they measure what they are meant to measure.

ability to measure what it is meant to measure—is to assess the convergent validity of the measure. Convergent validity is demonstrated by comparing two measures that are theoretically measuring the same phenomenon and are likely to be highly interrelated and highly correlated. Theoretically, the UCR and NCVS measure the social phenomenon of crime; therefore, they should show convergent validity. The study of convergence between the UCR and NCVS is one of the means available for assessing their respected validities.

Studying the convergence between the two series is important in terms of understanding the validity of the measurements of different crime categories measured by the two processes (Rosenfeld, Lynch, & Addington, 2007). It may be hypothesized that the validity of measurement is positively related to convergence and negatively related to divergence. The more the two series diverge on a crime category, the less they are considered reliable in terms of capturing and measuring that particular crime category. For example, the extreme discrepancy between the two series on rape and the minimal discrepancy on motor vehicle theft suggest that the measurement of rape is the more problematic and the measurement of motor vehicle theft is the most accurate.

Furthermore, if the two series are indeed converging, then the question arises as to whether they are converging because of changes in one series or in both. For example, the increase in the rate of the UCR noticed in the 1980s and 1990s was largely driven by the increase in the violent crime rate, which was generally attributed to the changes in domestic violence legislation and mandatory arrest policies (Catalano, 2006). Similarly, the rate of rape and assault with no injury were most affected by the methodological changes in the NCVS in 1992 (Rand, Lynch, & Cantor, 1997), while robbery and motor vehicle theft reports remained unaffected. The study of convergence might indicate the differential effects of the changes in the UCR and NCVS on changing rate differences between the two data series in terms of different categories of crime. Researchers have already reported on the crime-specific validity of the two measures and suggested using the UCR and the victimization data for different crimes (Booth et al., 1977). The study of convergence may shed more light on this crime-specific validity of the two measures and benefit future research in the field.

Researchers in this field are far from agreeing on an acceptable definition of *convergence* and a standard methodology for testing the degree of convergence between the UCR and NCVS. Considering the existence of different competing and often-conflicting definitions of convergence and the inconsistent results reported by relevant studies, this present research provides important methodological contributions to the literature on the subject of the convergence between the UCR and NCVS data series.

Limitations

The study of convergence between the UCR and NCVS has several limitations emanating from the data available for use. The study will use tools from time series analyses, available in econometrics, which require at least 50 observations on time series variables; however, since only 36 years of the victimization data are available, the time series analysis conducted to test the convergence phenomenon cannot be presented as definitive.

The second major limitation lies in the general lack of time series data for some predictor variables, data which are required for time series regressions to explain the convergence and identify the factors responsible for bringing the two series together. In addition, some of the variables for which time series data are available have missing observations, a serious problem that requires linear interpolations and extrapolations[3] to complete the series; however, such adjustments cause the data to lose a great deal of variability in an artificial ways. The details of the limitations of the study are further discussed in the last chapter following a complete presentation of findings and interpretation of same.

---

[3] Interpolation is the process of obtaining a value from a graph or table that is located between major points given, or between data points plotted. A ratio process is usually used to obtain the missing value. Extrapolation is the process of obtaining a value from a chart or graph that extends beyond the given data. The "trend" of the data is extended past the last point given and an estimate made of the value.

ORGANIZATION OF THE STUDY

This study is organized as follows. Chapter 2 presents historical and methodological accounts of the UCR and the NCVS, and speculates on the potential future directions of the two crime series. Chapter 3 includes the background drawn upon for developing the theoretical and methodological framework designed for the study. The research hypotheses are drawn from the review of the literature set forth in Chapter, 3 and are presented at the end of the chapter along with the principal research questions to be addressed. Chapter 4 consists of a discussion of the details of the data amassed, the measures of dependent and predictor variables, and the methods of analysis employed in this study. It also presents the descriptive statistics of all dependent and important predictor variables used in the analyses to follow. At the end of the chapter detailed descriptions of analytic strategies for testing research hypotheses are presented. Chapter 5 includes the results for the first four hypotheses which are tested to address the first two questions seeking to identify the reasons underlying the convergence between the two data series. Chapter 6 presents the results of the second part of the data analysis in which the last four hypotheses are tested to address the third research question which seeks to explain the changing differences of convergence between the two data series. Finally, Chapter 5 provides discussion of the findings, contributions and implications of the research, limitations of the study, future research suggestions, and conclusions.

SUMMARY

The following questions are currently relevant and need to be answered: Are the UCR and NCVS in the process of converging? What do researchers mean when referring to the convergence between the two data series? What factors were responsible for bringing the two highly discrepant data series together over the last 36 years? The purpose of this research is to address these questions by exploring and explaining the convergence between the two most important national crime data series maintained in the U. S. Examining the convergence between the UCR and NCVS data series offers meaningful insight into the dynamics of the relations between these two sets and explains the convergence by identifying the factors responsible for changing the rates of the two crime indexes and minimizing their divergence. The research set forth here provides important policy insights and methodological implications for improving the measures of the two crime measures and guiding future research on the subject of crime measurement in the U. S.

CHAPTER 2

UCR and NCVS: Historical and Methodological Review

The review of the literature in this section provides concise and brief descriptions of the nation's two data collection programs known as the Uniform Crime Reporting system and the National Crime Victimization Survey. In order to assess the data on national crime, the UCR, as a summary data collection program, began in the 1920s at the initiative of the law enforcement agencies in the United States (FBI, 2004). Over the years the UCR program has evolved, expanded, and gone through several noteworthy procedural changes. The authors of major crime policies and criminological researchers have made extensive use of the crime data provided by the program. The summary crime data provided by the UCR program, however, have limitations in terms of providing detailed information on the nature of crimes, offenders, and victims of crime. To deal with the shortcomings and limitations of the UCR and to address the problems of crime and law enforcement in the 21st century, an ambitious incident-based data collection program, currently known as the National Incident-Based Reporting System (NIBRS) has been envisioned to replace the UCR eventually (Maxfield, 1999).

The UCR and NIBRS provide information on official crime statistics, and official crime data reported by police are primarily based on the reporting of crimes to police by the people. Reporting of crime by the people is determined and affected by several individual, social, economic, political, and organizational factors (Black, 1970; Gottfredson & Gottfredson, 1988; Skogan, 1984).The crime data in the UCR and NIBRS are a function of the reporting and recording practices of American police agencies. They may or may not reflect all committed crimes as defined by the law. To calibrate the UCR and provide victim-oriented information on crime and crime statistics, the National Crime Survey (NCS) was initiated in 1972 to provide the national estimates of crime victimization according to Part I crimes (Biderman, et al., 1991). NCS has undergone several changes in the past, including rate-affecting major methodological changes[4] put into place in 1992 when the NCS became the NCVS.

The relationship between the official crime statistics provided by the UCR and the victimization estimates provided by the NCVS has been dynamic. Because the purpose of the current research is to understand and explain the trend of the relationship between the two data series in terms of their divergence and convergence, an overview of the two data collection programs is warranted. The literature review in this chapter, therefore, provides historical and methodological overviews of the two programs. In the first section, the historical development of the UCR, the development and current methodology of its data collection, and a short description of the NIBRS system are provided. In the second section the discussion is focused on the reporting of crime to police by the public. In the third section, a comprehensive but concise discussion on the NCVS is provided. The review in the third section includes a historical overview and the objectives of the NCVS process; the current survey methodology used in the NCVS; sample, design, data collection, and instruments featured in the survey; methodological changes made in the survey over time, the methodological changes of 1992 to the survey and its effects; changes beyond 1992; and future directions of the NCVS.

UNIFORM CRIME REPORTING (UCR)

The UCR, which began in 1927 at the initiative of the International Association of Chiefs of Police (IACP), started collecting crime data in

---

[4] The methodological changes of 1992 are considered rate affecting because they brought significant changes in the rates of estimated victimization in 1993. The rate-affecting changes consisted of changes made to the screening process, method of data collection, and significant definitions (Hubble, 1995).

1930 under the administration of the Federal Bureau of Investigation (FBI). The information presented in this section largely come from the *UCR handbook, 2004* published by the FBI. The IACP decided to include seven types of crimes which they felt were serious, prevalent, and well reported to police (Biderman et al., 1991). Homicide, rape, robbery, aggregated assault, burglary, larceny theft, and motor vehicle theft were initially known as index crimes and now are termed Part I offenses. The IACP declined to differentiate between felonies and misdemeanors in publication because of state-level differences in the definitions of felony and misdemeanor offenses (FBI, 2004). The IACP published a police records and statistics manual in 1929 and published the first monthly "Uniform Crime Reports for the United States and Its Possessions" in 1930, with a table labeled "Number of Offenses Known to the Police: January 1930." At the request of the IACP, the Congress authorized the Attorney General of the United States to collect the data, and the Attorney General handed the responsibility of administering the program to the FBI (FBI, 2004).

The UCR program has existed for over eight decades and has gone through refinement and expansion. The program began with 400 law enforcement agencies reporting from 43 states, and now over 17,000 agencies from 50 states, the District of Columbia, and some U.S. territories report to the program voluntarily (Barnett-Ryan, 2007). The program started collecting data on age, sex, and race in 1952; it created a National Crime Index in 1958; and it published the first National Crime Index in 1960, which included six Part I offenses and larceny theft over $50. The report published in 1960 included reported offenses from all 50 states, and in the same year the UCR published national statistics on law enforcement officers killed. The program started publishing the Supplementary Homicide Report (SHR) in 1962, and started collecting data on officers assaulted along with officers killed in 1972. The program included arson, with the other seven Part I crimes in 1982. The UCR program also collected ethnic data between 1980 and 1987, and started collecting statistics on hate crime in 1990 and statistics on bias against physical or mental disability in 1994. Now the program collects summary crime statistics on eight Part I crimes, including homicide, rape, robbery, aggregated assault, burglary, larceny theft, motor vehicle theft, and arson. The UCR program also reports arrests for 21 additional crime categories, known as Part II crimes in the UCR. The UCR series is now referred to as summary statistics in order to differentiate it from incident-based NIBRS. In 2004, the UCR program suspended the National Crime Index.

The UCR is a voluntary data collection program in which state, municipal, county, tribal, special, and federal law enforcement agencies participate. Local law enforcement agencies from 46 states participate through the state UCR programs, but others report directly to the national program. Different measures are taken by the program to ensure the optimal level of uniformity and precision in defining, classifying, and reporting data by the law enforcement agencies and state programs (FBI, 2004). Frequent training for individuals working in the state programs and law enforcement, audits of the data submitted by the agencies, and data quality control focused on dealing with outliers are the major steps taken by the UCR program to maintain the validity of the data (FBI, 2004). The program makes estimations of crime data for the agencies that, for some reason, either do not participate in the program or do not submit data for the entire year.

National Incident-Based Reporting System (NIBRS)

The NIBRS[5], which began in 1987 with a pilot demonstration conducted by the South Carolina Law Enforcement Division, is the ambitious future of the UCR and will transform the existing program from summary reporting to detailed incident-based reporting, providing information on incident, victim, and offender aspects of every crime included in the program. The NIBRS came as a response to the call from the law enforcement community for the evaluation of the UCR program and an expansion of the data-collection system to meet the needs of law enforcement in the 21st century. Data on 46 different offenses classified in 22 offense categories are collected under group A, and arrest data are collected for 11 offenses in group B. Not only does the NIBRS provide detailed incident-based statistics covering all three aspects of an offense, but it also covers every major criminal justice issue.

---

[5] The NIBRS data are not used in the study. A brief description of the NIBRS outlines the future development of official crime data collection program.

The NIBRS is different from the summary data-collection system on several accounts, apart from the depth and details noted. The NIBRS collects data on cybercrime, rape against men, and crime against society other than crime against property and persons. The NIBRS has also done away with the hierarchy rule of the summary system. The expansion of the NIBRS is slow because of its ambitious nature and the need for resources and technical expertise to participate effectively. However, over 6,000 law enforcement agencies from 31 states are participating in the NIBRS (FBI, 2004).

REPORTING CRIME TO POLICE

The UCR represents crime reported to police. Several relevant factors other than the reporting itself determine the rate reported by the UCR. The police have their formal and informal interpretations of the information provided by the public. The procedures for reporting crime to the UCR program are loosely related to the instructions provided in the UCR handbook. There is no standardization across police departments concerning recording and reporting crimes. Finally, no feedback comes from the FBI or the UCR program on the accuracy of reporting by the law enforcement agencies unless a major discrepancy is identified.

The reporting by the citizens, however, is the most important determinant and UCR data largely depend on crimes reported to police by victims and bystanders (Skogan, 1984). The UCR, which primarily reflects crimes known to police, has the components of crime reported to police and crime discovered by police, but crime recorded by police is chiefly a function of victims reporting (Langan & Farrington, 1998) because the role of police tends to be reactive (Black, 1970). Skogan (1984), using the victimization survey data from different developed countries, provided a detailed explorative discussion on the factors responsible for reporting of crimes to police. The central argument is that the cost-benefits calculus is the most important factor which victims and bystanders take into account while making a decision about reporting crime to police. Skogan (1984) provided a detailed list of factors and explained how those factors affect the cost-benefit calculation and determine the reporting of crimes to police. Determinants of reporting are seriousness, insurance, obligation and efficacy, attitude toward police, culpability of victims, demographics, relationship between victims and offenders, third-party reporting, and self-help. Serious crimes are more likely to be reported than less serious crimes.

Reporting of crimes by people increases when reports are required for insurance benefits claims. People also tend to report just so they claim to be responsible and good citizens. Culpability and a spoiled identity of the victim is also an important factor because a victim with no previous history is more likely to be comfortable in reporting a crime to police. Attitude toward police does not play an important role in reporting, but mutual hostility does stop people from going to police. Demography is another determinant of reporting. Women, older adults, Blacks, and educated people are more likely to report than men, younger adults, Whites, and less educated people. The relationship between a victim and an offender affects the reporting, with a crime by a nonstranger being more likely to be reported. Finally, being required to report to a third party, such as a school authority or company executive, and a culture of self-help reduce reporting to police.

Gottfredson and Gottfredson (1988) discussed decisions in criminal justice, including the decisions of victims to report crime to police. They referred to victims as the *principal gatekeepers* of the criminal justice system. The role of victims is more important in cases of simple assault and theft, and police in urban areas depend solely on victims for discovery of crimes (Gottfredson & Gottfredson, 1988). There are many determinants for reporting crimes to police, and the character of the victims plays an important role. Age, sex, race, income, seriousness of the offense, insurance coverage, cost-benefit calculation, fear of reprisal, and trust in the police are some of the important determinants.

Following Gottfredson and Gottfredson, Felson, Messner, Hoskin, and Deane (2002), in accordance with the rational choice perspective, assumed that victims are rational actors who consider the cost and benefits of making a decision to report crimes to police. Victims are more likely to report an incident to the police when the incentives are high and the costs are low. Three factors—self-protection, retribution, and protection of others—provide incentives in varying degrees for people to call police, depending on the seriousness of the incident. However, cost consideration is a more important factor in calling police than incentives. Fear of stigmatization and reprisal; unwillingness to send offenders for criminal prosecution, especially in the case of domestic violence; involvement in illegal activities; and opportunity cost are the factors that increase the perceived cost of calling police. Felson et al. (2002) examined the effects of self-protection; fear of reprisal; perceiving an incident as a trivial matter, a private matter, or unimportant for police; and protection of others on reporting behavior and reported that people are inhibited from calling police because of a desire for privacy, desire to protect the offenders, and fear of reprisal. The factors encouraging people to call police are the desire for self-protection, perception of the seriousness of incidents, and perception that the police view an incident as more serious.

The decision to call police is also affected by the social environment, more precisely neighborhood characteristics. Goudriaan, Wittebrood, and Nieuwbeerta (2006) argued that social cohesion, confidence in police effectiveness, and socioeconomic disadvantage play some role in victims' decision to report or not to report a crime to police. Victims' characteristics such as sex, age, income, education, and household types are also believed to be determinants of reporting and were controlled in the analyses of Goudriaan et al. (2006) in order to see the effects of neighborhood characteristics on reporting of crime. The study, which used data from a Dutch victim survey, reported a significant effect of neighborhood characteristics on the reporting of crime.

NATIONAL CRIME VICTIMIZATION SURVEY (NCVS)

The NCVS, known as the NCS before being redesigned in 1992, has existed for 36 years and has been established as a valid and alternative measure of crime and victimization in the United States. The NCS, which began as a household survey in 1972, drew upon a number of pilot studies, various reports on methodological research, and ongoing improvement of survey techniques (Rand, 2006). Its state-of-the-art methodology included panel-data-based design, with distinctive features of screening questions and interviews of all household members. The survey has gone through substantial changes that include rate-affecting and non-rate-affecting changes. Of all the changes made the most significant was a 1992 methodological change that changed the name of the survey from NCS to NCVS.

Historical Overview and Objectives

The UCR crime statistics had been criticized from the beginning for presenting only a fraction of known crime events (Biderman, et al., 1991), so in 1965 this concern was addressed by the President's Commission on Law Enforcement and Administration of Justice which decided to explore the feasibility and utility of a national crime victimization survey for the primary purpose of calibrating the UCR and providing an alternative measure other than providing information on victim characteristics and criminal events. In 1966 the Commission reviewed the results of victimization surveys in three cities, noting that the actual amount of crime in the United States was several times greater than reported in the UCR. It should be noted that the surveys of the three cities estimated the rate of personal crimes to be twice as high as did the UCR, and the rate of property crime to be more than twice as high (Biderman, 1967a). Furthermore, the Bureau of Social Science Research (BSSR) survey in three high and medium-crime precincts of Washington, DC reported even higher discrepancies between victim- and police-reported crimes (Biderman, 1967a).

These estimates revealed the presence of substantial unrecorded crime and fueled the discussion on the validity of official crime statistics, which arose from the belief that police ought to report all crimes that have occurred in their jurisdiction (Biderman & Riess, 1967). Biderman and Reiss (1967), who coined the term *dark figure of crime*, argued that there is a difference between the real and reported crime, and efforts to illuminate the dark figure of crime should consider the fact that crimes are not objectively observed universal events but rather are a function of institutional efforts (Biderman & Riess, 1967). Therefore, when the victimization survey was designed and administered by the Bureau of Justice Statistics in 1972 it sought to serve greater objectives than simply illuminating the dark figure of crime. The U. S. Bureau of Census, which was given the responsibility of conducting the survey because of its ability to conduct national-level surveys, outlined the following objectives and purposes of the victimization survey (U.S. Census Bureau, 2003):

- Provide an independent calibration for the UCR,
- Provide an alternative indicator of the crime problem,
- Provide measures of victim risk and change the concentration of the criminal justice system from offender to victims,
- Provide an insight into citizens' definitions of crimes.

The purpose of the current National Crime Victimization Survey is to provide personal victimization and property crime rates and collect information on incidents of crime, injuries and losses, victim characteristics, and the characteristics of offenders (U.S. Census Bureau, 2009). The objectives of the survey have changed with time, but the objectives of learning about crime and criminal justice through a national representative sample and clarifying the methodological distinctiveness of the victimization survey have remained unchanged. Groves and Cork (2008), after evaluating the original and dynamic objectives of the survey, outlined the following objectives that have been achieved thus far by the victimization survey. First, from the beginning, the survey provided assessment of the magnitude of the dark figure of crime. Second, victims who were practically ignored as participants in a crime before the survey have received prominence in the survey, and more is known about the characteristics of victims of crime. Third, the survey provided assessments of consequences faced by victims of crimes in terms of injuries and loses. Fourth, the survey provided information on the spatial aspect of crime events and the use of weapons. Finally, the survey also asked victims to provide profiles of offenders.

Current Survey Methodology

This section contains information available in annual BJS publications of *Crime Victimization in the United States*. The NCVS survey is a household survey that represents U.S. residential population at the age of 12 years and older, except for crew members of merchant vessels, Armed Forces personnel living in military barracks, and such institutionalized persons as correctional facility inmates. U.S. citizens residing abroad and foreigners visiting the country are also excluded.

Table 2.1. Number of Households and Persons Interviewed by Year

Year	Number of households interviewed	Household response rate	Number of persons interviewed	Response rate for persons
1996	45,000	93%	85,330	91%
1997	43,000	95%	79,470	90%
1998	43,000	94%	78,900	89%
1999	43,000	93%	77,750	89%
2000	43,000	93%	79,710	90%
2001	44,000	93%	79,950	89%
2002	42,000	92%	76,050	87%
2003	42,000	92%	74,520	86%
2004	42,000	91%	74,500	86%
2005	38,600	91%	67,000	84%
2006	38,000	91%	67,650	86%
2007	41,500	90%	73,600	86%
2008	42,093	90%	77,852	86%

Sample and design:
In 2008, the NCVS survey sample included approximately 48,000 designated addresses located in approximately 809 primary sampling units from throughout the United States (U.S. Census Bureau, 2009). A complex sampling procedure, involving stratified multistage cluster sampling, is used to draw a representative national sample. In the first stage of the sampling, primary sampling units (PSUs) are determined and selected through the stratification process. PSUs are based on population representing large metropolitan areas or counties or groups of counties. Some strata may be represented by a single PSU, and some may be represented by a group of PSUs, depending on the size of population. At the second level, each stratum is divided into four non-

overlapping frames (unit, area, permit, and group quarters), and samples are drawn from these frames using a random-sampling process. In January 2005, the survey introduced the first panel of samples based on the 2000 decennial census in continuing areas and, in January 2006, in new areas. The phase-in of the 2000 sample and the phase-out of the 1990 sample were completed in January 2008. In the 1972 survey 72,000 households were included in the sample, which kept decreasing primarily because of increasing cost. Table 2.1 displays information on households and individuals included in the sample of the survey from 1996 to 2008.

The survey uses 6-month reference periods and a bounding process in order to address the issue of recall and telescoping[6]. The bounding process and 6-months reference period give a unique nature to the NCVS, and if the reference period were to increase from 6 months to one year and the bounding process were removed, then the survey would lose its present nature (Rand, 2007). The entire sample is divided into six groups for field interviews, and persons are interviewed 7 times in a 3-year period. The first interview is used as a bounding in order to address the problem of telescoping and is not included in estimates. Each rotation or group is again divided further into six panels, and one panel is interviewed every month during the 6-month period. Every 6 months, a new group of households is entered into the sample, replacing a phased-out group that has been remained in the sample for 3 years. Respondents are always asked questions about victimization experiences in the previous 6 months before the interview, and the 6-month reference period is a powerful mechanism in the survey methodology to minimize the recall biases of respondents. All members of a sample household 14 years and older are interviewed directly, and 12- and 13-year-old members are interviewed through proxy, if desired, by a responsible member of the household.

---

[6] The NCVS employs a bounding technique to minimize the problem of recall and telescoping. Respondents to a survey may not recall the correct time of occurrence of incidents. This lapse is referred to as *telescoping*, which is related to limitations of recall. The bounding technique ensures that the information collected during one phase of an interview is used in the next phase so as to avoid duplication in estimating victimization (Rand, 2006).

Data collection and instruments:

In the beginning, all interviews were conducted in person using paper and pencil by the field surveyors. The development of communication technology, especially the phone, and cost considerations changed the process, and telephone interviews started replacing in-person interviews. The development of computer technology was another factor helping reshape the process of interviewing. In 2003, all household addresses became eligible for Computer Assisted Telephone Interviewing (CATI), and it was decided that the interviewers would use telephone interviews after the first in-person contact. It was also decided that if the first contact was not established during the first visit of the interviewers, all interviews could be done by telephone.

Although the Census Bureau-run CATI call center for calling households was discontinued as the expected cost saving was not realized, the interviewers were encouraged to use telephone for the second through the seventh interviews. CATI and Paper Assisted Personal Interviewing (PAPI) continued until June 2006, but at the beginning of July 2006 the NCVS began interviewing in a fully automated interviewing environment using computer-assisted personal interviewing (CAPI) and CATI data collection modes (U.S. Census Bureau, 2009). However, in July 2007, the NCVS discontinued using CATI for data collection and completely switched over to CAPI (U.S. Census Bureau, 2009).

The instruments for collecting data include two sets of questionnaires. The screening interview includes questions for determining whether a household or an individual has experienced any sort of criminal victimization in the past 6 months prior to the interview. This interview is conducted during the first contact. The basic screening interview does not ask respondents to classify victimization and avoids using legal language (Rand, 2006). All victimization experiences of a respondent in the reference period are recorded on separate incident reports. One person in one household is designated as the "household respondent" and is asked questions concerning victimization against the household. Proxy respondents for 12- and 13-year-old individuals are also asked the same screening questions.

At the second level, for each incident reported and recorded on an incident report during the screening process detailed interviews are conducted. In these interviews respondents are asked to provide detailed information on crime events, offenders, injuries and loses, and extent of reporting to police (Rand, 2007). At this stage, not only detailed information on victimization events is collected, but it is also classified into different categories. The NCVS tends to replicate the UCR and collects data on all Part I offenses of the UCR other than homicide and arson. The crime categories for which data are collected are rape or sexual assault, robbery, aggravated assault, simple assault, personal larceny, burglary, motor vehicle theft, and property theft. Any victimization not fitting under these categories is excluded. The NCVS also adds different supplements to the survey.

Along with crime victimization, the survey has included different supplements on additional topics of importance, such as crime in schools, contacts with law enforcement, identity-theft victimization, crime in the workplace, crime against persons with disabilities, hate-related victimization, and computer-related victimization or cybercrime (U.S. Census Bureau, 2009). Supplements on hate crime, cybercrime, and identity theft are the most recent additions.

There is a possibility that some respondents, especially victims of sexual abuse by non-strangers, are likely to face series victimization. In order to deal with the issue of series victimization and avoid causing victims difficulty in providing details about every victimization, the NCVS uses a special protocol called "series victimization." This protocol allows NCVS to report one victimization for six or more similar victimizations in a 6-month period.

Methodological Changes in the NCVS

The national victimization survey, which began in 1972, has undergone several changes in the last 36 years, changes that were driven principally by cost and methodological considerations. In 1972, the NCS consisted of three surveys—a national household survey, a household survey of major cities, and a survey of businesses. The panel for evaluation established in 1974 was given the responsibility of evaluating the survey. The panel submitted its report in 1976 (Penick & Owens, 1976) and brought about several methodological and procedural changes to the survey. The most important change was the discontinuation of the Commercial Victimization Survey and the City

Surveys. In 1992, the survey went through major methodological changes, but before 1992 several non-rate-affecting changes were incorporated into the survey. Those changes were focused largely on reducing cost and improving the questionnaire (Rand, 2006). The crime incident report, which was comprised of 4 pages and 20 questions in 1972, grew in size and by the time the newly designed questionnaire was implemented in 1993 it had 173 questions set forth in more than 24 pages (Rand, 2006).

Based on the recommendations of a redesign consortium, some changes were implemented in 1986 to include questions on victim-offender relationship, characteristics of crime incidents, and victims' interaction with the criminal justice system. Proxy respondents were used for 12- and 13-year-old respondents, but after 1986 they were directly interviewed unless parents insisted on a proxy. Major changes in the questionnaire of the survey were also implemented in 1989 and again in 1990.

The survey started with in-person interviews in 1972, but introduced telephone interviews for approximately one-half of the sample in 1980 for budgetary reasons. In 1984, a 20% sample reduction was introduced to manage costs and improve the design of the survey. The questionnaire was revised and redesigned in 1986 and 1989, and large-scale rate-affecting methodological changes were introduced in August 1991 and the name of the survey was changed from the National Crime Survey to the National Crime Victimization Survey. The redesigned questionnaire was fully implemented in July 1993. The sample size was reduced by 10% in 1992 and 12% in 1996 to manage the cost. The sample size was further reduced by 4% in 2002, 10% in 2005, and 16% in 2006. Further reductions in sample size were introduced in 2007 and 2008 in order to offset the growing costs.

Methodological Changes in 1992 and Their Effects

The methodological changes of 1992, acknowledged as rate-affecting changes, were primarily based on the recommendations of the panel for evaluation of the crime survey (Penick & Owens, 1976), established in 1974 by the National Academy of Sciences under the direction of the Department of Justice. To evaluate the recommendations of the panel and examine their feasibility, BJS sponsored a redesign research consortium which completed its work in 1985. The BJS and Census Bureau further examined the feasibility, cost effectiveness, and methodological advancements of the recommendations of the consortium and started phased implementation that finally culminated in a rate-affecting change in 1992. The most prominent feature of the redesign was the improved measures of sexual assault, rape, and domestic violence, which are generally considered to be the most difficult to define and measure. The NCVS divided the sample into two parts, administered the old and the new questionnaires, phased in the new questionnaires in half-sample areas from January 1992 through June 1993, and used redesigned methods in the entire sample from July 1993. Listed below are the major methodological changes implemented in 1992-1993 (U.S. Department of Justice, 1994).

- New screening questionnaire was introduced that extended the list of short cues and removed criminal terms and concepts found in the old screener.
- New screening questionnaire was introduced with specific cues on weapons used and explicit cuing for rape and other sexual assaults.
- New screening questionnaire also included cues for nonstranger offenders and place of incidents.
- Questions for estimating incidents of vandalism were included.
- Use of CATI for 30% of the sample was introduced.
- Threshold for series victimization was increased from three to six incidents.
- Sexual assault was added as a crime category measured by the survey.

The changes of 1992, as expected, greatly improved the measurement of certain crimes such as rape, sexual assault, and domestic violence. It also enhanced the recalling of some of the nonserious offenses. These changes in the estimates occurred due to the enhanced and explicit screening questionnaire (Rand, 2006). The effect of redesign was a statistically significant increase in all categories of crimes except robbery, motor vehicle theft, and personal theft in the national victimization estimates of 1993. Rape estimates increased by 157% and assault increased by 49% (Kinderman, Lynch, & Canter, 1997). Within the assault category, simple assault, especially with no injury, increased the most (Rand et al., 1997). Another effect of the redesign was an increase in estimates of crimes not reported to police because of explicit cues included in the screening questionnaire which helped respondents to recall less serious incidents. The differences between the NCS and NCVS on rape, aggravated assault, assault, and burglary were significant; therefore, BJS adjusted the NCS data using NCS/NCVS ratios (Rand et al., 1997).

Changes Beyond 1992 and Future Directions

The survey has continued to evolve after the redesign in 1992. However, the changes beyond 1992 have been focused on adding supplements for measuring different issues of crime problems and on cutting costs. In 1996, a 12% sample cut was implemented, and in 2000 the screening questionnaire was changed. Additional supplements measuring school crime, identity theft, hate crime, police public contact, stalking and harassment, and workplace risks were added.

In 2006, major changes were implemented and changed the estimate significantly, but the analysis of 2007 victimization survey by the statisticians of BJS and the Census Bureau concluded that the changes in 2006 caused a temporary anomaly (U.S. Census Bureau, 2009). The most important change in 2006 was the introduction of a new sample based on the 2000 Decennial Census to account for shifts in population and location of households that occur over time. The 2006 changes completely replaced the paper-and-pencil survey with the automated CAPI and CATI. In July of 2007, however, the NCVS discontinued using CATI for data collection and completely switched over to CAPI (U.S. Census Bureau, 2009).

The survey is facing challenges from increasing costs, changing demands, and a decreasing response rate (Groves & Cork, 2008; Lynch, 2011; Rand, 2007). The survey has to show dynamism in order to preserve its current stature and meet future law enforcement and research requirements. In order to deal with these challenges and modify the survey, the BJS requested the National Academies' Committee on National Statistics to convene a panel to review the programs of the Bureau of Justice Statistics, with a special request to give priority to the victimization survey. The panel submitted its report featuring both general and specific recommendations. The panel strongly recommended maintaining the quality of the only national victimization survey and urged Congress to provide sufficient funds for it. The two strongest recommendations of the panel were to change the reference period from 6 months to one year and to have subnational crime surveys. Changes in the sampling procedure, use of mixed-data collection modes, and inviting design suggestions were some of the other important recommendations emanating from the panel. Although the changes in the reference period and removal of the bounding process will change the current characteristics of the survey, the NCVS is more likely to be dynamic, flexible, and research-oriented as a result (Rand, 2007).

SUMMARY

This chapter provided a brief historical and methodological review of the UCR and NCVS because the purpose of the study is to understand and explain the convergence between the two data series. The UCR, a national crime data collection program that began in 1930 at the initiative of the IACP, collects summary data on eight Part I crimes and arrest data on Part II crimes through voluntary participation of over 17,000 local, state, special, and federal law enforcement agencies. It employs scientific methods to maintain uniformity and accuracy of crime statistics and publishes annual reports known as "Crime in the United States." The UCR data are summary data that have severe limitations in terms of their use in policy formulation and criminological research. To address the limitations of the summary data and deal with the growing complexity of law enforcement, the FBI has undertaken an ambitious endeavor to transform the summary data collection program of the UCR into an incident-based data-collection program called NIBRS. The NIBRS collects incident-based crime statistics on almost all categories of crime, but because of the ambitious nature of the program it is likely to be a number of years before it replaces the UCR.

The UCR and the NIBRS processes collect official crime statistics reported by law enforcement, and crime reported by law enforcement is crime known to police because it has the character of crime discovered by police and crime reported to police by the public. Official crime data are a function of crime reported to police and notification by police as the role of the police is primarily reactive. Reporting crime to the police is determined by several individual, social, and incident-related factors. Notification of crime by the police and reporting crime to the UCR and NIBRS program are again determined by several organizational and technical factors in police operations.

It has always been known that official crime statistics that depend on police data represent only a fraction of the total crime committed. To calibrate the official crime statistics, provide alternative estimates of crime, and give victims the opportunity to take part in estimating crime data, the NCS was implemented in 1972 to collect victimization data through a national household survey using sophisticated methods. The crime victimization data are collected by the NCVS though computer-based in-person interviews of a nationally representative sample of respondents over 12 years old. The crime victimization survey has gone through the process of maturation, development, and several methodological changes in the past, and changes are being contemplated for the future. The changes in the methods of the data collection have been motivated by the needs to improvement the ability to address current and future challenges and cost considerations. Of all major changes in the victimization survey, the changes incorporated in 1992 and 1993, when it was changed from the NCS to the NCVS, are the most important, being rate-affecting changes. The BJS is working on bringing further changes to the NCVS to address the future needs of research, universal problems related with household surveys, and the growing cost of the survey.

The purpose of the present study is to explore and explain the convergence between the UCR and NCVS data series, which showed a great deal of discrepancy in 1973 and are in the process of converging. Chapter 3 provides the review of the literature, dealing specifically with the divergence and convergence between the two series.

CHAPTER 3

Conception, Exploration, and Explanation of Convergence between the UCR and NCVS: Analytical Framework and Major Hypotheses

The review of the literature provided in this chapter is focused on the dimensions of the divergence and convergence between the UCR and NCVS data series and the factors that have determined their dynamic historical and present relationship. The purpose of the study is to explore and explain the convergence between the UCR and NCVS data series. The two crime data series, diverged greatly at the beginning of the victimization survey in 1973 (Skogan, 1974), but have gradually converged over the last 36 years.

Two important questions have been asked concerning these relations. First, why do the two data series diverge so much when they measure the same social phenomenon called crime? Second, are the two data series converging? Initially, researchers targeted the first question and attempted to explain the divergence between the two series. The divergence started declining with time, and as the two data series started showing the process of convergence researchers began to question why the two data series were converging and whether the two indicators were providing an accurate picture of crime in the country. It was also realized that the two data series are different and employ completely different methods of data collection, so it is possible that they should not converge. Different studies reported different and often conflicting findings, and the differing definitions of *convergence* and different methods of testing convergence became a topic of debate. A selective list of studies that explored and explained the divergence and convergence between the UCR and NCVS data series are presented in Appendix A.

This chapter includes discussion of these issues of convergence between the two data series. In the first section of the chapter the discussion is focused on the causes of the divergence between the UCR and NCVS data series. The discussion in the second section of the chapter is centered on the different aspects of the convergence between the two data series. A review of all major studies on the convergence between the UCR and NCVS data series is provided, and the issues of the definition of *convergence* and methods of testing convergence are also discussed. The review of the different methodologies adopted by various studies was used to develop the analytic strategy for the present research. In the third and last section of the chapter a theoretical framework for addressing the second question of the research that seeks to explain the convergence between the two series is presented.

UCR AND NCVS: WHY DO THEY DIVERGE?

The divergence between the UCR and NCVS data series could be attributed to two major factors (Biderman et al., 1991). One is how the reporting of crimes to police by people is influenced by several socioeconomic, political, demographic, organizational, and structural factors. The second cause of the divergence emerges from the uniqueness and specificity of the two measures that are characterized by differences in definition, collection, classification, and estimation. Studies exploring the causes of discrepancies between the two measures have used an array of explanatory variables that come from these two primary factors (Biderman et al., 1991; O'Brien, 1985 Rand & Rennison, 2002). The BJS provides explanations for the divergence between the UCR and NCVS data series, and according to Rand and Rennison (2002), "They use different data collection methods and measure an overlapping—but not identical—set of offenses against an overlapping—but not identical—population" (p. 48).

The most important reason for the divergence comes from the procedure through which the crime incidents are entered into the records of the UCR and the victimization survey. The UCR data are a function of reporting and recording rather than a real presentation of all crime incidents (Biderman & Reiss, 1967). The UCR program reports only crimes that are known to police while the victimization survey reports victimization incidents, both reported and not reported to police. Crime known to police includes crime reported to police and crime discovered by police. However, the role of the police in discovering crime is limited because the police tend to be more reactive than proactive (Black, 1970). Therefore, crime known to the police largely reflects reporting by citizens, and citizens' likelihood of reporting crimes to police depends on a large number of factors, similar to cost-benefit calculus (Felson et al., 2002; Gottfredson & Gottfredson, 1988; Skogan, 1984), demographic composition (Biderman et al., 1991), and neighborhood characteristics (Goudriaan et al., 2005).

The second reason for the divergence is that the two data series cover different populations (Biderman et al., 1991; O'Brien, 1985; Rand & Rennison, 2002). The UCR covers nearly the entire U.S. residential population while the NCVS reports victimization reported by the population over 12 years. Victimization of the population below the age of 12 is not reported by the victimization survey. The exclusion of children below 12 years of age, however, may not have a substantial effect on the overall estimate because very few children below the age of 12 become victims of personal Part I crimes reported in the NCVS (O'Brien, 1988). The NCVS excludes the population living on sea vessels and in institutions and members of the armed forces living in barracks. The UCR includes all these excluded habitations, although crimes committed in these places are not recorded in the UCR.

The third important reason for the divergence is a difference in the counting and categorizing protocols for the two data series (Rand & Rennison, 2002). In the UCR, *rape* is defined as "the carnal knowledge of a female forcibly and against her will" while the NCVS includes rape of both females and males. However, this discrepancy will be resolved once the UCR is completely replaced by the NIBRS, which includes rape against men. The basic counting unit of the NCVS is the victim, and the basic counting unit of the UCR is the offense. In case of rape and aggravated assault, the number of offenses is equal to the number of victims, but in case of other offenses the number of offenses is equal to the number of incidents. In the NCVS, the number of offenses in all crimes against persons is equal to the number of victims. The UCR also uses hotel and hierarchy rules[7] that are not followed by the NCVS.

Sampling and non-sampling errors of the NCVS are the fourth reason for the divergence between the UCR and NCVS. The estimates of the NCVS are based on sample data and confidence intervals are computed, whereas in the case of the UCR no adjustment is made for unreported data by different agencies or underreporting by police. The biggest source of non-sampling error in the NCVS is the telescopic effect (O'Brien, 1988). Although the bounding process is an effective methodological tool to minimize the effect of telescoping, the respondents' recalling victimization that occurred in the previous 6 months is not free from error. If the bounding process is removed and the reference period is increased from 6 months to one year, the non-sampling error due to telescoping will increase (Rand, 2007).

Fifth, the process of measuring series victimization in the NCVS is another reason for the discrepancies. According to series victimization, if a victim has experienced six or more similar but separate victimizations in the last 6 months and is unable to describe them separately, one report will be taken for the entire series of victimizations. This process may actually result in underestimating the actual number of victimizations.

Finally, the UCR is affected by the police "unfounding" crimes and by reporting errors. The UCR is not a mandatory program; therefore, all law enforcement agencies do not report to the UCR and do not follow the definition, classification, and reporting guidelines provided by the UCR program. Law enforcement agencies also have

---

[7] Hotel and hierarchy rules are counting protocols in the UCR. According to the hotel rule for scoring, if a number of dwelling units under a single manager are burglarized and the offenses are more likely to be reported to the police by the manager rather than the individual tenants, the burglary must be scored as one offense (FBI, 2004). According to the classifying and scoring rule of hierarchy, law enforcement agencies are required to identify and report the most serious crime in a multiple-offense situation in which several offenses have been committed at the same time and place. The hierarchy rule does not affect the prosecution. The offenses of justifiable homicide, motor vehicle theft, and arson are exceptions to the hierarchy rule (FBI, 2004).

the process of "unfounding" a crime that may bring some discrepancies between the two programs. A sizeable number of crimes reported by people are deemed unfounded by police because of wrong reporting, misunderstanding of the law, and lack of prima-facie evidence.

The preceding are the most important factors responsible for the divergence between the UCR and NCVS. The rates published by the UCR and NCVS also look different because of the use of different denominators. The NCVS uses a population over age 12 for calculating personal victimization rates and the number of households for calculating victimizations against the household. The UCR uses total residential population for calculating the rates of offenses.

CONVERGENCE BETWEEN THE UCR AND NCVS

The UCR and NCVS are both supposed to measure a social phenomenon called crime. Since both indexes measure the same underlying phenomenon, theoretically there should be a perfect correlation between the UCR and NCVS data, and some small divergence and discrepancies can be attributed to the procedural differences in measurement at play. However, the substantial discrepancies between the two data series have intrigued policy makers and scholars who have persisted in their attempt to understand why the two data series diverge. The victimization survey, which began in 1973, revealed that lower than 50% of offenses are reported through the UCR program (Skogan, 1974). The discrepancies between the UCR crime report and victimization reported by the NCS survey were too large to be attributed to the differences in measurement procedures. The discrepancies sparked a discussion in the media and among scholars regularly on the validity and similarity of the UCR and the victimization data. Serious questions were raised about the validity of official statistics. Scholars in the field have investigated this issue from different perspectives, and the focus of the discussion and methods of analysis have unfolded into a dynamic temporal process. Reporting of the first victimization survey data raised questions about the validity of official crime statistics; therefore, the earlier studies, which used cross-sectional data, focused primarily on exploring the comparative validity of the UCR and NCS data and reported in favor of one or the other.

The first influential study conducted by Skogan (1974) that used cross-sectional bivariate and multivariate analysis presented the spatial distribution of crime and victimization and opined that the UCR is a more valid measure of crime, although the victimization survey does not fully lack validity in his opinion. Booth, Johnson, and Choldin (1977) assessed the effect of similar independent variables and reported different correlations with two different measures. That study did not report in favor of one of the two crime measurements and concluded that the validity of a measure depends on the crime being measured. Decker (1977) reported considerable doubts on the accuracy of official crime statistics, while O'Brien, Shichor, and Decker (1980) reported that the NCS measure is more valid than the UCR and recommended that, if researchers have a choice, they should use the NCS instead of the UCR in their research.

Scholars tended to take two different and often contrary views while addressing the issues of comparability and convergence between the two data series. Some researchers, pointing at the lack of correlation between the two series, argued that the two series do not measure the same phenomenon (Menard, 1987; Menard & Covey, 1988) while others argued that both of the series measure the same phenomenon, but differently (Biderman et al., 1991; Blumstein et al., 1991; Catalano, 2006; Cohen & Lichbach, 1982; Cohen & Land, 1984; Gove, Hughes, & Geerken, 1985; McDowell & Loftin, 2007; O'Brien, 1990, 1996). The second group of scholars attributed the discrepancies to the differences in measurement procedures employed. Several studies, which reported the convergence between the two series, recommended detrending the series before estimating correlations (Blumstein et al., 1991; O'Brien, 1990, 1996) and making several adjustments in the denominator while calculating the crime rates (Blumstein et al., 1991; Biderman et al., 1991).

Two conclusions can be drawn by looking at the trend of the two data series between 1973 and 2007. First, both of the series can be seen to be converging over time (Catalano, 2006; McDowell & Loftin, 2007), and there is a sort of breakpoint in the NCVS (Rand, 2007). The series were maintaining a high level of discrepancy while converging at a very slow rate, and the convergence was generally occurring through marginal changes in the UCR data (O'Brien, 1996). After the breakpoint in the victimization data series, which coincides with the methodology changes in the victimization survey in 1993, the rate of convergence became faster and the two series can be seen as converging. The two series moved closer to each other after 1993, and this change is largely due to changes in reporting of victimizations in the NCVS. Most of the studies addressing the issue of convergence were published before the breakpoint, a time when convergence was almost negligible. The findings of those studies, which reported the lack of convergence between the two series and argued that the two crime measurements did not measure the same phenomenon, were primarily influenced by the limited years of data that lacked subsequent variability.

Very few studies (e.g., Catalano, 2006; McDowell & Loftin, 2007) had the advantage of more years of data and an increased rate of convergence after the breakpoint in 1993. Catalano (2006) tried to explain the convergence between the two series, but the focus of her study was limited to exploring the factors responsible for the convergence and the scope of her study was limited to the aggregated and disaggregated categories of violent crime. It is now incumbent upon researchers in the field to take up the challenge of explaining the convergence and identify correlates of convergence.

Debate on Methodology Explaining the Convergence

Researchers started doing trend analysis by using time series data to compare the trends of the UCR and the NCS by the end of 1980s and the beginning of 1990s (Blumstein et al., 1991; Menard, 1987; Menard & Covey, 1988; O'Brien, 1990). Different methodologies for comparing time series data were used by the various researchers who started a long debate centered on the issue of convergence and the use of the detrending method[8] in comparing the UCR with the NCVS

---

[8] *Detrending* is a statistical or mathematical operation of removing trends from time series data. Many alternative methods are available for detrending. Regressing a time series against a time trend or its single lagged value and differencing are popular methods of removing trends from time series. The use of the single lagged value or differencing methods of detrending is determined by the trend process present in a time series.

(Blumstein et al., 1991; Blumstein, 1992; Menard, 1991, 1992; O'Brien, 1990, 1991).

Menard and Covey (1988) used the UCR and NCVS raw data from 1973 to 1982 and conducted trend analysis to see whether the two series were correlated or converging over time. The study did not find convergence or comparability between the two data series except in some cases where a restrictive definition of the NCS crime has been used. Any restriction that reduces the number in the NCS reduces the discrepancy. The findings of the study did not support the findings of Gove et al. (1985), who concluded that the UCR data are a more valid measure of crime. O'Brien (1990), who used the NCS and UCR data from 1973 to 1986, reported conflicting results and concluded that the report of a lack of convergence between the two series by Menard (1987) and Menard and Covey (1988) was due to the use of raw crime rates in their time series analyses. Use of detrended crime rates by O'Brien (1990) showed a strong convergence between the two series and called into question the validity of the results of the studies that used raw crime rates in trend analysis. The differences in the use of analytical methods and conflicting results led to a continuing debate on the use of appropriate methodology in exploring the convergence between the two time series. An influential study by Blumstein et al. (1991) pointed out the shortcomings of studies reported by Menard and Covey (1988) and O'Brien (1990), and argued that these studies had focused on trend and deviation (detrended data) respectively, whereas the study of Blumstein et al. intended to assess the relative roles of both trend and deviance.

Menard (1990) responded to O'Brien's (1990) suggestion of using detrended data and raised a few questions in the process. First, what does convergence mean after detrending of the data? Although O'Brien (1990) had shown a high level of convergence, a close examination of convergence of detrended data revealed that the two series were quite different (Menard & Covey, 1988). Second, what is the substantive meaning of detrended data? To understand crime problems and evaluation research, detrended series are not going to be of much significance, but crime trend is going to be important. Third, what is the applicability of time series data after detrending? In this situation, detrending the rates does not advance the research. In time series modeling, detrending is used to make data stationary, which is an important assumption in time series modeling. Menard (1990) argued that time series modeling requires 50 or more observations (Box & Jenkins, 1970; McCleary, Hay, Meidinger, & McDowall, 1980), and only 17 years of data were available. Menard (1990) strongly opposed the idea of using time series analysis for the NCS data and argued that the use of detrending in time series modeling, especially in ARIMA, has mathematical but not substantive meaning.

Blumstein et al. (1991) reported a strong consistency between the UCR and NCS robbery and burglary data and concluded that both of the series measure the same crime phenomena. Blumstein et al. (1991) also argued that the previous studies had generally used trends in the analysis and ignored the deviation. Ignoring the deviation or misunderstanding the meaning of trend deviation has serious consequences in understanding the convergence. Menard (1992) commented on the findings of Blumstein et al. (1991) and argued that Blumstein and his colleague had exaggerated the convergence and understated the divergence between the two series. Menard further argued that the use of first differencing is a more acceptable method of detrending time series data than using residual gain scores. The use of residual gain scores as a deviation from the trend is done by Blumstein et al., assuming the linearity of the relationship; however, the trends in the UCR and NCS rates are not linear except for the case of burglary. Menard also pointed out that selection of the two offenses—robbery and burglary—may have been done deliberately to make a strong case of the convergence between the two series because these two offenses converge more than any of the others do.

Menard (1992) suggested using test-retest or Cronbach's alpha to establish reliability of the correlations between the two measures. A reliability score of less than .8 would mean that the two series do not measure the same phenomenon. Except for motor vehicle theft, the correlations are well below the limit of .8 for all other crimes, including robbery and burglary, which show greater correlation than aggravated assault, rape, simple assault, and theft. In short, the results presented by Blumstein et al. (1991) did not support the use of the UCR and NCVS as measures of the single underlying phenomenon (Menard, 1992). Blumstein et al. (1992), while replying to Menard's comment on Blumstein et al. (1991), argued that Menard's assessment was narrow and based on minor technical issues. He further argued that the efforts of Blumstein et al. (1991) were focused on reconciling and providing an argument that the two series measure the same underlying phenomenon of crime with different measurement processes. Blumstein et al. (1992) replied systematically to all issues raised by Menard, but the core augment was that both of the series measure the same phenomenon with different processes and some degree of imperfection, both lack complete validity, and both are required for different research and policy purposes; in same, measures are complementary.

McDowell and Loftin (1992), who entered the debate to introduce some moderation, argued that the controversy over the convergence is inevitable largely because of the extremely limited years of time series data available, causing them to lack variability and have autocorrelation problems even after detrending. They evaluated the findings of Menard and Covey (1988) and Blumstein et al. (1991) and argued in favor of studying and accepting the differences noted as complementary (Biderman et al., 1991) rather than making artificial adjustment to minimize differences. They also cautioned about using the methods of differencing and controlling time for detrending the data because they had great effects on the results.

Meaning of Convergence

The concept of convergence must be understood in this context because several scholars have conceptualized and explained convergence in somewhat different ways. One way to define *convergence* is as the crossing of two trend lines. In case of the UCR and victimization survey series, when UCR and NCVS rates with or without adjustment cross each other they converge. This definition of convergence is used in the field by the researchers comparing different related series, such as trends in male and female crimes (Austin, 1993). However, some researchers (e.g., O'Brien, 1999) did not accept this definition of convergence because it is not only difficult but also impossible for the two lines representing male and female crime to cross. O'Brien (1999), while comparing male and female crimes, accepted the definition of *relative convergence*. According to the definition of relative convergence, the ratio of two lines remains constant over time. If the two series are not moving away from each other over time, the null hypothesis of no convergence or divergence may be rejected. If the series are moving together they converge, and if they are moving apart they diverge. Furthermore, O'Brien (1999) defined *convergence* as the cointegration of the two data series.

A comprehensive discussion on the meaning of convergence was presented in McDowell and Loftin (2007), who explicated four different definitions of convergence found in the literature and discussed each one in detail. Convergence has been seen as identical rates, as identical rates after adjustment, as correlated rates, and as long-term equilibrium. Convergence as identical rates is the most stringent of all, and convergence as long-term equilibriums and convergence as identical rates after the adjustments are the least demanding (McDowell & Loftin, 2007). Convergence as correlated rates is generally considered the most acceptable definition and is less demanding than convergence as identical rates but more demanding than the other two definitions. McDowell and Loftin, (2007) provided discussion on the merits and problems associated with the different definitions and used convergence as long-term equilibrium in their study for exploring the convergence between the two series (McDowell & Loftin, 1882; McDowell & Loftin, 2007).

All definitions of convergence have problems of practical significance. The first definition of convergence is too stringent, and in view of specificity and differences involved with the two series this definition is clearly unrealistic. However, convergence as identical rates after adjustments and convergence as long-term equilibrium are the least demanding definitions and may become overly fuzzy and lose their practical significance (McDowell & Loftin, 2007).

Convergence as correlated rates has been the most popular definition to use with cross-sectional and time-series data. The first problem associated with this definition is the issue of detrending and differencing, especially when time-series data are used. The second problem is the threshold of correlation coefficient for determining whether the two series are converging. Since convergence as correlated rates has been the most popular definition of convergence, it would be helpful to see how some of the important research that adopted the correlational definition has used this definition for exploring convergence, and to determine what conclusions have been drawn as a consequence. Studies using the correlated rates definition of convergence have used cross-sectional and time-series data for comparing the rates of different aggregated and disaggregated crime categories of the UCR and NCVS (McDowell & Loftin, 2007).

Cross-sectional studies:

The earlier studies that adopted the correlated rates definition for exploring convergence and used cross-sectional data yielded rather inconsistent results. Almost all of them used the 26 City Victimization Survey data (Booth et al., 1977; Cohen & Land, 1984; Decker, 1977; Gove et al., 1985; Nelson, 1980; O'Brien et al., 1980; Skogan, 1974). The Central City Household Surveys that were conducted in 1972 and 1975 were designed to collect victimization information on selected crimes in 26 cities.

Although using the UCR and victimization survey data for cross-sectional comparison between different geographic areas has been considered valid and useful (Skogan, 1974), all correlational convergence studies are not free of analytical problems. First, they produced inconsistent results. Second, they used different crime categories that inhibit comparison between the results of the different studies. Third, the conclusions about the comparability between the UCR and victimization survey by studies based on the 26 cities survey data were not valid as the 26 City Victimization Survey used a one-year reference period and lacked the bounding process. Finally, as McDowell and Loftin (2007) pointed out, the UCR measures crimes that occurred in a particular geographic area whereas the victimization survey measures crimes reported by people from a geographic area.

Time series studies:

The other set of studies that adopted correlated rates definition of convergence used time-series data of the UCR and NCS/NCVS (Biderman et al., 1991; Blumstein, et al., 1991, 1992; Menard, 1991, 1992; Menard & Covey, 1988; McDowell & Loftin, 1992, 2007; O'Brien, 1990, 1991, 1996, 1999; Biderman et al. 1991; Steffensmeier, Zhong, Ackerman, Schwartz, & Agha, 2006). The severe limitation of these studies, especially the earlier ones, is that they used less than an adequate number of years of data for time-series analysis. However, the results between the earlier studies which used few years of the data and recent studies which used longer series are not very different (McDowell & Loftin, 2007).

Different studies have used different definitions of *convergence*, and most of the definitions are correlational. Studies have used cross-sectional and time-series data and estimated correlational coefficients in order to determine whether the two series were converging. Several studies using time-series data have used differencing or time control, first, and detrended the data before calculating correlation coefficients and assessing the convergence between the two data series (e.g., Biderman et al., 1991; Blumstein et al., 1991, 1992; McDowell & Loftin, 1992, 2007; O'Brien, 1990, 1991, 1996, 1999; Steffensmeier, et al., 2006). However, some studies have opposed the idea of detrending the time series before estimating the correlations between the two data series (Menard, 1991, 1992; Menard & Covey, 1988). Menard (1991), while commenting on O'Brien (1990), asked a question: "What does convergence mean after detrending of the data?" If the trend is removed, then it may not be possible to see whether the two series—the UCR and NCVS—have identical long-term trends.

Bernard and Durlauf (1995), while explaining the convergence of per capita output between 15 OECD countries, provided a time-series definition of convergence and common trends. According to their definition of convergence, "Countries i and j converge if the long-term forecasts of output for both countries are equal at a fixed time t" (p. 99). According to this definition of convergence, two time series will be said to be converging if their differences tend to be zero as the forecasting horizon tends to infinity. Oxley and Greasley (1995) developed the time-series definition of convergence of Bernard and Durlauf and came up with the definitions of *catching-up* and *long run convergence*. According to the catching up definition of Oxley and Greasley (1995), if the UCR and NCVS are two time series, i and j, and their log crime rate is denoted as y_i and y_j, then catching up would imply the absence of a unit root in their difference y_i - y_j. Long run convergence, which is more demanding than catching up, implies the absence of a unit root in their difference y_i - y_j and the absence of a time trend in their deterministic process.

Another time series definition of convergence that is often used in the discipline is convergence as long-term equilibrium. Cointegration analysis of time series is employed to test the convergence as long-term equilibrium. McDowell and Loftin (2007) used the definition of long-term equilibrium-based convergence and performed cointegration analyses between UCR and NCVS rates for rape, robbery, assault, burglary, motor vehicle theft, and larceny theft. They rejected the null hypothesis of no cointegration for all categories except robbery. O'Brien (1999) performed cointegration analysis between men and women crime rates for homicide, robbery, aggravated assault, burglary, larceny, and motor vehicle theft and reported no cointegration between men and women crime rates for any of the crime categories.

The preceding discussion on the definition of convergence between the UCR and NCVS informs us that convergence as correlated rates has been the most frequently adopted definition of convergence used in the literature to explore the convergence between the UCR and NCVS. The correlated rates definition of convergence, however, has serious conceptual and methodological limitations for understanding the convergence between the two time series. The present study, in view of the above discussion, uses a combination of methods for exploring the convergence of the two UCR and NCVS data series. A detailed description of the methods used to explore the convergence of the UCR and NCVS data series is provided in Chapter 5.

FACTORS LEADING TO THE CONVERGENCE BETWEEN THE UCR AND NCVS

Perhaps the easiest way to understand the factors leading to the convergence between the two series is to look into the factors responsible for the divergence in the first place, and then to see how the causes of divergence have changed over time and brought the two series closer to each other. From the beginning in 1973, the NCS reported more than twice the numbers that the UCR did on almost every category of index crime (Catalano, 2006; Skogan, 1974). However, the discrepancy between the two series became reduced substantially over time. The UCR and NCVS ratio for aggregated total crimes of aggravated assault, robbery, burglary, motor vehicle theft, and larceny theft was 1:3.87 in 1973 and became 1:1.72 in 2007. Because the divergence was attributed to the two major factors—reporting and recording of crime at the level of the police and uniqueness and specificity of measurement—the explanation of the convergence will be best understood by examining the changes in reporting crime to police, recording and reporting practices of police, and methodological changes in the UCR and NCVS (Biderman et al., 1991). Changes in the overall household surveys, including response rate and use of information technology, are other factors that may be responsible for the changes in the NCVS.

The convergence between the two series is a result of changes both in the UCR program and the victimization survey. The changes in the UCR crime rates have occurred largely because of changes in police reporting and notification of crimes, which are affected by several institutional, organizational, and procedural factors (O'Brien, 1996). The victimization survey data have gone through substantial changes in these years because of methodological changes, maturation, and format changes in the household surveys and responses. The divergence between the two series arise from the fact that a large number of crimes that are likely to be less serious are not reported to police and the two series measure the problem of crime differently. Thus, it is hypothesized that the convergence between the two series is a function of increased police productivity, changes in reporting by people, and changes in the process of crime measurement (Catalano, 2006, 2007; O'Brien, 1999). The factor of increased police productivity and changes in reporting by citizens are limited to the changes in the UCR data and the percentage of reported crime data in the NCVS, while changes in measurement processes have affected both of the UCR and NCVS.

Police Productivity

Police productivity, in this specific context, related to the reporting and recording of crime (O'Brien, 1999). Reporting and recording of crime by police depend on how often victims report to the police and how readily police record crimes reported to them (Langan & Farrington, 1998). Reporting of crime to police by citizens again depends on several factors. Calculation of cost benefits of reporting, seriousness of the offense, fear of reprisal, attitude toward police, privacy issues, desire to protect others, desire to protect the offender from legal punishment, demographic characteristics of the victim, victim-offender relations, neighborhood characteristics, level of community policing, third-party reporting, and self-help are some of the important determinants which influence the decisions of victims to report crime to the police (Felson et al., 2002; Gottfredson & Gottfredson, 1988; Goudriaan et al., 2005; Skogan, 1984).

The second aspect of police productivity is related to the recording and notification of crime by police. Black (1970) reported that the production of crime rate by the police is determined by their reporting, and reporting in turn is influenced by the legal seriousness of crimes, complainants' preferences, rational distance between offenders and victims, and complainants' deference to police. Police reporting and recording of crime is influenced by a series of internal and external factors. Internal organizational factors which affect the reporting of police are related to changes in police professionalization, changes in the demographic characteristics of a police force, use of technology, and changes in police responses to certain social issues such as domestic disturbances and hate crime. Langan and Farrington (1988) concluded that police now record more crime than ever, and the factors responsible for the increased level of recording are developed professionalization in the police, computer use, electronic reporting, increased response of police to certain issues such as domestic violence, and the growing threat of civil suits and tort claims against the police.

While discussing the increase of violent crime rates between 1973 and 1992, as measured by the UCR, O'Brien (1999) argued that the increase in the violent crime rate in the UCR is not because of the actual increase in crime, but rather because of the increased police productivity which he defined as the systematic recording and reporting of crime. His police productivity thesis was supported by two facts. First, homicide remains almost stable and second, the UCR and NCVS show different trends for rape. If the changes in violent crime for the period can be attributed to a real crime increase, then the homicide rate, which is least affected by the recording and reporting process, should also increase. Similarly, rape should show a similar trend between the UCR and NCVS. On the basis of this evidence, O'Brien (1999) argued that the upward trend in violent crime between 1973 and 1992 is not because of an increase in crime but because of an increase in police productivity. The increase in police productivity was achieved by improvement in police record keeping and computerization; increase in the number of police officers per 100,000 in the population; increase in the number of civilians in police special units, such as domestic violence unit; an increase in participation of local police agencies in the UCR; and an increase of people involved in dispatching and record keeping.

Thus, a clear and linear relationship between police reporting and recording of crime and organizational and technological changes in police departments can be hypothesized. Increase in the police-public ratio is one of the most important organizational changes in the police that predict an increased rate of crime reporting and recording. Levitt (1998) tested the thesis of reporting bias and concluded that each additional officer is associated with an increase of roughly five index crimes because victims are more likely to report crime when they perceive a strong likelihood of a crime being solved. Ready availability of a police officer near a crime scene also increases reporting. Furthermore, Marvell and Moody (1996) presented a detailed review of studies that had examined the relationship between police and crime. The review of literature presented in the study showed that 29 out of 36 studies examining the relationship between the number of police officers and crime had reported a significant positive relationship. The results of the study also supported the findings of the majority of the studies done in this area and found that crime reporting increased with the number of police officers. Total expenditure on police is another important component of police productivity. A continuous overall growth and growth in the percent of total state and local budget may give an indication that the resources are being provided to increase police professionalization and police productivity.

The number of civilians and patrol officers in police departments is another personnel characteristic that affects reporting and recording by police (Catalano, 2006; O'Brien, 1999). Patrol officers are known as the backbone of the police force, and most reporting and arrests are done by patrol officers. Increasing the number of patrol officers is likely to increase police reporting of crime. The main reasons for using civilians in the police are to bring specialized skills and to free patrol officers for field duties. Increasing the number of civilians in the police force is also likely to increase reporting and recording of crimes and bring expertise in dealing with computers and data management.

The demographic composition of a police force is also hypothesized to have an effect on reporting and recording by police. A more representative police force is likely to have better relations with the community. The problem of the relationship between police and a minority community and the problem of language barriers may stop people from reporting victimization. A diverse and representative police force is assumed to develop a better police-community relationship and reduce the language barrier, thereby encouraging people to report. Finally, education and training are the other personnel characteristics of the police department that may improve reporting and recording. Better educated and better trained police officers are more likely to be comfortable with report writing and dealing with computers and data archives.

Technological development, especially the use of computers by police, has had a great impact on police productivity (O'Brien, 1999). Computerization is helping police in many ways, such as crime mapping, crime analysis, record maintenance and access, dispatching, and reporting. Computer-aided dispatch (CAD), mobile computers, online incident reporting, and remote access to the data are the most important features of computerization that are directly helping in the reporting and recording of crime. Computer-aided dispatch is helpful in transmitting accurate information to the patrol officers. Remote access to the data through the network may have positive effects on discovering and reporting crimes, although it is not possible in the absence of mobile computers. The use of mobile computers or portable computers mounted in a vehicle is an important development and is required for computer-aided dispatch and access to the data system stored in the hard drive or available on the network. Reporting an incident online minimizes the time gap between the occurrence of an incident and the reporting and brings effective and quick follow-up by police supervisors.

Among the factors responsible for increased police productivity, institutional changes are important. Domestic violence legislation and mandatory arrest policies for police departments, coupled with the creation of special domestic violence units, can be assumed to have an effect on the cases of assault and aggravated assault reported to police (Catalano, 2006; Dugan, Nagin, & Rosenfeld, 2003).

Population Characteristics

Demography is another determinant of reporting (Skogan, 1984). The changing demographic composition of the U.S. may explain some of the divergence between the two series. Females are more likely to report than males. Older people are more likely to report crimes to police than are younger people. Blacks are more likely to report than are Whites. Well educated people are also more likely report to police than poorly educate dpeople. There is no evidence available, but it is assumed that Hispanics are less likely to report mainly because of language difficulties and immigration issues. The demographic composition of the U.S. population, therefore, is hypothesized to be an important factor in changing police productivity by affecting the reporting of crime to police.

Changes in Measurement

The process of measurement is an important factor, and changes in methods of recording, counting, and categorizing are likely to affect the convergence between the two series (Catalano, 2006; Rand & Rennison, 2002). As far as the UCR is concerned, the number of state UCR programs and yearly participation of law enforcement agencies in the UCR program may affect the estimates of total crimes in the program. However, changes in methodology are more important in regards to the NCVS because the NCVS is a household survey that is continuously changing and growing. Changes in overall survey technology and response rates have effects on all surveys. The NCVS has been affected by these universal changes as well as changes from within. The NCVS has continuously incorporated changes in the methods of data collection, but the most important changes in the NCVS survey methodology occurred in 1992. These changes were known to be rate-affecting changes because they brought statistically significant changes in the estimates of all crimes except robbery and motor vehicle theft.

Attitudes of People toward Crime and Police

The attitudes people have toward crime and the police are important determinants of crime being reported to the police, and people's attitudes are influenced and changed by social changes in American life (Baumer & Lauritsen, 2010). Citizen's attitudes toward crime are reflected in public punitiveness and fear of crime. The growing population of prison inmates and strong support for tough crime policies may be seen as indications of a growing punitiveness and, to some extent, fear of crime. Fear of crime is difficult to measure and is affected by the larger environment. A change in fear of crime changes the reporting of crime by people and notification by police (Baumer & Lauritsen, 2010). In terms of people's attitudes toward police, although not playing an important role, mutual hostility stops people from going to police (Skogan, 1984). Attitude toward police plays an important role in calling police. People in some inner city neighborhoods believe in taking care of themselves rather than calling police because they feel that police are not interested in providing protection and they do not trust police (Anderson, 1999). The community policing approach, which focuses on building partnerships and solving problems, is primarily a trust-building exercise. Trust building by police increases the legitimacy of police, and people develop confidence in the ability of police to solve problems and be impartial. This resulting trust is likely to increase reporting of crime to police.

Mobile Phone Use

The use and popularity of cell phones has changed the way people communicate and report crimes to police. Cell phone technology has changed communication in several ways. The numbers of traditional landline phones were limited by the number of households, to some extent, while cell phones have removed that limitation because its use is based on individuals rather than households. More cell phone use is likely to produce higher connectivity and more frequent communication that may have positive effects on calling 911 and reporting crime to police. Second, the use of cell phones has solved the problem of spatial limitation. One does not have to look for a telephone box or landline phone in order to make a call and report a crime to the police. This change is especially true in the case of bystanders and witnesses calling and reporting crimes to police. It is, therefore, assumed, that cell phone usage, by increasing the number of phone connections and removing the spatial limitation of making calls, has changed the communication between citizens and the police and affected the reporting of crime positively. However, many people switched from easy-to-locate home phones to the more convenient cell phones. According to an estimate, more than 60% of the calls to local 911 centers now come from cellular phones (Mullins, 2008). It will be interesting to see the effects of cell phone usage by citizens reporting crime to the police in the data series.

Figure 3.1. Convergence between the UCR and NCVS

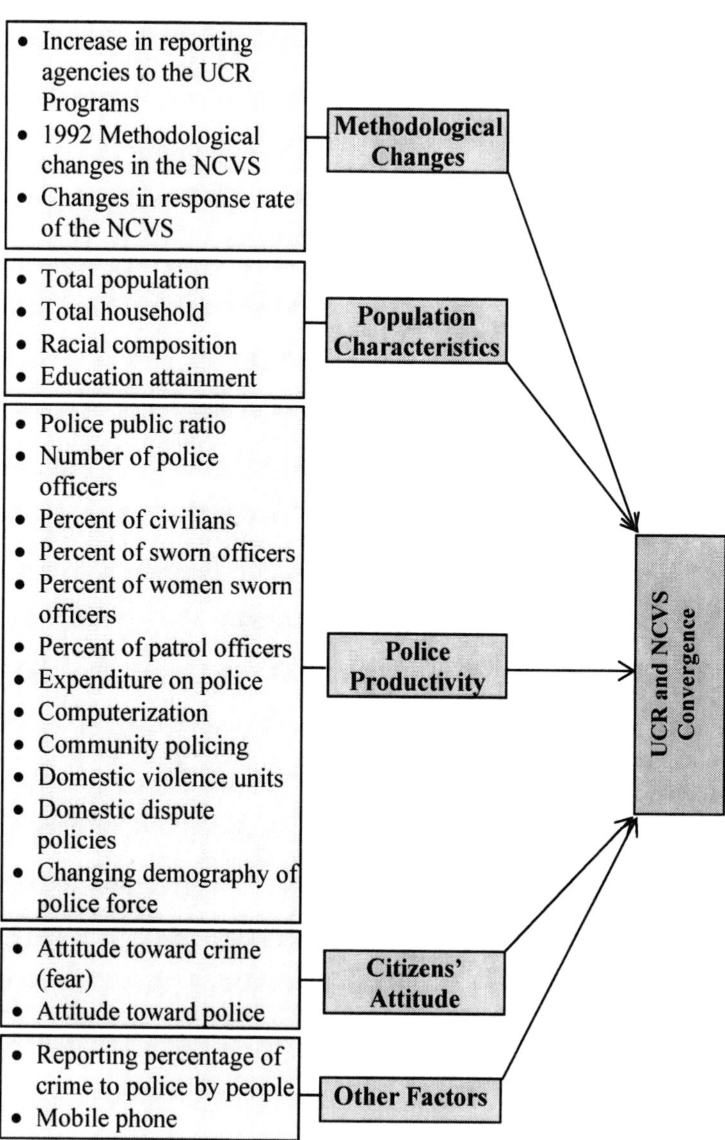

The potential factors for reducing the discrepancies between the two series, as indicated in the preceding discussion, are many and arise from social, organizational, and technological sources. The discrepancies between the two series have been reduced by the increase in the UCR and decrease in the NCVS rates. The UCR rates may increase because of an increase in crime and increase in reporting of crime to police, as well as police notification and recording process for crimes. The NCVS, on the other hand, is a national sample survey and more sensitive to the changes in the methods of data collection. Therefore, it is hypothesized that increased police productivity, change in people's attitude toward crime and police, demographic characteristics of the population, changes in the process of measurement, and changes in communication technology, especially mobile phone use, are the factors potentially responsible for the convergence of the two data series, as shown in Figure 3.1.

RESEARCH HYPOTHESES

A review of the literature on the convergence between the UCR and NCVS shows that the studies exploring and explaining the convergence between the two series have produced different and sometimes conflicting results. Studies have generally reported convergence between the two series, but some of the studies have reported a complete lack of convergence. Furthermore, the studies reporting convergence have reported different results for different categories of crime. The differences in results in the studies are largely due to the use of different methods by different studies. The studies have used either total crime or rate per 100,000 population. The studies using rates have either depended on the rates provided by the programs, which used different denominators, or calculated their own rates using common denominators for the UCR and NCVS rates. More importantly, the studies have used different definitions of convergence and different statistical techniques to explore and explain the convergence. Debates on the definition of *convergence* and the methodology are still not resolved. In view of the continuing debates and different and conflicting results, the first purpose of the present research is to explore the convergence between the two series and to see whether the discrepancies between the two series have decreased significantly and whether the series have shown convergence in recent years.

The discrepancies between the two series have apparently decreased over time because of an increase in UCR rates and a decrease in NCVS rates. The studies investigating the convergence between the two series, however, have reported that the increase in UCR rates has been responsible for the convergence between the two series, at least prior to early 1990s. Increasing crimes as well as reporting crimes to police may have been responsible in increasing crime rates reported by the UCR program. The percentage of crimes reported by people, as estimated by the NCVS, has consistently improved over time. Thus, it can be inferred that improvement in reporting crimes to police is also a responsible factor along with increase in crime for the increased UCR crime rates reported by the law enforcement agencies. What changes in the relationship between the UCR and NCVS, in terms of convergence, are expected if UCR rates are adjusted for the increased reporting of crimes to police?

Studies explaining the convergence between the two series have used an array of explanatory variables and reported somewhat different results. The initial convergence, as reported by the studies, took place because of significant increase in UCR rates, but after methodological changes in 1992, the NCVS rates have shown continuous decrease, and the discrepancies between the two series decreased because of decreases in NCVS rates and increases in UCR rates. Variables related with population changes; demographic characteristics; police, institutional, and legal mechanisms; methodological changes in the UCR and NCVS; and public attitude have been used to explain the changes in UCR and NCVS rates responsible for convergence.

The literature review provided in Chapter 2 and, especially, in Chapter 3, helped in developing formal research hypotheses for addressing the research questions. The following hypotheses were developed and are tested through the data analyses set forth in Chapter 5 and Chapter 6.

Q1: Has the discrepancy between the UCR and NCVS data series significantly decreased so that the two series are in the process of converging?

H_1: The UCR and NCVS data series will have come closer to each other, moving toward convergence during the period of 1973-2008.

Researchers have continuously reported positively concerning convergence between the two series, and the two series appeared to have decreased in their discrepancies over time.

H_2: The UCR and NCVS data series display different levels of convergence for different aggregated and disaggregated categories of crime. Reporting of different crimes to police and notification of crimes by police are different depending on such factors as seriousness, victim offender relations, and attitudes of people toward crime and police.

H_3: Aggregated and disaggregated categories of violent crime should show stronger convergence than property crime categories. Violent crimes are considered more serious than property crime, and improvements in police practice in terms of recording and reporting crimes to the UCR are more likely to improve the measurement of violent crimes. Similarly, improvements in design of the NCVS were more successful in improving measurements of violent crime categories such as aggravated assault. Violent crime categories, therefore, are more likely to decrease the discrepancies between the UCR and NCVS.

Q2. Does the adjustment of UCR rates for the reporting of crimes to police, as estimated by the NCVS, affect the convergence of the two series?

H_4: Adjusted UCR rates for the reporting of crimes to police and NCVS rates for different crime categories are likely to show different levels of convergence. UCR rates primarily depend on the reporting of crime to police by citizens, which is perhaps the most important reason for the discrepancies between the two series. Reporting percentages estimated by the NCVS show substantial improvement and variability.

Q3. What factors have changed the UCR and NCVS rates substantially and have been responsible for the convergence of the UCR and NCVS data series?

H_5: Changes in population and demographic characteristic are likely to have affected the convergence of the UCR and NCVS data series. Changing demography in terms of racial composition is likely to affect the reporting of crime, and improvement in educational attainment is likely to improve reporting of crime to police, thus improving convergence between the two series.

H_6: Police productivity should positively affect the convergence of the UCR and NCVS data series. Police productivity consists of several organizational and technological factors and is likely to increase police reporting and recording of crime, thus increasing UCR rates and reducing the discrepancies between the UCR and NCVS.[9]

H_7: Citizens' attitudes toward crime and the police should positively affect the convergence of the UCR and NCVS data series. Attitudes toward crime can be measured in terms of fear of crime, which is likely to affect the reporting of crime to police. Trust in police is another dimension of citizens' attitude that affects the reporting of crime to police.

H_8: Changes in measurement procedures, especially in the NCVS, should positively affect the convergence of the UCR and NCVS data series, especially after 1993.[10]

---

[9] Police productivity hypothesis (O. Brien, 1999) argues that the convergence between the two series was largely, at least in the initial years, facilitated by the increase in UCR rates and increase in UCR rates was primarily caused by increase in police productivity rather than increase in crime. Police productivity is a sum of increase and development in crime reporting and recording practices of police. The factors responsible for increased police productivity include but are not limited to changes in employment; demographic composition of employees; civilianization; per capita police officers and per capita expense of police; technological development, such as computerization, data management tools, mobile computer, and computer-aided dispatch; changes in operational strategies, such as community policing and domestic violence specialized units; and institutional changes, such as mandatory arrest policies. These factors are reported to increase the efficiency of police reporting and recording of crimes by law enforcements.

[10] Both of the data collection programs have gone through the process of maturation and development and incorporated several methodological changes of defining, collecting, classifying, and reporting crime rates. Increase in the state UCR programs and reporting agencies have certainly improved the estimate of UCR rates. Rates affecting changes of the NCVS have brought significant changes in the estimation of victimization after 1993. These methodological changes in the UCR and NCVS have shown positive relationships with continuously decreasing discrepancies between the two series.

SUMMARY

The review of the relevant literature in this chapter is focused on the results and methodology of exploring and explaining the divergence and convergence between the UCR and NCVS data series. This review was conducted to develop the theoretical and methodological understanding in order to undertake the present research that seeks to explore and explain the convergence between the UCR and NCVS data series.

The official crime rates published by the UCR were always suspected of being far below the actual magnitude of crime committed, and that concern was addressed by the Presidential Commission on Law Enforcement and Administration of Justice of 1965 which sponsored the three-city victimization surveys as pilot studies to estimate the discrepancies between the official crime rates and actual victimization and to explore the feasibility of implementing a national victimization survey. The city surveys reported a crime rate more than twice as high as that of the UCR (Biderman, 1967), so the national victimization survey NCS came into existence, which revealed a huge dark figure of crime in the UCR by reporting substantial discrepancies between the UCR and NCS data series. The discrepancies intrigued policy makers, law enforcement officials, and researchers alike. Efforts were undertaken to explain the divergence between the two data series, and discrepancies were generally attributed to the procedural uniqueness and specificity of the two data collection processes because they used different data-collection methods to measure overlapping but nonidentical sets of offences for overlapping but nonidentical populations (Rand & Rennison, 2002).

The most important reason for the divergence is non-reporting of a huge number of crimes, especially less serious crimes, to police. The NCVS, a household survey, estimates total victimizations reported by the respondents, whereas the UCR reports only crime known to police. Other important factors causing the divergence are the different populations covered by the two data-collection programs, use of different counting and categorizing protocols, sampling and non-sampling error of the NCVS, and issues such as the series victimization protocol of the NCVS and unfounding of crimes by police.

The divergence raised the issue of validity for both of the data series. If both of the data series measure the same phenomena, then why are they so divergent, and which one is more valid? Researchers took two different views on the issue. Some researchers argued that both of the series measure the same phenomena and the divergence could be attributed to the procedural differences between them. Others refused to attribute such a huge divergence to the procedural differences and argued that the two sets do not measure the same phenomena. The first group of researchers supported their argument by providing evidence of convergence between the two series, but the second group of researchers questioned the methods of testing convergence and provided evidence against the convergence, leading to a debate on methodology for testing the convergence hypothesis. Initial studies used cross-sectional data and used correlation coefficients to argue in favor of the convergence. Later studies began using time-series data and time-series analysis for studying the convergence between the two series. Different methods of detrending were employed, but the analyses remained focused on estimating correlations. Few studies have used the time-series technique of cointegration, but the limitation of the number of years of data available probably discouraged people from using time-series modeling for testing the convergence.

The series have apparently come closer, and the discrepancies have decreased substantially over the past 36 years. Studies have attempted to provide explanations for the process of convergence between the two series. The initial convergence primarily occurred because of the increase in the UCR rates after 1973, but the convergence after 1993 is generally attributed to the sharp decrease in the victimization estimates of the NCVS. These phenomena have been explored, and several responsible factors, especially for the increase in the UCR, were identified. These factors include development of police productivity, changed demography of police employment, changed population characteristics, community policing, changing attitudes of people toward crime and police, changes in technology and communication, and changes in the methods of data collection by the UCR and NCVS.

The review of the literature set forth in this chapter and Chapter 2 helped in developing theoretical and methodological understanding to undertake the study and address the research questions posed. The research hypotheses for the research questions were presented after the review of the literature in the two chapters. Chapter 4 includes a description of the data and methods for testing the hypotheses and addressing the research questions. The results of the convergence test analyses are presented in Chapter 5, and the results of the regression models for explaining the convergence are presented in Chapter 6. The discussion, conclusions, and implications are presented in Chapter 7.

CHAPTER 4

Data, Measurement, and Analytic Strategy

DATA

The present study, in order to address the research questions and test the hypotheses, required two different sets of the data. The first is the time-series data on crime and victimization estimates from the UCR and NCVS, and the second consists of different time-series variables responsible in affecting the relationship between the UCR and NCVS. The data for the study, therefore, are drawn from several sources that include UCR, NCVS, Law Enforcement Management and Administrative Statistics (LEMAS), U.S. Census, General Social Survey (GSS), and *Cellular Telephone Industries Association* (CTIA) - The Wireless Association. Several police-related variables were drawn from the LEMAS data series. Population characteristics, educational attainments, law enforcement employment, and expense for police-related variables are drawn from The U.S. Census Bureau. The variable of reporting crime to the police was drawn from the NCVS, and the variable of reporting agencies to the UCR was drawn from the UCR. Fear of crime, which is used as proxy measure for the attitudes of people toward crime, was drawn from the GSS, and the cell phone connections variable was drawn from the CTIA.

Linear interpolation and extrapolation were used for missing observations in some of the series. Fear of walking at night in the neighborhood and cell phone subscriptions were the two series for which many observations were missing and, thus, were interpolated and extrapolated. Apart from these two, many other variables had one or two missing observations which were interpolated or extrapolated through linear interpolation and extrapolation using commands in the STATA. Details about the data and sources follow.

Uniform Crime Reports

The Uniform Crime Reporting Program is administered by the FBI, and all participating state programs report summary crime data on eight Part I offenses and arrest data on part II offenses in accord with the classification and reporting guidelines of the UCR. The summary data on aggravated assault, robbery, burglary, motor vehicle theft, and larceny theft from 1973 to 2007 are drawn from *Crime in United States* (CIUS), annual reports published by the programs. Apart from the summary data on the six crime categories, data on reporting agencies to the program are also drawn from the CIUS of the UCR program.

National Crime Victimization Survey

BJS publishes "Criminal Victimization in the U.S.," an annual report since 1973 that provides national estimates on criminal victimizations reported by the respondents of the survey. The BJS classifies the data and makes several adjustments to them before they are published. The reports were used to draw victimization data because this study requires only summary data and the reports provided the most valid summary data on criminal victimization. The NCVS collects criminal victimization data on violent and property crimes committed against persons and households. The criminal victimization reports include data on violent crimes (rape or sexual assault, robbery, aggravated assault, and simple assault), property crimes (burglary, motor vehicle theft, and property theft), and personal theft (pocket picking and purse snatching).

The victimization survey has been dynamic, and the 36-year history of the survey is characterized with continuous methodological improvements and changes. Most of the changes are considered non-rate-affecting changes (Rennison & Rand, 2007) focused on improving the validity and cost effectiveness of the survey. However, the rate-affecting changes of 1992 were comprehensive and changed the rates for all categories, affecting convergence with the UCR. In order to make the NCVS comparable with the NCS, BJS adjusted the pre-1992 victimization data.

Adjustment with the pre-1993 victimization data:
The data on victimization prior to the methodological change in 1992 were adjusted using the adjustment ratios provided by the Bureau of Justice Statistics (Rand et al., 1997). The adjustment using NCVS/NCS ratios was applied to only aggravated assault, burglary, and larceny theft because robbery and motor vehicle theft did not show significant differences between pre- and post-1993 victimization rates (Rand, et al., 1997). The ratios of the NCVS/NCS for aggravated assault, burglary, personal larceny and household larceny are 1.23, 1.20, .75, and 1.27.

Census

Data on population, demographic characteristics, educational attainment, law enforcement employment, and expense of police-related variables were drawn from the *Statistical Abstract of the United States*, published by the U.S. Census Bureau since 1878. The *Statistical Abstract of the United States includes data from* the Census Bureau, Bureau of Labor Statistics, Bureau of Economic Analysis, and many other federal agencies and private organizations. It is considered an authoritative and comprehensive summary of statistics on the social, political, and economic organization of the United States. The U.S. Census Bureau provides estimates of residents, civilians, and total population. Estimates of the resident population exclude the U.S. Armed Forces overseas, as well as civilian U.S. citizens whose usual place of residence is outside the United States. For calculating the rates of crime and victimization, residential population estimates are used in the present study.

Law Enforcement Management and Administrative Statistics

Law Enforcement Management and Administrative Statistics is a national survey of law enforcement agencies in the U.S. that began in 1987. The survey is conducted every 3 to 4 years. The survey includes over 3,000 state and local law enforcement agencies, with more than 100 sworn officers and a nationally representative sample of smaller agencies. Data were obtained on the organization and administration of police and sheriffs' departments, including agency responsibilities, operating expenditures, job functions of sworn and civilian employees, officer salaries and special pay, demographic characteristics of officers, weapons and armor policies, education and training requirements, computers and information systems, vehicles, special units, and community policing activities (BJS, 2003). The survey has been conducted in 1987, 1990, 1993, 1997, 1999, 2000, and 2003. Police organizational and operational variables were drawn from all seven LEMAS data series for the current study. The LEMAS data were available only from 1987 to 2003 while this study is using time-series dependent variables from 1973 to 2008. This discrepancy may be problematic in terms of using the LEMAS variables in time-series regression modeling and analysis of convergence between the UCR and NCVS data series.

The General Social Survey

The General Social Survey began in 1972 as the single largest survey for collecting data on social attitudes in the United States. The GSS 1972-2008 cumulative data file that has 5,364 variables was used to draw variables in the study.

Cellular Telephone Industries Association

The first commercial cellular service began on Oct. 13, 1983, in Chicago Illinois and in the Baltimore-Washington area in December 1983 (CTIA, 2009). The data on cell phone subscriptions were drawn from the CTIA survey[11]. CTIA began tracking the number of subscribers in the United States beginning in January of 1985.

---

[11] CTIA, the Wireless Association's semi-annual wireless industry survey, develops industry-wide information drawn from operational member and non-member wireless service providers. It has been conducted since January 1985, originally as a cellular-only survey instrument and now including PCS, ESMR, and AWS types of licensees.

MEASURES

Dependent Variables

Convergence studies have used total number of crimes (Catalano, 2006), raw rates of crimes (Decker, 1977; O'Brien, 1990, 1996), and adjusted rates of crimes (Biderman et al., 1991; Blumstein, 1991; McDowell & Loftin, 2007) as their dependent variables. The studies that used number of crimes rather than crime rate argued that, because the two data collection programs are different and they calculate rates differently, using raw counts rather than rates was more appropriate (Catalano, 2006). The two series are definitely not comparable because of large components of variations specific to them (McDowell & Loftin, 2007); therefore, using rates provided by the two programs are problematic in any convergence study. To mitigate this problem, several studies made possible adjustments to the nominator and denominator of the rate computation formula of both of the series (Biderman et al., 1991; Blumstein et al., 1991; McDowell & Loftin, 2007). The present study adjusted the rates because there are strong differences between the UCR and NCVS in the ways they make their calculations. Using raw count makes less sense because it does not provide opportunity for any adjustment, and raw numbers may be less informative and sometimes difficult to comprehend, especially when comparing the two series and explaining convergence.[12]

This study uses five Part I crimes as well as aggregated violent, property, and total crime categories in the analyses. The five crimes used in the study are aggravated assault, robbery, burglary, motor vehicle theft, and larceny theft. The aggregated category of violent

---

[12] The total UCR crime rate is computed using the following formula: total number of crime/total U.S. residential population x 100,000. The total crime index includes an aggregated value of violent and property crimes as defined in the study and reported annually to the program. Other aggregated crime rate variables—violent crime and property crime—and disaggregated crime rate variables—aggravated assault, robbery, burglary, motor vehicle theft, and larceny theft—are calculated using the same formula.

crime is computed by combining aggravated assault and robbery, and the aggregated category of property crime is computed by combining burglary, motor vehicle theft, and larceny theft. Following are the rationales for using only five Part I crimes and an aggregation of violent and property crimes in the analyses.

<u>Reasons for using only six Part I crimes and aggregated measure crime</u>: Part I crimes are serious, more accurately reported, and recorded by police. Only Part I crime data are reported by the UCR. In the case of Part II crimes, only arrest data are reported.

- The NCVS measures seven crimes that include rape, robbery, aggravated assault, burglary, motor vehicle theft, assault, and simple theft. Aggravated assault, robbery, and assault are violent offenses, and burglary, motor vehicle theft, and simple theft are property offenses.
- Rape, aggravated assault, robbery, burglary, and larceny theft are the only categories that are measured and reported by both of the programs.
- Rape is the only Part I crime that is not included in the study because of measurement problems and inconsistency. The 1992 methodological changes brought significant changes in reporting of rape data; therefore, it was decided not to use rape in the study. Because the purpose of the study was to explore the trends and convergence between the two series over time, inclusion of rape would be problematic given this fundamental change in crime classification for rape.
- Although robbery is an offense described as a property crime as well as violent offence, it is considered violent in this study because violence is considered more serious than loss of property and the perception of seriousness has considerable effects on the reporting and recording of crime. The UCR also classifies robbery as a violent offense, although NCVS classifies robbery as a property offense.
- If robbery as a violent crime shows a different trend of convergence than other violent offenses, the property offense argument can be used and analysis can be presented as to why robbery is unique and different. Although robbery is classified as a

violent crime by the UCR and is treated as a property crime by the NCVS, it is neither a property nor a violent offense in the strict sense of the definitions. Robbery is committed for criminal gains of goods or money and not for the purpose of inflicting injury, but violence is used to achieve the goal of gaining goods or money. If we look at robbery from the aspect of the motive, it can be defined as a property offense because gaining illegitimate property is the sole motive of committing robbery. However, if it is seen from the aspect of the seriousness index, robbery may be defined as a violent crime. Personal violent victimization is considered more serious than the loss of property, and use or threat of violence is the key element of robbery. This is the very reason the UCR defines robbery as a violent crime.

- The UCR uncovers proportionately more nonstranger violent crimes while the victimization survey uncovers more nonstranger crimes and more crimes in general (Menard & Covey, 1988). These results suggest that more property nonstranger crimes are reported by the victimization survey whereas more violent nonstranger crimes are discovered by UCR. This is one of the reasons for the trend of convergence between aggregated crimes of property and violence.
- It is hypothesized that convergence between the violent and property crimes will show different patterns. Furthermore, the convergence between the two series may have different explanations for the categories of violent and property offenses. This assumption is based on the fact that property crimes are defined, reported, and recorded differently than violent crimes because property crimes are generally committed by strangers and perceived to be less serious.
- Apart from reporting and recording, certain correlates of property crimes may not be significantly correlated with violent crime, and that may have an effect on long-term trends. Evidence is available that the public's economic perceptions and consumer confidence have a significant effect on property crime rates, including robbery (Blumstein & Rosenfeld, 2008; Rosenfeld & Fornango, 2007).
- Many crimes, especially robbery, burglary and motor vehicle theft, are not compatible in the two series, but they are used in this study because the study did not compare different categories of offenses

between the two series cross sectionally. The study sought to understand the **trend** of violent and property crimes over the period of 36 years, and differences between the measurements of different crimes in the two series remain constant over that period.

The preceding discussion provides the rationales for using five disaggregated Part I crimes for the convergence analysis. The discussion also provides justification for not using rape, considering robbery as a violent crime, and using the aggregated violent and property crime categories.

<u>Reasons for using an aggregated category of property crime</u>:
Violent crimes in the UCR and NCVS are commonly considered to feature fewer measurement issues than property crimes. Validity of the measurement of property crimes is challenging, and probably because of the measurement and validity issues involved prior, studies have primarily focused on violent crimes in convergence studies. Only burglary and motor vehicle theft categories of property crimes have been used in prior studies because they are frequently reported and have fewer measurement issues in comparison with larceny theft. The present study used larceny theft in addition to burglary and motor vehicle theft and an aggregated category of property crimes. The following discussion provides the rationales for using larceny theft and an aggregated category of property crimes.

- Property crimes are more difficult to discover and investigate because they are generally committed by strangers, and except for pocket picking and purse snatching there is generally no contact between a victim and an offender.
- They are less likely to be reported by people and discovered by police in comparison with the reporting and discovery of violent crimes.
- All studies examining the convergence of the two series have generally focused on serious violent crimes and ignored nonserious property crimes because of the ambiguity involved in defining, reporting, and recording such crimes. The present study fills the gap in the literature in an effort to determine whether the two series behave differently when compared for violent and property crimes.

The problem of ambiguity related to property offenses, especially less serious offenses, may not have affected the results of the analyses because these factors remain constant in the time-series data of the UCR and NCVS.

- The most important reason for not using property crime, most notably larceny theft, is the difficulty in differentiating crime against commercial and business establishments in the UCR (Biderman et al., 1991). However, the current study used larceny theft and the aggregated category of violent crimes that include larceny theft for the following reasons. First, the purpose of the study is to explore and explain the convergence between the two crime series using time-series data from 1973 to 2008. The ambiguity in measurements of larceny theft by the UCR and NCVS and the problem of the identification of larceny theft committed in commercial and business establishments are constant factors. In cross-sectional analysis, these difficulties in measurement and comparability may seriously affect the findings, but in time-series analyses they will not have substantial effects. Second, prior studies have excluded larceny theft, although this crime category contributes more than 50% to the total Part I crimes in the UCR (Biderman et al., 1991). Thus, when the general population compares the two series for overall crime, the larceny theft category plays the most important role in determining the relationship between the two series and affecting the perception of people. Third, if the disaggregated categories of motor vehicle theft and burglary have been continuously used, despite the ambiguity, in identifying household and commercial crimes, then larceny theft can and should be used as well.

Independent Variables

This study explored and used several predictor variables in the time-series regression models to explain the convergence between the UCR and NCVS data series. The first set of the variables is population and such relevant demographic characteristics as age, sex, race, and educational attainment which are likely to affect reporting of crime to police. The second set of variables is related to the police productivity phenomenon that is affected by several organizational and technological factors in police operations (Catalano, 2006; O'Brien, 1996). The third set of variables comes from the methodological changes in the victimization survey and the UCR. The fourth set of variables concerns the attitudes of people, especially attitudes toward crime and police that may affect reporting of crime to police (Catalano, 2006). Finally, some other variables, such as the number of mobile phone subscriptions and reporting percentages of crimes to police, were included in the study. Descriptions of the dependent and explanatory variables explored and used in the study are provided in Appendix B.

DESCRIPTIVE STATISTICS

Descriptive statistics of all dependent variables and independent variables used in the analyses are presented in Tables 4.1 and 4.2. An examination of the descriptive statistics of UCR rates shows a wide variability across all categories. UCR burglary rates show the highest variability, followed by UCR aggravated assault and UCR robbery rates. UCR larceny rates show the least amount of variability, followed by UCR motor vehicle theft rates. The variability among aggregated categories of violent crime, property crime, and total crime is higher than the variability in larceny theft and lower than UCR burglary, UCR aggravated assault, and UCR robbery rates. The variability of the UCR violent rate is, however, higher than the variability in UCR property and total crime rates.

NCVS rates have shown continuous decrease overall, whereas UCR rates show increase until the beginning of the 1990s, and then continuous decrease. The pattern of variability in NCVS rates is similar to the pattern of variability in UCR rates. The NCVS burglary rate, as with the UCR burglary rate, shows the highest variability, followed by NCVS aggravated assault and NCVS robbery rates. Similarly, NCVS motor vehicle theft and NCVS larceny theft rates show comparatively lower levels of variability, but unlike UCR larceny theft NCVS larceny theft does not show the lowest variability. In the case of NCVS, motor vehicle theft and larceny theft show similar variability, whereas variability in the UCR larceny theft rate is lower than the variability in the UCR motor vehicle theft rate. Another difference between the UCR and NCVS is that all three aggregated categories—violent, property, and total crime—show similar variability in the NCVS while the UCR violent rate shows substantially higher variability than UCR property and UCR total crime rates.

Table 4.1. Descriptive Statistics of the Dependent Variables

Variable	*N*	Mean	*SD*	Minimum	Maximum
UCR aggravated assault rate*	36	322.48	67.08	198.36	441.90
UCR robbery rate	36	200.13	41.68	136.71	272.74
UCR burglary rate	36	1123.64	310.47	722.48	1684.14
UCR motor vehicle theft rate	36	486.94	82.70	314.69	659.00
UCR larceny theft rate	36	2776.42	347.69	2051.17	3229.07
UCR violent crime rate	36	522.61	93.14	380.72	706.11
UCR property crime rate	36	4387.00	646.96	3212.50	5353.38
UCR total crime rate	36	4909.62	710.04	3632.40	5902.97
NCVS aggravated assault rate	36	734.09	239.24	282.49	993.42
NCVS robbery rate	36	403.35	129.98	176.24	601.83
NCVS burglary rate	36	2411.22	1014.47	1050.84	3866.72
NCVS motor vehicle theft rate	36	549.62	152.26	322.19	837.72
NCVS larceny theft rate	36	8192.28	2371.65	4378.68	11715.91
NCVS violent crime rate	36	1137.44	366.58	478.94	1564.54
NCVS property crime rate	36	11153.12	3467.64	5758.25	15993.53
NCVS total crime rate	36	12290.56	3820.31	6237.19	17489.16

* Crime rates per 100,000 population are calculated by using total residential population.

Between 1973 and 2008, the number of households increased from 68 million to 121 million, and the U. S. residential population increased from 210 million to 304 million, for a total increase in the residential population of 50% and a total increase in number of households of over

77%. This comparatively higher increase in households has significantly affected the victimization estimates provided by the NCVS which uses household numbers as a denominator to calculate the rate of victimization. It was, therefore, decided to use total residential population to calculate rates in the present study to make UCR and NCVS rates comparable.

The second set of explanatory variables used in this study is the demographic characteristics of the U.S. population. The growth of different population groups has been substantially different during the study period, and the changing demographic composition may have some effects on crime and reporting of crimes to police. Growth in the White population was recorded at 9% and in the Black population at 13% growth, while the Hispanic population had a recorded growth of over 200% during the 36-year period.

Educational attainments of the U.S. population have substantially changed over time, possibly having an effect on the problem of crime and reporting of crime. Forty percent of the population had less than a high school education in 1973, a statistic that decreased significantly to 13% in 2008. Similarly, only 13% of the population had 4 years of college in 1973, but 38% had 4-year college degrees in 2008. The population with only a high school education decreased, and the population with some college education increased moderately during the same period. The population with less than a high school education decreased by over 200%, while the population with 4-year college degrees increased by over 200%. The population with only high school degrees showed a moderate decrease, while the population with some college increased by 61% during that time. The variables of the population with less than a high school education and the population with 4 years of college showed the highest variability. The third set of variables is related to law enforcement employment and expenses. Employment of police in terms of number and composition has gone through major changes in the past 36 years. Total employment in police departments has increased significantly, with over 150% growth during the study period. The police-to-population ratio that indicates the number of employees in law enforcement for every 1000 people was 1.9 in 1973 and became 3.4 in 2008. The growth in law enforcement employment, however, has been primarily characterized by the growth in female sworn officers and civilians in police departments. The percentage of female sworn officers in the total number sworn officers grew by over 150% during the period. Only 11% of the sworn officers were female in 1973, but by the end of 2008 the percentage of female sworn officers was over 27%. Another interesting feature of employment for police is the proportion of civilians in police forces. The percentage of civilians grew by over 100% during the period being studied, growing from 15% of total law enforcement employment in 1973 to 31% in 2008. The variables of the percentage of sworn officers who are female and the percentage of law enforcement employees who are civilians have the highest variability, and the variable of the percentage of the all law enforcement employees who are sworn officers has shown the lowest variability. The total expenses of maintaining police forces grew 14 times between 1973 and 2008. The exponential growth of the total expenses for police is better reflected in the growth of per capita expense for police. The United States spent approximately $36 on the police for every person in 1973, and $354 in 2008. The per capita expense of police grew over nine times during the study period.

Furthermore, the number of law enforcement agencies reporting to the UCR program has had an effect on the validity and accuracy of crime rates reported by the program. In 1973, only 6,615 agencies reported crime statistics to the program, but by 2008 the total number of agencies reporting to the program had increased to 13,865. Over the years, the UCR and NCVS have gone through several changes in terms of design for collecting crime data. Redesigning, therefore, is a critically important factor to be taken into consideration to explain the convergence of the two series. The present study, however, has included only the redesign of the NCVS in 1992 because those are considered the rate-affecting changes which influenced the estimated rates of victimization in 1993.

The attitude of people toward crime is an important factor that is likely to affect the reporting of crime to police. A proxy measure of the attitude toward crime used in this study is fear of crime, which is measured by the GSS by asking respondent whether they would be afraid to walk alone at night. A linear interpolation and extrapolation technique was used for missing observations for the fear of crime variable. On average, 39% of respondents feared walking alone at night. In 1973, 40% were afraid of walking alone at night, and in 2008 only 32% were afraid of walking alone at night. However, the lowest percentage of people (30.2) being afraid of walk alone at night was in 2004, and the highest percentage (45.4) was registered in 1994.

Table 4.2. Descriptive Statistics of the Independent Variables Used in the Analyses

Variable	*N*	Mean	*SD*	Minimum	Maximum
Year	36.00	18.50	10.54	1.00	36.00
Total household (in millions)	36.00	95.62	15.37	68.30	121.14
Total population (in millions)	36.00	253.75	28.88	209.80	304.06
% White	36.00	83.58	2.32	79.80	87.23
% Black	36.00	12.25	0.49	11.34	12.85
% Hispanic	36.00	9.49	3.27	5.05	15.44
% below high school	36.00	23.57	8.01	13.40	40.20
% with high school	36.00	35.39	2.51	31.20	38.90
% with some college	36.00	16.08	1.78	11.40	18.40
% with 4 years college	36.00	24.95	8.44	12.60	38.20
Total employees in police (in 100,000)	36.00	7.19	2.00	4.06	10.24
% sworn officers	36.00	74.72	4.83	68.80	85.00
% female employees	36.00	21.78	5.00	10.80	27.20
% civilians	36.00	25.29	4.83	15.00	31.20
Total expenses to police (in millions)	36.00	44982.82	31093.15	7624.00	107700.00
UCR reporting agencies	36.00	11673.72	1514.41	6615.00	13865.00
NCVS redesign in 1993	36.00	0.44	0.50	0.00	1.00
% afraid to walk at night	36.00	39.21	4.21	30.20	45.40
% aggravated assault reported to police	36.00	56.25	3.66	47.50	64.20

Table 4.2. Descriptive Statistics of the Independent Variables Used in the Analyses (Continued)

Variable	*N*	Mean	*SD*	Minimum	Maximum
% robbery reported to police	36.00	56.24	4.41	50.10	71.20
% burglary reported to police	36.00	50.87	2.64	46.00	57.90
% motor vehicle theft reported to police	36.00	75.02	5.93	66.10	86.10
% larceny theft reported to police	36.00	27.97	2.56	23.00	33.60
% violent crimes reported to police	36.00	56.23	3.17	49.52	63.11
% property crimes to police	36.00	35.16	2.35	30.85	40.30
% total crimes reported to police	36.00	37.10	2.35	32.85	41.95
Cell phone connections (in millions)	36.00	56.84	83.76	0.00	270.33

The NCVS estimates the percentage of crimes reported to police by the public. The reporting of crime can also be considered a more direct measure of the attitudes of people toward crime. The reporting percentage variable has been included in the study although it may be highly correlated with the fear variable because both of them are assumed to be measuring public attitudes toward crime. Reporting percentages for all categories have increased from 1973 to 2008. Aggravated assault and larceny theft categories have shown the most improvement in terms of reporting, and burglary has shown minimum change. Therefore, reports of aggravated assault and larceny theft are the variables that show the most variability, whereas the variable of burglary reporting variable shows the least variability. In terms of reporting percentage, motor vehicle theft remained the highest reported category of crime and larceny theft remained the least reported category.

ANALYTIC STRATEGY

The analysis scheme for the research focuses on addressing the research questions through testing the research hypotheses. At the beginning of the analyses, the rates of aggregated and disaggregated crime categories for both the UCR and NCVS were calculated using the same denominator of total residential population of the United States. The adjustment of the NCS data was done to make them compatible with NCVS data. This adjustment is accomplished by re-estimating the victimization numbers using the NCS/NCVS ratios provided by the BJS (Rand et al., 1997). The rates of crime and victimization are calculated per 100,000 residents. Descriptive statistics for all dependent and important independent variables included in the analyses appear in Table 4.2.

The first two questions of the study explore the convergence of the UCR and NCVS rates and the convergence of the adjusted UCR rates and NCVS rates for the disaggregated crime categories of aggravated assault, robbery, burglary, and larceny theft and the aggravated crime categories of violent, property, and total crime. The question of whether the two series are converging is addressed by testing the following hypotheses through a combination of different statistical techniques.

H_1: The UCR and NCVS data series will have come closer to each other, moving toward convergence during the period of 1973-2008.

H_2: The UCR and NCVS data series display different levels of convergence for different aggregated and disaggregated categories of crime.

H_3: Aggregated and disaggregated categories of violent crime should show stronger convergence than property crime categories.

H_4: Adjusted UCR rates for the reporting of crimes to police and NCVS rates for different crime categories are likely to show different levels of convergence.

The convergence between the UCR and NCVS data series has been tested using different cross-sectional and time-series analyses (McDowell & Loftin, 2007). McDowell and Loftin provided a survey of all major convergence studies and classified them into four categories. The four types of *convergence* are convergence as identical rates, convergence as identical rates after adjustments, convergence as correlational rates, and convergence as long-term equilibrium.

Convergence as identical rates and convergence as identical rates after adjustment may not be appropriately applied because the UCR and NCVS have different methods of measuring overlapping, feature different sets of crimes, and tap different sets of populations (Rand & Rennison, 2002). Most of the studies have used correlational and time-series definitions of convergence as a consequence. An overview of some of the known convergence studies (Blumstein et al., 1991; Catalano, 2006, 2006; McDowell & Loftin, 1992, 2007; Menard & Covey, 1988; O'Brien, 1990, 1991, 1996, 1999) indicated that they used time-series data and adopted cross-sectional and time-series definitions of convergence for exploring the convergence between the UCR and NCVS for different categories of crime. Some studies that used the correlational definition (Blumstein et al., 1991; Menard & Covey, 1988; O'Brien, 1990, 1991, 1996) used time-series data of the UCR and NCVS and estimated correlation coefficients with non-detrended and detrended or differenced rates. Studies that explored convergence between the two data series in a time-series environment employed the cointegration technique and estimated long-term equilibrium between the UCR and NCVS for different crime categories (McDowell & Loftin, 2007; O'Brien, 1999, 2003).

None of the definitions of convergence and techniques used for testing the convergence can be accepted as complete. Correlational studies of convergence that used cross-sectional and time-series data and estimated correlation coefficients between the UCR and NCVS at one point in time or across time failed to indicate the trend of the relationship between the two data series. Cointegration analysis, the most commonly used technique adapted for time-series analysis of convergence, has indicated the equilibrium between the two data series. The long-term equilibrium definition of convergence defines convergence in loose and the least-demanding terms because cointegration of the two series is only an indication of their influencing one another and moving together. Apart from the issues related with correlational and long-term equilibrium definitions of convergence in terms of understanding the convergence of the UCR and NCVS data series, the debate on the use of crime rates and detrended or differenced crime rates in estimating correlation coefficients is still unresolved. In view of these issues and problems, a strategy that combines different important methods to explore the convergence of the UCR and NCVS data series was used in this study. The first three hypotheses were tested using the following methods for the estimation of UCR and NCVS rates.

The first method resulted in a graphical analysis of the relationship of trends or convergence between the two series. In the graphical analysis, UCR and NCVS series for all crime categories were plotted against time. This analysis provided an overview of the comparative movements of both data series and showed the relationship of trends between them.

The second method used in the study was correlational. The correlation coefficients between the two series for all categories of crime rates and differenced crime rates were estimated for the entire period of 36 years from 1973 to 2008. In the second step of the correlational analysis, the series were broken into 18 separate series, each having 18 observations. Correlation coefficients between the UCR and NCVS for all categories in all the series were estimated.

The third method used was bivariate OLS regression estimation, in which crime rate and logged crime rate differences between the UCR and NCVS were regressed. Significant and negative regression coefficients were considered to be indicative of convergence.

The fourth method was use of time-series techniques. In the first step of the time-series analyses of the convergence, rate differences and logged rate differences between the UCR and NCVS for all categories of crime used in the study were regressed over time. In the second step of the time-series convergence analyses, cointegration analyses were conducted for all the categories.

To test the fourth hypothesis, all methods mentioned above were applied to adjusted UCR and NCVS rates. Reporting of crime by citizens and police productivity in terms of official reporting of crime are considered important factors that changed UCR rates and facilitated the convergence of the UCR and NCVS (Catalano, 2006, 2007; O' Brien, 1996, 2003). The NCVS estimates percentages of crimes reported to police by the public. The study used the reporting percentage to adjust the UCR rates and repeated the convergence analyses with the adjusted UCR rates to see whether the changes in the reporting of crimes to police have had some effects on the convergence of the two series.

The third research question guiding this study is explanatory in nature and seeks to provide explanations for the changing relationship trend between the UCR and NCVS. The discrepancies between the two crime series have apparently decreased over time, and the studies have consistently reported a growing convergence between the two series. Several factors have been identified in the literature as being responsible for reducing the discrepancies between the two series. The primary reason for the convergence of the two series was increase in the UCR rates, at least prior to the redesign of the NCVS. The factors identified as responsible for increased UCR rates are increased police productivity, institutional and legal changes, changes in the UCR program, changed population and demographic characteristics, and attitudes of people toward crime and the police. Police productivity, which was consistently found to be an important factor in increased UCR rates, includes changes in employment in terms of increase in number of police per capita, civilianization of police, percentage of sworn police officers who are female, increased use of computers and data management systems, increased educational level of police officers, development in communication technology, increase in community policing, and new management tools. The question of explaining the convergence through several relevant explanatory variables is addressed by testing the following hypotheses.

H_5: Changes in population and demographic characteristics are likely to have affected the convergence of the UCR and NCVS data series.

H_6: Police productivity should positively affect convergence of the UCR and NCVS data series.

H_7: Citizens' attitudes toward crime and the police should positively affect the convergence of the UCR and NCVS data series.[13]

---

[13] The attitude of citizens toward police is difficult to measure, and fear of crime, to some extent, can be used as a proxy measure of attitude toward crime. A time series of fear of crime is available in the GSS data, but a time series from 1973 to 2008 for trust in police is not available. The LEMAS and the GSS data sets include a trust-in-police variable, but the LEMAS is available only for a few years, and the GSS has not measured the trust-in-police variable on an annual basis. Therefore, it was decided to drop the trust-in-police variable from

H_8: Changes in measurement procedures, especially in the NCVS, should positively affect the convergence of the UCR and NCVS data series, especially after 1993.

The strategy used for addressing the third question and testing the related hypotheses is identification and estimation of time-series regression models with multiple predictors. The process of modeling was focused on building the best fitting, most efficient model. The theoretical relevance of the independent variables and their contributions in predicting the dependent variables were the criteria used for building models. The rate differences between the UCR and NCVS were regressed over time, and single lagged value of dependent variables for all categories of disaggregated and aggregated crimes included in the study before estimating models with predictors in order to see the effects of time and check for autoregressive process. Three separate regressions for all dependent variables (rate differences between the NCVS and UCR for all eight disaggregated and aggregated categories), each having three models, were estimated. Only predictor variables were used in the first set of models. Predictor variables along with trend variables are used in the second set of models, and predictor variables along with single lagged dependent variables are used in the third set of models. Population characteristics, educational attainment, law enforcement expense and employment, redesign of the victimization survey, fear of crime, and the reporting percentages of the crime variables are used in the models. The biggest limitation of the model-building process was the limitation of time-series variables and direct measures of certain constructs.

SUMMARY

In answering the research questions and testing the related hypotheses, this study draws time-series data from different sources. The UCR and NCVS are the main sources of the data for the study. The UCR collects crime data from local, state, special, and federal law enforcement agencies, and the NCVS estimates crime victimization through a national household survey. Other sources of the data from which

---

the analyses and include only citizens' attitudes toward crime measured as fear of crime in the GSS.

several explanatory variables have been drawn to explain the convergence include the U.S. Census Bureau, GSS, LEAMAS, and CTIA. Prior to the data analyses, some adjustments to the data were made, and UCR and NCVS rates were calculated using the same denominator and rate formula. Linear interpolations and extrapolations were completed with some of the variables to provide missing data points, but some knowingly relevant variables were dropped because of the unavailability of sufficient observation points for time-series analysis.

The data analyses for testing the hypotheses and addressing the research questions were conducted in two parts and are presented in Chapters 5 and 6. The first part of the analyses explores the convergence of the two series, and the second part explains the convergence. The analytic strategies in the first part include graphic presentations, correlation estimation, regression, and cointegration between the two time series. The analytic strategies in the second part include regression modeling of the time-series data.

CHAPTER 5

Are the UCR and NCVS Converging?

One of the research questions of this study addressed the relationship between the UCR and NCVS in terms of their convergence. The study attempted to address this question by testing a set of hypotheses focused on exploring the convergence of different disaggregated and aggregated crime rates of the UCR and NCVS. The second research question, an extension of the first research question, addressed the convergence between adjusted UCR rates and NCVS rates.

The first method adopted for visualizing the relationship of the trends between the two series is graphical analysis. In the graphical analyses, UCR and NCVS series for all crime categories are plotted against time. This analysis provides an overview of comparative movements of both of the series and shows the relationship of trends between them.

The second method adopted in the study is correlational. The correlation coefficients between the two series for all categories of crime rates and differenced crime rates are estimated for the entire period of 36 years from 1973 to 2008. In the second step of the correlational analyses, the series are broken into 18 separate series, each having 18 observations. Correlation coefficients between the UCR and NCVS for all categories in all the series are estimated.

The third method is bivariate OLS regression. The rate differences and logged rate differences between the UCR and NCVS for all categories of crime used in the study are regressed over time, with significant and negative regression coefficients considered indicative of convergence.

The fourth method is cointegration analysis, which is purely a time-series analysis of convergence or long-term equilibrium. Three steps of cointegration analysis are adopted in the present study. First, the two series with their rate difference series, known as rate spread, are plotted against time. Second, the Augmented Dickey-Fuller test of unit root for the logged differences of the two series is conducted. Finally, a more formal cointegration test, known as the Engle-Granger Test of cointegration, is conducted.

GRAPHIC ANALYSIS OF CONVERGENCE

The first step toward testing the convergence is to have UCR and NCVS series for different crime categories plotted together against time. Time-line graphs of the two series with crime rates, differenced crime rates, and logged crime rates for all crime categories are presented in Figures 5.1, 5.2, and 5.3. The plotting of UCR and NCVS time-series together across the years gives an idea about the temporal movement of the series and the trend of the relationship between them.

The purpose of presenting graphs of differenced rates is to show the relationship between the two series after the trend is removed because several studies have concluded in favor of the convergence based on strong correlations between detrended or differenced series (Blumstein et al., 1991; O'Brien, 1990, 1996).[14] The purpose of presenting graphs with logged series is to see the trend of relationship

---

[14] Time series have either deterministic or stochastic trends. In the case of a deterministic trend, the movement of a series is nonrandom and change can be predicted. In the case of a stochastic trend, changes do not take a linear direction, and movement of a series is random. An overview of the graphs (Figure 5.1) shows that long-term movements of all the series of the UCR and NCVS are random, thus the series are stochastic. The presence of unit roots in all the series is evidence of the presence of stochastic trends. The description of unit root test and results for all the series have been provided further in the chapter.

after the variances have been stabilized through logarithmic transformation of the series.[15]

Figure 5.1 shows a substantial change in the relationship between the two series for the aggravated assault category. UCR and NCVS aggravated assault rates came together in 2007, although the NCS reported an almost 5 times higher rate of aggravated assault than the UCR in 1973. This change occurred because of a substantial increase over time in the UCR aggravated assault rate and a decrease in the NCVS aggravated assault rate. The UCR aggravated assault rate increased almost 122% between 1973 and 1993, although the rate of increase fell off after 1993 so that the total increase from 1973 to 2008 was 38%. The NCVS aggravated assault rate did not decrease between 1973 and 1993 but remained stable, but after 1993 a sharp decrease was recorded reflecting a 71% decrease between 1973 and 2008. One important feature of the NCVS aggravated assault rate is that it showed the greatest fluctuation in 1993 because methodological changes in the NCVS in 1992 affected this category the most. The graphs with differenced aggravated assault rates in Figure 5.2 show that the aggravated assault rate becomes stationary after the first differencing, although variability of both of the series, especially the NCVS, has slightly increased over time.

The second violent crime of robbery showed a different trend and relationship than those of aggravated assault (Figure 5.1). The discrepancy between the UCR and NCVS for robbery was smaller in the beginning, although the two series still maintained divergence. The UCR robbery rate kept increasing until 1992, which was the main reason for the reduced discrepancy. The decrease in the NCS robbery

---

[15] Time series are transformed to make variance more stable for statistical analyses. The logarithmic transformation of a series is often useful in analysis if it has a value greater than zero, it grows exponentially, and/or its deviance is proportional to its level; that is, the variance is unstable. All UCR and NCVS series used in the analyses included in this study have values greater than zero, and they show exponential growth with unstable variance. Therefore, in order to stabilize the variance of the series, it was decided to use natural logs of all the UCR and NCVS series in the analysis. Logged UCR and NCVS series are plotted in Figure 2, which indicates that logarithmic transformation has stabilized the series that justifies the use of logged series in the analysis.

rate until 1992 was, however, higher than the decrease in the NCS aggravated assault rate as well as the total NCS rates. The total decrease in the UCR robbery rate from 1973 to 1993 was about 145%, and the total decrease in the NCVS robbery rate was 63% with the overall decrease in the NCVS rate for the same period being only 20%. The robbery graph for the differenced rates (Figure 5.2) indicates a reduced discrepancy between the series while the NCVS shows greater variability than the UCR. The robbery graph for the logged series (Figure 5.3) shows greater convergence and lower variability.

UCR and NCVS burglary rates still maintain a discrepancy, although they started coming closer to each other early on. The UCR burglary rate, unlike aggravated assault and robbery, which kept increasing until the mid- and early-1990s respectively, started decreasing after 1980. The UCR burglary rate increased by 36% between 1973 and 2008, but recorded a decrease of 56% between 1980 and 2008. The total decrease in the UCR burglary rate between 1973 and 2008 was 40%. The NCVS burglary rate remained almost unchanged from 1973 through 1980, but started decreasing gradually after 1980. The UCR burglary rate showed a 73% decrease from 1981 to 2008. Because of these changes, the UCR and NCVS came closer together. The graph for burglary (Figure 5.1) also shows that the NCVS burglary rate was unaffected by the 1992 methodological change. The graph with differenced data for UCR and NCVS burglary rates (Figure 5.2) shows that the series become almost mean stationary after the first differencing. The UCR and NCVS burglary series show greater variability in the pre-1990 era, but after 1990 both series, especially the UCR burglary rate, became almost flat. The burglary graph with logged rates in Figure 5.3 indicates that the UCR and NCVS series moved together and maintained that distance.

Motor vehicle theft graphs, both nondifferenced and differenced (Figures 5.1 and 5.2), show that this category is different from other crime categories in terms of the relationship between the UCR and NCVS. The UCR and NCVS motor vehicle theft rates showed minimal discrepancy from the beginning of the victimization survey and moved together with some exceptions. The nondifferenced graph demonstrates that both of the series were high between 1985 and 1995. UCR and NCVS motor vehicle theft series are unique because they show a structural break in 1991, when both suddenly rose. Methodological changes in the NCVS did not have any effect on motor vehicle theft because the series does not show a fluctuation in 1993. Another important feature shown in the nondifferenced graph is that the NCVS motor vehicle theft rate remained below the UCR rate from 1996 to 2007, with one exception in 1997 when the NCVS motor vehicle theft rate went slightly higher than the UCR rate. The differenced graph of motor vehicle theft shows higher variability than the other categories, and the first differencing keeps the series from being perfectly stationary because the series still show slight downward trend. The pattern of the relationship between the UCR and NCVS motor vehicle theft rates remained unchanged after the series were logarithmically transformed. The probable cause of this result could be a lack of exponential growth and a high level of variance instability in UCR and NCVS motor vehicle theft series.

The larceny theft graph (Figure 5.1) shows that the UCR and NCVS larceny theft rates are the most discrepant of all. The NCVS larceny theft rate in 2008 was more than twice the UCR larceny theft rate. The decrease in the NCVS larceny theft rate from 1973 to 2008 was 56%, which is substantial but less than the decrease in other categories. More importantly, the UCR larceny theft rate showed only a 6% increase between 1973 and 2008. The NCVS larceny theft series shows a fluctuation in 1993 that indicates an effect of the methodological changes in terms of larceny theft measurement in the victimization survey. The differenced larceny theft graph (Figure 5.2) indicates that the first differencing did not remove the trend completely, so the series are still showing some downward trend. The variability in the NCVS larceny theft rate is higher than the variability in the UCR larceny theft rate, which is almost flat. The graph showing the logged UCR and NCVS larceny theft rates (Figure 5.3) indicates that the logarithmic transformation of the series reduced the discrepancy and variability, but the series have been highly discrepant and still maintain divergent.

Figure 5.1. UCR and NCS/NCVS Crime Rates, 1973-2008.

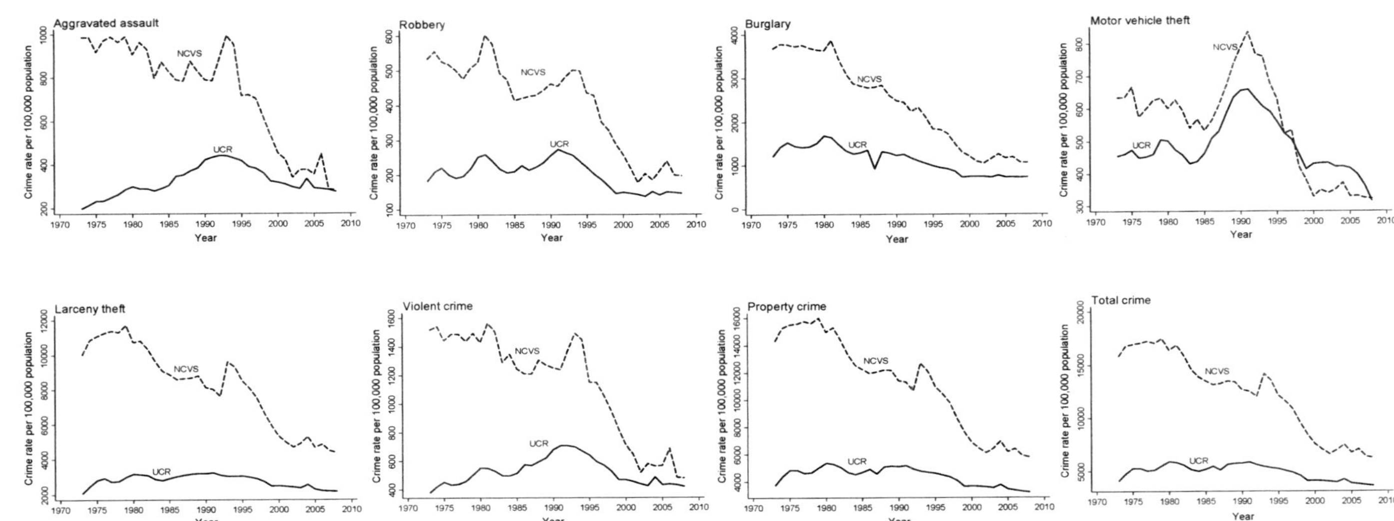

Figure 5.2. UCR and NCS/NCVS Differenced Crime Rates, 1973-2008.

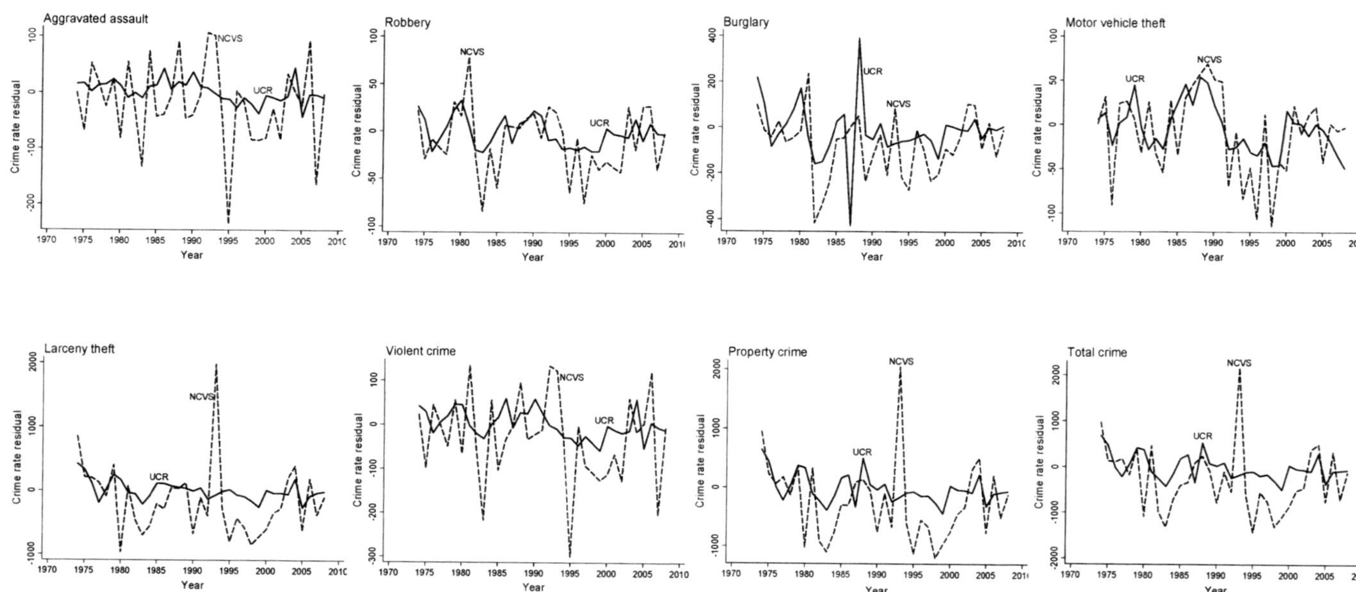

Figure 5.3. UCR and NCS/NCVS Logged Crime Rates, 1973-2008.

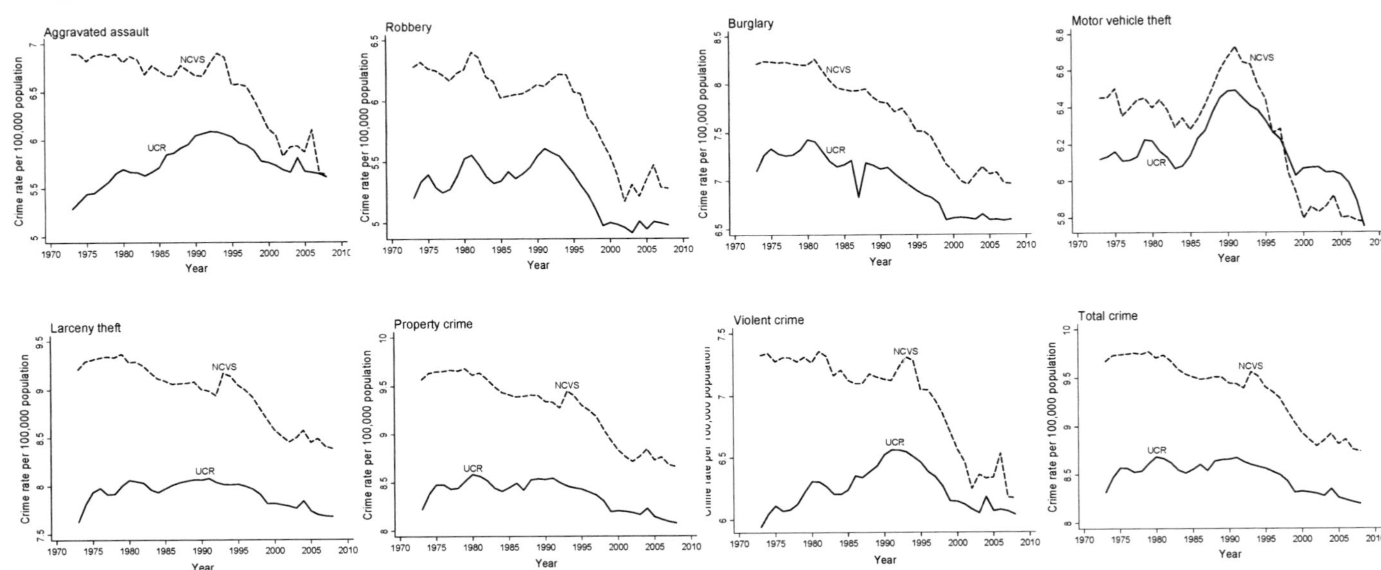

An examination of the graphs for the aggregated categories of violent, property, and total crime (Figures 5.1, 5.2, and 5.3) does not provide any unique or valuable information. The violent crime, aggravated assault, and robbery graphs are quite similar to each other. The aggravated assault category shows more discrepancy than robbery in the beginning, and robbery, unlike aggravated assault, which converged in 2007, is still divergent. The violent crime category graph synthesizes the aggravated assault and robbery categories because they are almost equal in number. The property crime category is different in that it is primarily dominated by larceny theft. In this study, the UCR larceny theft rate represented 55% of the total property crime in 1973 and 67% in 2008. Similarly, the NCVS larceny theft rate represented 70% of the total property crime in 1973 and 76% in 2008. The total crime category in this study was also dominated by larceny theft to some extent because of its extremely large number in comparison with other categories. This is perhaps the most important reason that larceny theft has been included in the study, despite all the issues involved with the measurement of larceny crime. The graphs of differenced aggregated series show that the first differencing did not remove the trends from the property and total crime categories, although it reduced the trend in the violent crime category. The graphs with logged violent, property, and total crime categories show that the property and total crime categories have been less discrepant with higher variability than violent crime, although the violent crime series have come closer, and the property and total crime categories still maintain divergence.

CORRELATIONAL ANALYSES OF CONVERGENCE

The second analytical method to explore the relationship between the UCR and NCVS is to estimate the correlation coefficients between different UCR and NCVS disaggregated and aggregated crime rates series. Convergence as correlated rates is one of the popular definitions used in cross-sectional and time-series studies (McDowell & Loftin, 2007). Studies using correlational definitions estimated correlations between UCR and NCVS crime rates or between several known correlates of crime and UCR and NCVS crime rates (McDowell & Loftin, 2007). Studies using a correlational definition of convergence with time-series data used non-detrended and detrended rates and demonstrated different and sometimes opposite results. Studies using detrended data adopted different methods for detrending, such as differencing first and using residual scores (Blumstein et al., 1991; O'Brien, 1990).

Table 5.1. Correlation between Nondifferenced and Differenced UCR and NCVS Crime Rates

	r	
Crime category	**Nondifferenced rates**	**Differenced rates**[a]
Aggravated assault	0.0170	0.2155
Robbery	0.8359	0.4396
Burglary	0.9496	0.3725
Motor vehicle theft	0.8445	0.6198
Larceny theft	0.5858	0.3841
Violent crime[b]	0.3713	0.2493
Property crime[c]	0.8043	0.3844
Total crime[d]	0.7643	0.3796

[a] Crime rates detrended through the process of first differencing

[b] Violent crime category includes aggravated assault and robbery.

[c] Property crime category includes burglary, motor vehicle theft and larceny theft.

[d] Total crime category includes aggravated assault, robbery, burglary, motor vehicle theft, and larceny theft

Detrending of a time series is conducted to make it stationary because nonstationary time series produce spurious relationships. The question is whether detrending of the series is required in order to estimate correlations. This was the main argument of Menard (1991) against the methods of Blumstein et al. (1991) and O'Brien (1991). What is the appropriate method of detrending a time series so as to remove a trend and make the series stationary? Menard (1992) and O'Brien (1992) recommended using the differencing method first. The method of transforming a nonstationary time series into a stationary time series depends on the trending process in the series. If a series has a stochastic trend, then differencing is the correct method. However, if a series has a deterministic trend, then detrending through other methods is the correct method of transforming a nonstationary series into a stationary series (Gujarati, 2004; Stock & Watson, 2003). The present study used the differencing method first because both series have stochastic trends and unit roots. It was decided to estimate correlations between differenced and nondifferenced rates of all UCR and NCVS crime categories in order to provide a more balanced picture without taking side in the debate of non-detrended and detrended correlational definitions of convergence between the UCR and NCVS (see Table 5.1).

Table 5.1 presents the correlations between the UCR and NCVS for all categories of crime included in the study for the period from 1973 to 2008. In contrast to the results of prior studies which examined the convergence between the two series in the early 1990s and reported high correlations between detrended UCR and NCVS rates compared to non-detrended rates (Blumstein et al., 1991; O'Brien, 1991), the present study found higher correlations between nondifferenced rates of the UCR and NCVS than between differenced rates. If a .8 threshold as suggested in the literature is maintained, then robbery, burglary, and motor vehicle theft are the only categories in which the UCR and NCVS have converged. In addition, property crime as an aggregated category seems to be converging because of high correlations between the series for burglary and motor vehicle theft. Larceny theft, which is more divergent than the other categories (as seen in Figures 5.1, 5.2, and 5.3), also shows a high correlation of .58. The correlation coefficient for the aggravated assault category is extremely low, and because of this, the correlation between the UCR and NCVS for the aggregated category of violent crime is low. Thus, the correlations between differenced rates are substantially lower than the correlations between nondifferenced rates for most of the crime categories. The correlation coefficients for none of the differenced rates are close to the threshold of .8. The correlations between the series decrease substantially when the trend is removed through the first differencing. Motor vehicle theft becomes the highest correlated series, and the correlation coefficient of burglary, which was the highest for nondifferenced data, drops below that of larceny theft.

There are several problems in using the correlational definition in examining the convergence of the UCR and NCVS data series. First, correlation between two time series indicates the strength and the direction of the association rather than convergence. Series with greater discrepancies at the beginning will show a lack of correlation even if they have come closer to each other over time. For example, the aggravated assault series, which have converged recently, show extremely low correlation because of the earlier great discrepancy. Conversely, the series that have maintained stability in terms of discrepancies over time will show stronger correlation. For example, burglary, which shows the highest correlation, has still maintained divergence, but because UCR and NCVS burglary rates have shown stability in their relationship and moved together they show a high correlation. Similarly, robbery rates also show a strong correlation because UCR and NCVS robbery rates have moved simultaneously, maintaining divergence. Therefore, the correlation between the two series for the entire period from 1973 to 2008 may not show the changing relationship or convergence between the two series. In order to address this problem to some extent it was decided to split the series in the middle by creating 18 series with gradual increases of a year for every subsequent series, and the estimate the correlations between the UCR and NCVS to see the changing relationship over time.

Split Series Correlation

First, the series was split into two equal parts with 18 observations each; then, the entire series was divided into 18 consecutive series having 18 observations with incremental increases of one year. The first series has observations from 1973 to 1991, and the 18th series has observations from 1990 to 2008. Separate correlations were estimated for all 18 series having 18 observations in order to see the trend of the correlation between the two data series over time. The changes in direction and strength of association between the UCR and NCVS on different aggregated and disaggregated crime categories over time give an idea of the convergence between the two series. Subsequently, similar correlations were estimated for differenced UCR and NCVS series, and the results are presented in Tables 5.2 and 5.3.

The correlation between the UCR and NCVS aggravated assault rates, as shown in Table 5.2, is negative for the period of 1973-1991 (-0.79). Thus, the rate of one series was increasing while another was decreasing. Figure 5.1 clearly shows a gradual increase in the UCR aggravated assault rate and a decrease in the NCVS aggravated assault rate from 1973 until the early 1990s. The negative correlation between the two series keeps decreasing, and for the series of 1981-1999 the correlation coefficient is almost zero. The correlation coefficient after that time is positive and gradually increases to become .86 in 2008. After the 1990s, the UCR and NCVS aggravated assault series move together in a similar direction, with a sharp decrease in the NCVS rate and a moderate decrease in the UCR rate (see Figure 5.1).

The correlation between the UCR and NCVS robbery rates has always remained positive and showed continuous increase. The correlation coefficient for the series of 1973-1991 was almost zero but increased continuously to .94 for the last four series. The correlation of robbery shows substantial increase for the first seven series, but then it starts stabilizing. The UCR and NCVS show high correlation on burglary and motor vehicle theft rates. The correlation between the two series for burglary and motor vehicle theft categories are almost perfect for the series of 1990-2008, although the correlation between the UCR and NCVS for these categories were high for the series of 1973-1991. The larceny theft category is somewhat similar to the aggravated assault category. This category started with negative correlation for the series of 1973-1991, but displays strong and positive correlation for the later series.

Table 5.2 shows some of the information about the patterns of correlations between the UCR and NCVS. First, all categories showed extremely high correlation coefficients (more than .9) for the last series of 1990-2008. Second, the correlation coefficients gradually increased in all the series over time. Third, aggravated assault, larceny theft, and all three aggregated categories initially showed a negative correlation, which became positive and stronger with time. Fourth, the robbery, burglary, and motor vehicle theft series showed positive and strong correlations from the beginning, although the correlations between the two series for these categories also improved substantially with time. Finally, the trend of the correlation in Table 5.2 suggests convergence between the UCR and NCVS on all five Part I crimes and three aggregated crime categories because the correlations between the two series on all crime categories increased gradually and reached close to perfect positive correlations.

Table 5.2. Trend of Correlations between UCR and NCVS Rates, 1973-2008

Data Range	*r*							
	Aggravated assault rate	Robbery rate	Burglary rate	Motor Vehicle theft rate	Larceny theft rate	Violent crime rate	Property crime rate	Total crime rate
1973-1991	-0.7876	0.0521	0.6766	0.8657	-0.3720	-0.6786	-0.1156	-0.2477
1974-1992	-0.6831	0.1179	0.7771	0.8941	-0.5303	-0.5829	-0.0937	-0.2877
1975-1993	-0.4345	0.1958	0.8095	0.9103	-0.5282	-0.3843	0.0190	-0.2110
1976-1994	-0.3389	0.2203	0.8240	0.9244	-0.4893	-0.3012	0.0721	-0.1643
1977-1995	-0.3523	0.2994	0.8514	0.9122	-0.4654	-0.2842	0.1590	-0.0641
1978-1996	-0.3005	0.4180	0.8814	0.8781	-0.3110	-0.1993	0.3635	0.1692
1979-1997	-0.2410	0.5722	0.9022	0.8857	-0.0007	-0.0875	0.5736	0.4308
1980-1998	-0.1197	0.7060	0.9095	0.8776	0.3029	0.1186	0.6934	0.6029
1981-1999	0.0440	0.7803	0.9146	0.8914	0.5135	0.3338	0.7541	0.6980
1982-2000	0.2550	0.8289	0.9054	0.9036	0.6467	0.5276	0.7983	0.7640
1983-2001	0.4526	0.8838	0.9019	0.9237	0.7392	0.6890	0.8393	0.8213
1984-2002	0.5995	0.9061	0.9052	0.9444	0.8349	0.7872	0.8877	0.8797
1985-2003	0.7715	0.9372	0.9095	0.9771	0.9012	0.8878	0.9240	0.9238
1986-2004	0.8612	0.9358	0.9067	0.9868	0.9214	0.9217	0.9347	0.9376
1987-2005	0.9014	0.9402	0.9028	0.9892	0.9310	0.9359	0.9394	0.9429

Table 5.2. Trend of Correlations between UCR and NCVS Rates, 1973-2008 (Continued)

Data Range	*r*							
	Aggravated assault rate	Robbery rate	Burglary rate	Motor Vehicle theft rate	Larceny theft rate	Violent crime rate	Property crime rate	Total crime rate
1988-2006	0.9204	0.9440	0.9887	0.9907	0.9302	0.9461	0.9529	0.9560
1989-2007	0.9496	0.9438	0.9873	0.9858	0.9318	0.9573	0.9529	0.9567
1990-2008	0.9610	0.9424	0.9847	0.9682	0.9314	0.9610	0.9514	0.9557

Table 5.3. Trend of Correlations between Differenced UCR and NCVS Rates, 1973-2008

Data Range	*r*							
	Aggravated assault rate	Robbery rate	Burglary rate	Motor Vehicle theft rate	Larceny theft rate	Violent crime rate	Property crime rate	Total crime rate
1973-1991	-0.0073	0.5300	0.3743	0.6094	0.5419	0.1379	0.4906	0.4692
1974-1992	-0.0410	0.4717	0.3878	0.6601	0.5563	0.0621	0.5165	0.4844
1975-1993	-0.1258	0.4131	0.2989	0.6516	0.0787	-0.0294	0.1130	0.0927
1976-1994	-0.0427	0.4341	0.2902	0.6598	0.0280	0.0448	0.0791	0.0787
1977-1995	0.2109	0.4957	0.3003	0.6598	-0.0025	0.2632	0.0906	0.1052
1978-1996	0.1546	0.4765	0.3004	0.7057	0.0607	0.2281	0.1322	0.1443
1979-1997	0.1573	0.5245	0.2979	0.6809	0.0888	0.2621	0.1417	0.1570

Table 5.3. Trend of Correlations between Differenced UCR and NCVS Rates, 1973-2008 (Continued)

Data Range	r							
	Aggravated assault rate	Robbery rate	Burglary rate	Motor Vehicle theft rate	Larceny theft rate	Violent crime rate	Property crime rate	Total crime rate
1980-1998	0.1861	0.4955	0.2897	0.7451	0.0410	0.2651	0.1166	0.1360
1981-1999	0.2708	0.5087	0.2709	0.7438	0.2515	0.3558	0.2736	0.2960
1982-2000	0.3151	0.4613	0.3142	0.7560	0.2357	0.3665	0.2653	0.2893
1983-2001	0.3133	0.4508	0.2629	0.7505	0.2336	0.3674	0.2469	0.2725
1984-2002	0.3131	0.3648	0.2109	0.7421	0.1845	0.3341	0.1857	0.2042
1985-2003	0.2712	0.3365	0.1933	0.7298	0.1551	0.3115	0.1640	0.1841
1986-2004	0.2877	0.3753	0.2143	0.7670	0.2501	0.3302	0.2348	0.2590
1987-2005	0.3113	0.3074	0.2065	0.7663	0.3153	0.3113	0.2763	0.2983
1988-2006	0.2924	0.3698	0.4490	0.7398	0.2869	0.3216	0.3202	0.3358
1989-2007	0.2123	0.3431	0.5258	0.6776	0.2713	0.2476	0.3045	0.2972
1990-2008	0.2221	0.3085	0.5608	0.5154	0.2553	0.2484	0.2956	0.2885

The correlation trend in Table 5.2 is different from the correlation in Table 5.1, which presents estimated correlation coefficients between UCR and NCVS series for the entire period from 1973 to 2008. In Table 5.1, only robbery, burglary, and motor vehicle theft show correlation coefficients over .8. Larceny theft shows a moderate correlation of .56, and aggravated assault shows a weak correlation of .02 when the correlations are estimated for the entire period. However, when the correlations were estimated after splitting the time series, the aggravated assault and larceny theft categories also displayed substantial increase and showed positive and extremely strong correlations. The correlations, however, become weaker after the series are differenced (Table 5.3).

CONVERGENCE TEST THROUGH REGRESSION OF UCR AND NCVS RATE DIFFERENCES ON TIME

One simple way to see whether the two crime rate series are converging is to regress the crime rate difference between the two series on time. If the regression coefficient is negative and significant, then it can be concluded that the series are coming closer or the difference between the two series is significantly reducing over time. The NCVS and UCR are denoted as y and z, and the following regression models have been estimated.

$$y_t - z_t = \beta_0 + \beta_1 t + u_t \qquad (5.1)$$
$$l_n y_t - l_n z_t = \beta_0 + \beta_1 t + u_t \qquad (5.2)$$

In Equation 5.1, the rate difference between the NCVS and UCR is regressed on the time variable, and in Equation 5.2, the logged rate difference between the NCVS and UCR is regressed on year. A negative and significant regression coefficient in Equation 5.1 would indicate that the difference between the NCVS and UCR crime rates is getting significantly smaller with time, and a negative and significant regression coefficient in Equation 5.2 would indicate that the ratio between the NCVS and UCR crime rates is getting smaller with time. If the difference and ratio between the NCVS and UCR crime rates have significantly reduced over time, a conclusion can be made in favor of convergence between the two series, or in other words, the series have significantly come closer to one another and are in the process of converging. The regressions were estimated for each category of crime using the rate difference and logged rate difference variables as dependent variables and the year variable as the independent variable. The results of the regressions are presented in Tables 5.4 and 5.5.

Table 5.4. Results of Bivariate OLS Regressions for Different Crime Categories

Crime category	Coefficient	*SE*	*t* statistics	*p* value
Aggravated assault	-22.6121	1.0842	-20.86	0.000
Robbery	-8.6067	.5988	-14.37	0.000
Burglary	-67.5904	2.3184	-29.15	0.000
Motor vehicle theft	-7.5641	.7979	-9.48	0.000
Larceny theft	-198.2202	10.5274	-18.83	0.000
Violent crime	-31.2188	1.5885	-19.65	0.000
Property crime	-273.3747	11.9517	-22.87	0.000
Total crime	-304.5936	13.1676	-23.13	0.000

Table 5.5. Results of Bivariate OLS Regressions for Different Crime Categories with Logged Rates

Crime category	Coefficient	*SE*	*t* statistics	*p* value
Aggravated assault	-.0413	.0016	-25.28	0.000
Robbery	-.0185	.0016	-11.29	0.000
Burglary	-.0181	.0012	-13.94	0.000
Motor vehicle theft	-.0157	.0014	-10.63	0.000
Larceny theft	-.0229	.0013	-17.14	0.000
Violent crime	-.0323	.0015	-21.23	0.000
Property crime	-.0206	.0011	-18.40	0.000
Total crime	-.0217	.0011	-19.48	0.000

The regression results displayed in Table 5.4 show that the regression coefficients on the year variable, in the case of all regression estimates in which differences between NCVS and UCR rates for all crime categories were regressed against year variable are negative and statistically significant; the *p* values are less than 001 in all cases. The rate differences between NCVS and UCR significantly decreased between 1973 and 2008, and both series have come closer for all the crime categories. Table 5.5 presents the results of the regressions with dependent variables of difference between logged rates of the NCVS and UCR. The regression coefficients for all categories are again negative and significant. The ratio between the UCR and NCVS, therefore, has significantly decreased between 1973 and 2008. Based on the results presented in Tables 5.4 and 5.5, it can at least be concluded that discrepancies between the UCR and NCVS series for all crime categories included in the study decreased significantly between 1973 and 2008. They either converged or were in the process of converging.

COINTEGRATION ANALYSES OF CONVERGENCE

Convergence as long-term equilibrium is purely a time-series definition of *convergence*. Several methods are used in the literature for testing convergence in a time-series environment. One method, which is often used in neoclassical economics, was first suggested by Bernard and Durlauf (1995). According to this method, two series are said to be converging if the difference between them tends to be zero as the forecasting horizon tends toward infinity. This method uses the Dickey-Fuller (DF) test for testing the convergence hypothesis.

The second method that tests the long-term equilibrium in a cointegration framework of time series, however, seems to be more commonly used in the discipline for testing the convergence between the UCR and NCVC (McDowell & Loftin, 2007) and between crime rates for men and women (O'Brien, 1999). Two time series are said to be cointegrating when they have stochastic trends and they move together closely over the long run. According to cointegration theory, two variables will be cointegrated if they have a long-term or equilibrium relationship between them (Gujarati, 2004). The theory

Figure 5.4. UCR and NCVS Rates and Rate Difference, 1973-2008

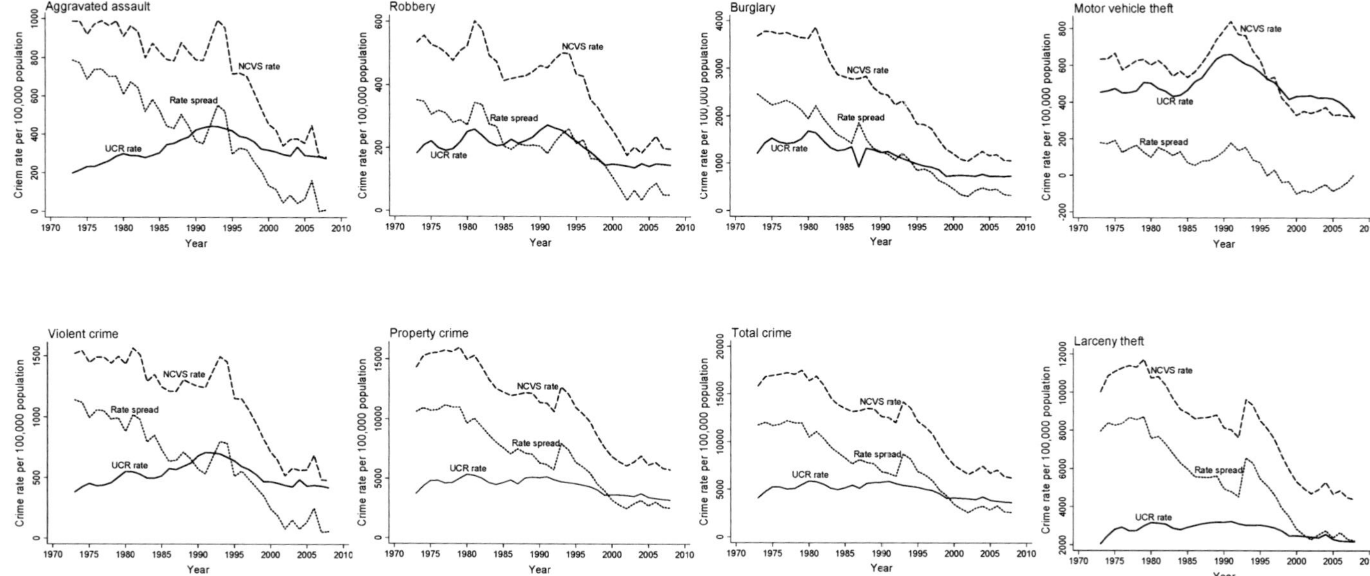

behind cointegration is that if the two or more series are influenced by the same factor they are pulled and kept together by that factor, and any divergence is temporary. The series can diverge for a period, but they eventually come back together. In other words, two nonstationary series are said to be cointegrated if their nonstationarity has a common source. The UCR and NCVS measure the same social phenomenon called crime. Although the real crime rate is not known, the UCR and NCVS programs make efforts to improve their measurement and come close to measuring the total crime committed. This similarity is likely to force both of the series—UCR and NCVS—to remain close to each other. Since both have stochastic trends and both are influenced by the common force of total crime committed, cointegration analysis for testing long-term equilibrium may be considered an acceptable time-series method to explore the convergence between the two series.

In the time-series analysis environment, this study has used three steps of testing cointegration between the UCR and NCVS, although a number of methods are suggested in the literature (Gujarati, 2004). First, the rate spreads were plotted against time. Second, Augmented Dickey-Fuller (ADF) tests of unit root for logged differences of UCR and NCVS crime rates for different crime categories were conducted. Finally, Engle-Granger test, a more formal statistical test of cointegration, was conducted.

Rate Spread Plots

Rates of the UCR and NCVS and differences between them are plotted in Figure 5.4. Rate spread between NCVS and UCR rates should be flat if the two series are perfectly cointegrated. The rate spreads for all categories have been continuously decreasing and showing a downward trend. The UCR and NCVS series, except for motor vehicle theft and to some extent burglary do not move together, but their differences have been continuously decreasing. Initially, the divergence was reduced because UCR rates were increasing, but after the mid-1990s the UCR rates either remained stable or started decreasing. The divergence between the two series decreased more quickly after the mid-1990s, and this decrease was possible because of a steep decline in NCVS rates. The rate spread plots displayed in Figure 5.4 clearly indicate a lack of cointegration, although the divergence between the two series for all categories of crime decreases substantially.

The ADF Test of Logged Differences between UCR and NCVS Rates

The Dickey-Fuller test provides a method for determining whether two series are cointegrated (O'Brien, 1991). If the difference between two logged series has a unit root, then the two series are not cointegrated, and if the difference between two logged series does not have a unit root and both of the series are integrated on the same order, then the series may or may not be cointegrated. This simple test can determine whether the two series are potentially cointegrated, although the test may not be enough to conclude that two series are cointegrated.

The logged differences between UCR and NCVS rates for all categories were calculated, and the ADF tests of unit root were conducted. The following models using the constant only and using the constant and trend were estimated and run for all the categories where y and z represent NCVS and UCR series.

$$\Delta\ (Y_t - z_t) = \beta_0 + \delta(Y_{t-1} - z_{t-1}) + \Delta\gamma\ (Y_{t-1} - z_{t-1}) + u_t \qquad (5.3)$$
$$\Delta\ (Y_t - z_t) = \beta_0 + \beta T + \delta(Y_{t-1} - z_{t-1}) + \Delta\gamma\ (Y_{t-1} - z_{t-1}) + u_t \qquad (5.4)$$

The ADF test was used in the place of DF because the series have autocorrelation problems.[16] The following null hypothesis of unit roots

---

[16] In time series data, the value of a variable at one period is usually correlated with its value in the next period. The correlation of a series with its own lagged variable is known as *autocorrelation* or *series correlation.* Therefore, checking a time series for autocorrelation and incorporating modifications into the analysis is essential. Autocorrelation or serial correlation of the series has been checked through a correlogram that presents autocorrelation function (ACF) and partial autocorrelation function (PAF). The numbers of lags used in the correlogram analyses was 16, the STATA default. In all the series, autocorrelation coefficients are more than .8 at the first lag, which start decaying as the number of lags increases. In most of the series after 7-8 lags, the autocorrelation coefficients start hovering around zero and then start moving toward negative values. The correlograms clearly show that all the UCR and NCVS series used in the analyses have a problem of autocorrelation. In other words, they are correlated with their lagged values. Correlograms of all the series also provide evidence that the series are nonstationary.

Table 5.6. Results of Augmented Dickey Fuller Test of Unit Root with Single Lag on Logged Differences between UCR and NCVS, 1973-2008

Crime category	ADF test statistics	1% critical value	5% critical value	10% critical value
Aggravated assault	-0.766	-3.689	-2.975	-2.619
Model with constant	-3.984	-4.297	-3.564	-3.218
Model with constant and trend				
Robbery	-1.093	-3.689	-2.975	-2.619
Model with constant	-2.695	-4.297	-3.564	-3.218
Model with constant and trend				
Burglary	-1.063	-3.689	-2.975	-2.619
Model with constant	-4.107	-4.297	-3.564	-3.218
Model with constant and trend				
Motor vehicle theft	-1.275	-3.689	-2.975	-2.619
Model with constant	-1.441	-4.297	-3.564	-3.218
Model with constant and trend				
Larceny theft	-1.363	-3.689	-2.975	-2.619
Model with constant	-3.095	-4.297	-3.564	-3.218
Model with constant and trend				
Violent crime	-0.743	-3.689	-2.975	-2.619
Model with constant	-3.510	-4.297	-3.564	-3.218
Model with constant and trend				
Property crime	-1.205	-3.689	-2.975	-2.619
Model with constant	-3.093	-4.297	-3.564	-3.218
Model with constant and trend				
Total crime	-1.147	-3.689	-2.975	-2.619
Model with constant	-3.152	-4.297	-3.564	-3.218
Model with constant and trend	-0.766	-3.689	-2.975	-2.619

in logged differences of NCVS and UCR series for all categories was tested through the ADF test, and the results are presented in Table 5.6.

H_0: $\delta = 0$

In the ADF test, the null hypothesis of unit root is rejected if the test statistic is less than the ADF critical value at a determined level of significance. When the null hypothesis of unit root is rejected, a series is said to be stationary with no unit root problems, and if the null hypothesis of unit root is not rejected, a series is nonstationary with a unit root problem. According to the results of the tests, the ADF test statistics are less than the critical values only for aggravated assault, burglary, and the aggregated category of violent crime. In the case of both aggravated assault and burglary, the values of the test statistics for the model using the constant and trend are smaller than the critical value at 5% and 10%, and in the case of violent crime the value of the test statistic is smaller than the critical value of 10%. The burglary model using the constant and trend, however, shows a lower test value than all others. The null hypothesis of unit root in the case of all three categories is rejected; thus, the logged differences of aggravated assault, burglary, and violent crime series are stationary and do not have unit root problems. Therefore, it can be concluded that the UCR and NCVS are not cointegrated for all categories except for aggravated assault, burglary, and violent crime, which may or may not be cointegrated.

Cointegration: Engle-Granger Test

The Engle-Garner test of cointegrating between the UCR and NCVS for different crime categories was conducted in four steps. First, ADF tests of stationarity were conducted to determine whether all the series have unit roots and are integrated on the same order. Second, one series was regressed against the other, and residuals were saved. Third, ADF tests of unit root were conducted on residuals. Finally, error correction models were estimated.

Nonstationarity test:

Prior to running formal cointegration tests, it was necessary to test the series for stationarity and order of integration. Details about the stationarity check and transformation of a time series are provided in Appendix C. The results of ADF tests for all the series presented in Table 5.7 shows that the test statistics of all the crime categories are greater than the critical values; therefore, the null hypothesis of nonstationarity cannot be rejected, and it must be concluded that all series used in the analyses are nonstationary and have unit root problems.

Table 5.7. Augmented Dickey Fuller Tests of Stationarity for All UCR and NCVS Series

Crime category	ADF test statistics	1% critical value	5% critical value	10% critical value
UCR aggravated assault	-1.607	-3.689	-2.975	-2.619
UCR robbery	-1.478	-3.689	-2.975	-2.619
UCR burglary	-0.611	-3.689	-2.975	-2.619
UCR motor vehicle theft	-1.117	-3.689	-2.975	-2.619
UCR larceny theft	-1.120	-3.689	-2.975	-2.619
UCR violent crime	-1.306	-3.689	-2.975	-2.619
UCR property crime	-0.610	-3.689	-2.975	-2.619
UCR total crime	-0.655	-3.689	-2.975	-2.619
NCVS aggravated assault	-0.083	-3.689	-2.975	-2.619
NCVS robbery	-0.652	-3.689	-2.975	-2.619
NCVS burglary	-0.621	-3.689	-2.975	-2.619
NCVS motor vehicle theft	-0.649	-3.689	-2.975	-2.619
NCVS larceny theft	-0.259	-3.689	-2.975	-2.619
NCVS violent crime	-0.097	-3.689	-2.975	-2.619
NCVS property crime	-0.187	-3.689	-2.975	-2.619
NCVS total crime	-0.172	-3.689	-2.975	-2.619

In order to make the series stationary first, the first difference operator was used and the ADF tests were repeated with first differenced series. The results of the ADF tests for all first differenced series are presented in Table 5.8. According to the results, the null hypotheses of nonstationarity for all series except UCR aggravated assault, UCR motor vehicle theft, and NCVS motor vehicle theft can be rejected because the test statistics are smaller than the critical values. It is, therefore, concluded that all the series except UCR aggravated assault, UCR motor vehicle theft, and NCVS motor vehicle theft become stationery after the first differencing. To make the remaining three series stationary, a second differencing was used, and the ADF tests were repeated with second differenced UCR aggravated assault, UCR motor vehicle theft, and NCVS motor vehicle theft series. The results, presented in Table 5.9, show that the test statistics in all three series are greater than the critical values; therefore, the null hypotheses of nonstationarity can be rejected. The results show that the series, which did not become stationary after the first differencing, became stationary after the second differencing.

Table 5.8. Augmented Dickey Fuller Tests of Stationarity for All First Differenced UCR and NCVS Series

Crime category	ADF test statistics	1% critical value	5% critical value	10% critical value
UCR aggravated assault	-2.524	-3.696	-2.978	-2.620
UCR robbery	-3.790	-3.696	-2.978	-2.620
UCR burglary	-5.690	-3.696	-2.978	-2.620
UCR motor vehicle theft	-2.243	-3.696	-2.978	-2.620
UCR larceny theft	-4.955	-3.696	-2.978	-2.620
UCR violent crime	-2.831	-3.696	-2.978	-2.620
UCR property crime	-4.818	-3.696	-2.978	-2.620
UCR total crime	-4.554	-3.696	-2.978	-2.620
NCVS aggravated assault	-4.833	-3.696	-2.978	-2.620
NCVS robbery	-3.039	-3.696	-2.978	-2.620
NCVS burglary	-4.019	-3.696	-2.978	-2.620
NCVS motor vehicle theft	-2.338	-3.696	-2.978	-2.620
NCVS larceny theft	-3.696	-3.696	-2.978	-2.620
NCVS violent crime	-3.990	-3.696	-2.978	-2.620
NCVS property crime	-3.616	-3.696	-2.978	-2.620
NCVS total crime	-3.621	-3.696	-2.978	-2.620

Table 5.9. Augmented Dickey Fuller Tests of Stationarity for Second Differenced UCR Aggravated Assault, UCR Motor Vehicle Theft, and NCVS Motor Vehicle Theft

Crime category	ADF test statistics	1% critical value	5% critical value	10% critical value
UCR aggravated assault	-6.606	-3.702	-2.980	-2.622
UCR motor vehicle theft	-4.512	-3.702	-2.980	-2.622
NCVS motor vehicle theft	-5.802	-3.702	-2.980	-2.622

<u>ADF test of residuals of cointegration regressions between UCR and NCVS rates</u>:

The most common method suggested and used to test the cointegration between two series is to run ADF or DF tests for residuals from cointegration regressions between two series (Engle & Granger, 1991; Gujarati, 2004; O'Brien, 1999). When a nonstationary time series is regressed on another nonstationary time series and the residuals series does not have a unit root, the two series are said to be cointegrated. The two nonstationary series NCVS and UCR are represented as y and z, and they are integrated on the order one and contain a unit root. Both nonstationary series were first regressed:

$$y_t = \beta_0 + \beta_1 z_t + u_t \tag{5.5}$$

The equation can also be written as

$$u_t = y_t - \beta_0 + \beta_1 z_t \tag{5.6}$$

Residuals that are u_t were then subjected to ADF tests of a unit root. The decision to run ADF tests with a single lag was based on the residuals being autocorrelated, which was determined through Autocorrelation Function (ACF) tests for residuals series saved from the regression analyses of the nonstationary series of the UCR and NCVS for all categories. Results of the ADF tests for residuals series are presented in Table 5.10. According to the results, the null hypothesis of a unit root can be rejected only in the case of burglary because the test statistic in that case is less than the ADF critical values.

Table 5.10. Augmented Dickey Fuller Test Results of Residuals of Cointegration Regression between UCR and NCVS Rate

Crime category	ADF test statistics	1% critical value	5% critical value	10% critical value
Aggravated assault	-1.633	-3.689	-2.975	-2.619
Model with constant	-0.831	-4.297	-3.564	-3.218
Model with constant and trend				
Robbery	-2.377	-3.689	-2.975	-2.619
Model with constant	-2.222	-4.297	-3.564	-3.218
Model with constant and trend				
Burglary	-4.303	-3.689	-2.975	-2.619
Model with constant	-4.283	-4.297	-3.564	-3.218
Model with constant and trend				
Motor vehicle theft	-1.533	-3.689	-2.975	-2.619
Model with constant	-0.122	-4.297	-3.564	-3.218
Model with constant and trend				
Larceny theft	-2.359	-3.689	-2.975	-2.619
Model with constant	-2.302	-4.297	-3.564	-3.218
Model with constant and trend				
Violent crime	-2.504	-3.689	-2.975	-2.619
Model with constant	-2.413	-4.297	-3.564	-3.218
Model with constant and trend				
Property crime	-1.787	-3.689	-2.975	-2.619
Model with constant	-1.303	-4.297	-3.564	-3.218
Model with constant and trend				
Total crime	-2.335	-3.689	-2.975	-2.619
Model with constant	-2.204	-4.297	-3.564	-3.218
Model with constant and trend	-1.633	-3.689	-2.975	-2.619

In case of all other categories, the ADF test statistics are greater than the critical value; therefore, the null hypothesis of unit root or nonstationarity cannot be rejected. In other words, the residuals saved from the cointegration regression between NCVS and UCR rates have unit root problems in all crime categories included in the analyses except burglary. Therefore, it can be concluded that the UCR and NCVS series are cointegrated only for burglary and not cointegrated for other categories of crime. The cointegration test results presented in Table 5.10 show that the ADF test statistics for robbery, larceny theft, and violent crime are slightly less than the 10% critical value, but far below for aggravated assault, motor vehicle theft, and the property crime categories.

The results from three methods of cointegration tests—plotting of spreads, ADF tests of logged differences of UCR and NCVS series, and ADF tests of residuals of cointegration regression between nonstationary series of the UCR and NCVS—are clearly mixed. According to the rate spread plots, the UCR and NCVS are not cointegrated for any category because none of the rate spreads (differences between UCR and NCVS rates) is flat, although the rate spread of burglary is flatter than the others. According to the ADF tests of logged differences of UCR and NCVS rates, the UCR and NCVS are cointegrated only for aggravated assault, burglary, and the violent crime category. However, the last test is considered a more formal test of cointegration, and according to the results of the last test the UCR and NCVS are cointegrated only for burglary. The results in the second test partially support the results in the third test because the ADF test value for burglary is the lowest. It can be inferred from the results of the cointegration test that robbery, larceny theft, and violent crime are in the process of cointegrating, and aggravated assault, motor vehicle theft, and property crime are the least cointegrated crime categories.

<u>Error correction model</u>:

Two series that are cointegrated or have a long-term equilibrium relationship may have a disequilibrium relationship in the short term. The two cointegrating series having a short-term disequilibrium relationship, however, are brought together by an error-correction mechanism. In the error correction model, the first difference of one of the two cointegrated series is regressed against the first difference of another series and one lagged value of the residuals from the cointegration equation between the two series. The error correction equation for two cointegrated series—NCVS and UCR rates—can be written as following:

$$\Delta y_t = \alpha_0 + \alpha_1 \Delta z_t + \alpha_2 u_{t-1} + \varepsilon_t \quad (4.7)$$

where Δ is the first difference operator, ϵ is the error term, and u_{t-1} is the one period lagged value of the error term of the cointegration equation between the y and z series. Table 5.11 presents the results of the error correction analysis between the UCR and NCVS crime rates for the categories of crimes.

Table 5.11. Results of Error Correction Models between the UCR and NCVS Rates for Different Categories of Crimes

Variables	Coefficient	*SE*	*z*
Aggravated assault			
Dependent variable ΔUCR			
Error correction term	-0.0853	0.0400	-2.13
ΔUCR_{t-1}	0.1056	0.1693	0.62
$\Delta NCVA_{t-1}$	0.0463	0.0440	1.05
Dependent variable ΔNCVS			
Error correction term	0.0142	0.1697	0.08
ΔUCR_{t-1}	0.4208	0.7180	0.59
$\Delta NCVA_{t-1}$	-0.1350	0.1865	-0.72
Robbery			
Dependent variable ΔUCR			
Error correction term	-0.1854	0.1112	-1.67
ΔUCR_{t-1}	0.4881	0.1676	2.91
$\Delta NCVA_{t-1}$	0.0363	0.0731	0.50
Dependent variable ΔNCVS			
Error correction term	0.4473	0.2408	1.86
ΔUCR_{t-1}	1.1689	0.3629	3.22
$\Delta NCVA_{t-1}$	-0.1388	0.1584	-0.88

Table 5.11. Results of Error Correction Models between the UCR and NCVS Rates for Different Categories of Crimes (Continued)

Variables	Coefficient	*SE*	*z*
Burglary			
Dependent variable ΔUCR			
Error correction term	-0.9833	0.2308	-4.26
ΔUCR_{t-1}	0.0557	0.1658	0.34
$\Delta NCVA_{t-1}$	0.0148	0.1373	0.11
Dependent variable ΔNCVS			
Error correction term	-0.1914	0.3494	-0.55
ΔUCR_{t-1}	0.1048	0.2510	0.42
$\Delta NCVA_{t-1}$	0.0636	0.2078	0.31
Motor vehicle theft			
Dependent variable ΔUCR			
Error correction term	-0.1272	0.0891	-1.43
ΔUCR_{t-1}	0.6740	0.1898	3.55
$\Delta NCVA_{t-1}$	-0.0168	0.1062	-0.16
Dependent variable ΔNCVS			
Error correction term	0.0352	0.1739	0.20
ΔUCR_{t-1}	1.1899	0.3707	3.21
$\Delta NCVA_{t-1}$	-0.2689	0.2074	-1.30
Larceny theft			
Dependent variable ΔUCR			
Error correction term	-0.1882	0.0795	-2.37
ΔUCR_{t-1}	0.2288	0.1456	1.57
$\Delta NCVA_{t-1}$	0.0187	0.0394	0.47
Dependent variable ΔNCVS			
Error correction term	-0.0325	0.3884	-0.08
ΔUCR_{t-1}	0.0707	0.7115	0.10
$\Delta NCVA_{t-1}$	0.0363	0.1927	0.19

Table 5.11. Results of Error Correction Models between the UCR and NCVS Rates for Different Categories of Crimes (Continued)

Variables	Coefficient	*SE*	*z*
Violent crime			
Dependent variable ΔUCR			
Error correction term	-0.1046	0.0591	-1.77
ΔUCR_{t-1}	0.2751	0.1618	1.70
$\Delta NCVA_{t-1}$	0.0558	0.0520	1.07
Dependent variable ΔNCVS			
Error correction term	0.1304	0.2041	0.64
ΔUCR_{t-1}	0.8810	0.5588	1.58
$\Delta NCVA_{t-1}$	-0.1303	0.1797	-0.73
Property crime			
Dependent variable ΔUCR			
Error correction term	-0.2463	0.1035	-2.38
ΔUCR_{t-1}	0.1370	0.1514	0.91
$\Delta NCVA_{t-1}$	0.0483	0.0594	0.81
Dependent variable ΔNCVS			
Error correction term	0.0249	0.3375	0.07
ΔUCR_{t-1}	0.2989	0.4936	0.61
$\Delta NCVA_{t-1}$	0.0086	0.1937	0.04
Total crime			
Dependent variable ΔUCR			
Error correction term	-0.2090	0.0938	-2.23
ΔUCR_{t-1}	0.1425	0.1541	0.92
$\Delta NCVA_{t-1}$	0.0535	0.0599	0.89
Dependent variable ΔNCVS			
Error correction term	0.0601	0.2999	0.20
ΔUCR_{t-1}	0.3196	0.4924	0.65
$\Delta NCVA_{t-1}$	0.0323	0.1914	0.17

The coefficients of error correction terms are the most important indicators to understand the error correction mechanism because they show how quickly a series moves backs to its equilibrium with another integrating series after it is pushed away by an external shock. The error-correction coefficients in all categories of crime for the UCR and NCVS are small except for UCR burglary (-0.9833) and, to some extent, NCVS robbery (0.4473). These categories, especially UCR burglary, adjust to the shock and return to the equilibrium more quickly than other crime categories. Conversely, NCVS motor vehicle theft (-0.1272) and larceny theft (-0.0325) have the most gradual and slow movement back to the equilibrium. The error correction mechanism of UCR series is responsible for the cointegration of the UCR and NCVS burglary series. In case of robbery, which is in the process of cointegrating, the error mechanism of the NCVS series is playing an important role.

CONVERGENCE ANALYSIS WITH ADJUSTED UCR RATES

The second research question, which is an extension of the first question, asks whether the adjustment of UCR rates for the reporting percentages of crimes to police, as estimated by the NCVS, will affect the convergence between the two series. One important finding in the literature is that the convergence between the UCR and NCVS has been greatly influenced by the changes in reporting and recording of crime. The UCR data are a function of reporting and recording rather than a real presentation of all crime incidents (Reiss & Biderman, 1967). The UCR crime rates are determined by the reporting of crime by people, discovery of crime by police, and recording and reporting practices of law enforcement. The NCVS data on citizens' reporting crime to police reveals that nonreporting of crime is the biggest reason for the divergence between the UCR and NCVS. In 1973, only 52% of aggravated assaults, 51% of robberies, 46% of burglaries, 67% of motor vehicle thefts, and 23% of larceny thefts were reported to police according to the respondents in the victimization survey. The reporting percentage, however, kept increasing with time, and in the 2008 victimization survey, respondents reported 62% of aggravated assaults, 60.5% of robberies, 56.2% of burglaries, 79.6% of motor vehicle thefts, and 33.6% of larceny thefts. Reporting percentages for all categories have increased over 10% in the past 36 years. The trend of percentages for reporting people crime to the police, as reported in the victimization survey, is shown in Figure 5.5. This increase might have been possible because of increased police productivity, changed attitudes of people toward the police and crime, and improved measures of data collection.

The temporal variability in reporting data supports the police productivity hypothesis and changed attitude of people toward crime and the police. Studies have reported police productivity as an important factor for increase in UCR rates until the beginning of the 1990s. They have also reported an increase in the UCR rates as one of the determining factors in reducing the divergence between the two series (Catalano, 2006; O'Brien, 1996). Recent studies have provided support in favor of the police productivity thesis and the role of increased police productivity in terms of affecting UCR rates and facilitating convergence between the two series (Catalano, 2006).

Although increased police productivity is an important factor in increasing UCR rates, people reporting crime to the police reflects the attitude of people toward crime and the police and is the most important determinant of UCR crime rates. The decision of people to report crime to the police is influenced by several factors, such as a personal cost/benefit calculus, demographic composition, police-public relations, development in communication technology, and so on. In view of the above facts and the availability of a direct and reliable measure, it was decided to test the convergence between the two series after adjusting the UCR rates for the reporting. In the absence of a direct and clear measure of police productivity, it was also decided not to adjust UCR rates for police productivity.[17]

---

[17] There is no direct measure of police productivity available. In the case of reporting crime to the police, the NCVS provides a direct measure by asking the respondents about reporting crime to police. In view of this, it was decided to adjust UCR rates only for the reporting of crime. Several variables conceptualized as part of police productivity—employment composition, especially civilianization of the police department; expenditure of law enforcement per capita sworn officers; computerization and record management; and many other factors—present problems for measurement and are unavailable for the entire period of the study. It was, therefore, decided to include some of them in the models explaining convergence, but not to use them for adjusting UCR rates.

Figure 5.5. Percentage of Reported Crimes to Police in NCVS, 1973-2008

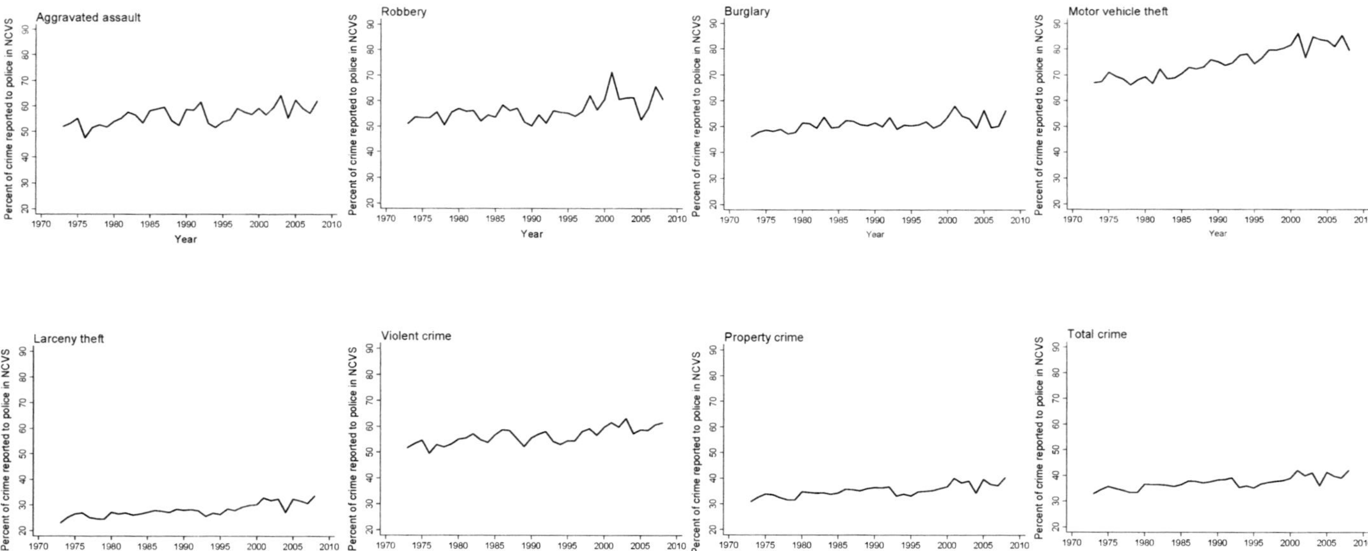

Figure 5.6. UCR, NCVS, and Adjusted UCR Rates for Aggravated assault, Robbery, Burglary, Motor Vehicle Theft, Larceny Theft, Violent Crime, Property Crime, and Total Crime, 1973-2008

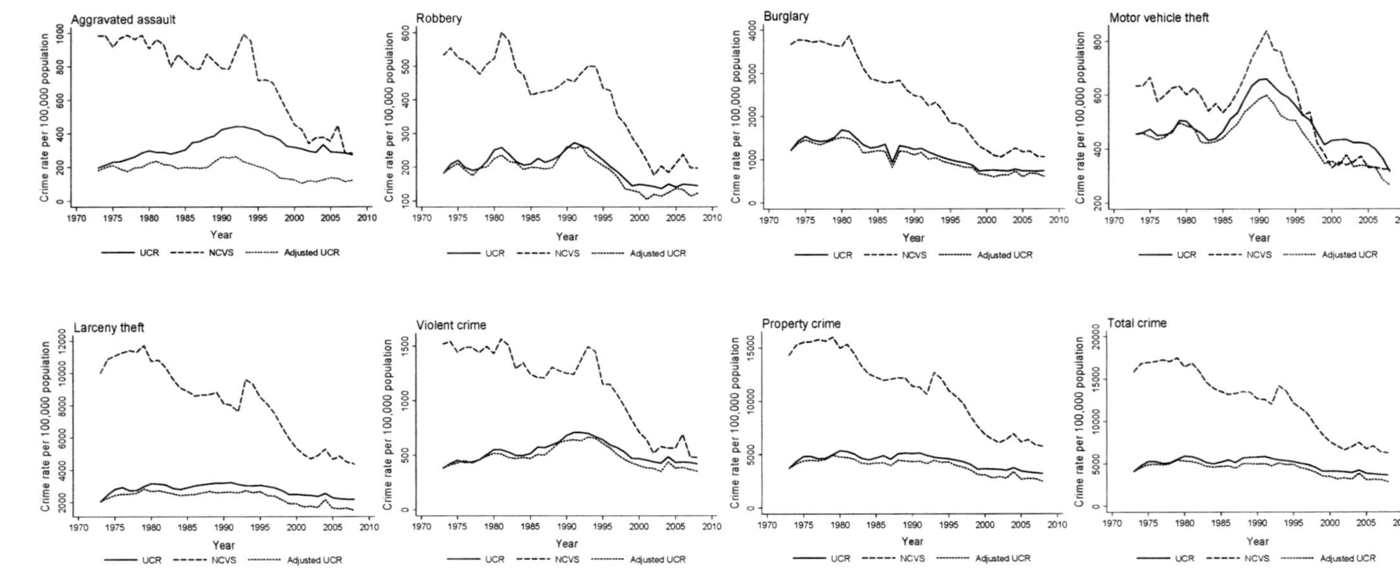

It is hypothesized that that the level of convergence between the two data series would be different if the UCR rates were adjusted for reporting percentages before the convergence test was conducted. For testing this hypothesis and addressing the second research question, the UCR crime rates were adjusted for reporting, and then the major steps of the convergence analyses were repeated. To adjust the UCR for reporting, reporting percentages in the 1973 victimization survey were taken as a base (100%), and then reporting percentages in subsequent years were calculated in terms of the percentages of the base. Then the UCR crime rates from 1974 to 2008 were adjusted by multiplying them by the calculated percentages for every year.

Graphic Analysis

Rates of the UCR, NCVS, and adjusted UCR for all disaggragated and aggragated crime catagories were plotted against time (see Figure 5.6). Adjusted UCR rates were continously lower than UCR rates for all disaggragated and aggragated catagories. The differences between UCR and adjusted UCR rates do not seem to be different for different catagories. When the UCR is adjusted for reporting, the divergence between the UCR and NCVS increases for all catagories. This increase occurs because the adjustment of the UCR rates for the reporting percentages of crime reduces the UCR rates. The reduction in the UCR rates after adjustments for reporting supports the police productivity thesis which attributes some of the increase in the UCR to improvements in the reporting and recording practices of police. The trends in the UCR and adjusted UCR rates are similar and, thus, indicative of the reliability of the UCR and police reporting data in the NCVS. In all categories, except burglary, the discrepancy between the UCR and the adjusted UCR increased over time.

Correlational Analysis

The correlations between the adjusted UCR and NCVS and correlations between the UCR and NCVS for all disaggregated and aggregated categories are presented in Table 5.12. Although the graphs in Figure 5.6 indicate that the UCR and NCVS become more divergent after UCR rates are adjusted for reporting, the correlational analyses between the two series for the period of 1973-2008 tell a slightly different story. The correlations between the adjusted UCR and NCVS are higher for all categories than the correlations between the UCR and NCVS. The correlation coefficients for all categories are positive and over .8, except for the aggravated assault and violent crime categories.

Table 5.12. Correlation between Adjusted UCR and NCVS Crime Rates and UCR and NCVS Crime Rates

Crime category	*r*	
	Adjusted UCR and NCVS	UCR and NCVS
Aggravated assault	0.1920	0.0170
Robbery	0.8533	0.8359
Burglary	0.9642	0.9496
Motor vehicle theft	0.9542	0.8445
Larceny theft	0.8282	0.5858
Violent crime[a]	0.5411	0.3713
Property crime[b]	0.9129	0.8043
Total crime[c]	0.8918	0.7643

[a]Violent crime category includes aggravated assault and robbery.

[b]Property crime category includes burglary, motor vehicle theft and larceny theft.

[c]Total crime category includes aggravated assault, robbery, burglary, motor vehicle theft, and larceny theft.

The conflicting picture presented by the graphic and correlational analyses and the increase in correlation coefficients after adjustment of the UCR rates for the reporting of crime to police, however, reiterate the fact that correlational analyses do not provide true assessments of convergence or divergence between the two series; rather they simply indicate how the two series have been moving together without fluctuation or changes. The two series continuously came closer because of the increase in the UCR and the decrease in the NCVS rates. The adjustment of the UCR for the rate of reporting reduces the increase of the UCR which in turn increases the correlation coefficients between the adjusted UCR and NCVS in comparison with the correlation coefficients between the UCR and NCVS.

In order to show the trend of correlations between the adjusted UCR and NCVS, the estimated correlation coefficients of the split series are presented in Table 5.13. The overall picture remains the

Table 5.13. Trend of Correlations between Differenced UCR and NCVS Rates, 1973-2008

Data range	*r*							
	Aggravated assault rate	Robbery rate	Burglary rate	Motor vehicle theft rate	Larceny theft rate	Violent crime rate	Property crime rate	Total crime rate
1973-1991	-0.6767	0.0324	0.7805	0.8960	-0.0013	-0.6088	0.4363	0.2677
1974-1992	-0.5984	0.0641	0.8404	0.9140	0.0089	-0.5247	0.6032	0.4278
1975-1993	-0.2780	0.1247	0.8519	0.9093	0.1432	-0.2918	0.6833	0.5246
1976-1994	-0.1437	0.1368	0.8592	0.9351	0.2572	-0.1843	0.7172	0.5662
1977-1995	-0.2106	0.2033	0.8720	0.9287	0.3173	-0.2001	0.7312	0.5747
1978-1996	-0.1809	0.3119	0.8919	0.9217	0.5027	-0.1299	0.8095	0.6934
1979-1997	-0.1009	0.4595	0.8988	0.9298	0.6405	0.0032	0.8497	0.7617
1980-1998	0.0010	0.6324	0.8967	0.9411	0.6583	0.2154	0.8515	0.7794
1981-1999	0.1354	0.7267	0.9011	0.9553	0.7649	0.3981	0.8720	0.8252
1982-2000	0.3405	0.8032	0.8935	0.9595	0.8369	0.5912	0.8994	0.8697
1983-2001	0.5177	0.8950	0.8931	0.9744	0.8958	0.7632	0.9254	0.9122
1984-2002	0.6526	0.9005	0.9086	0.9732	0.9320	0.8340	0.9545	0.9452
1985-2003	0.7830	0.9262	0.9110	0.9796	0.9561	0.9042	0.9683	0.9643
1986-2004	0.8447	0.9244	0.9047	0.9798	0.9458	0.9249	0.9635	0.9594
1987-2005	0.8933	0.9231	0.9005	0.9816	0.9534	0.9431	0.9661	0.9639
1988-2006	0.9241	0.9277	0.9891	0.9829	0.9537	0.9587	0.9794	0.9771

Table 5.13. Trend of Correlations between Differenced UCR and NCVS Rates, 1973-2008 (Continued)

Data range	*r*							
	Aggravated assault rate	Robbery rate	Burglary rate	Motor vehicle theft rate	Larceny theft rate	Violent crime rate	Property crime rate	Total crime rate
1989-2007	0.9386	0.9334	0.9865	0.9801	0.9553	0.9675	0.9796	0.9776
1990-2008	0.9424	0.9321	0.9847	0.9721	0.9559	0.9682	0.9774	0.9761

same, with no substantial differences present. The aggravated assault series in this case also moves from a highly negative correlation to a highly positive one.

The mean correlation of the 18 series between the adjusted UCR rates and NCVS aggravated assault rates is higher. In addition, the variance between correlations of the 18 series is higher in the case of the adjusted UCR and NCVS aggravated assault rates than between the UCR and NCVS aggravated assault rates.

In case of robbery, burglary, and motor vehicle theft, there do not seem to be noticeable differences between correlations with and without the adjusted UCR. In case of larceny, the patterns of correlations between the UCR and NCVS and the adjusted UCR and NCVS are different. The larceny theft category shows a different trend of correlation when the UCR rates are adjusted for reporting percentage. The first series shows a negative correlation, which quickly becomes positive and keeps increasing until the last series. The property and total crime categories are greatly influenced by the larceny theft category because the correlations between the adjusted UCR and NCVS for property and total crime categories are positive and higher than the correlation between the UCR and NCVS.

Convergence Test through Regression of Rate Differences on Time

The differences and logged differences between adjusted UCR and NCVS rates were regressed against the year variable, and the results are presented in Tables 5.14 and 5.15.

Table 5.14. Results of Bivariate OLS Regressions for Different Crime Categories

Crime category	Coefficient	*SE*	*t* statistics	*p* value
Aggravated assault	-21.5125	1.0341	-20.80	0.000
Robbery	-8.2068	.6034	-13.60	0.000
Burglary	-67.1894	2.3268	-28.88	0.000
Motor vehicle theft	-5.0507	.8898	-5.68	0.000
Larceny theft	-186.3539	9.8477	-18.92	0.000
Violent crime	-29.6194	1.5225	-19.45	0.000
Property crime	-261.7192	10.8288	-24.17	0.000
Total crime	-291.0436	12.0170	-24.22	0.000

Table 5.15. Results of Bivariate OLS Regressions for Different Crime Categories with Logged Rates

Crime category	Coefficient	*SE*	*t* statistics	*p* value
Aggravated assault	-.03741	.00159	-23.47	0.000
Robbery	-.01443	.00173	-8.31	0.000
Burglary	-.01518	.00129	-11.75	0.000
Motor vehicle theft	-.00880	.00142	-6.20	0.000
Larceny theft	-.01578	.00110	-14.26	0.000
Violent crime	-.02836	.00139	-20.28	0.000
Property crime	-.01574	.00078	-19.94	0.000
Total crime	-.01707	.00081	-20.91	0.000

These results show that all the regression coefficients are negative and statistically significant because the *p* values for all categories are less than .001. Similarly, the regression coefficients in Table 5.15 are also negative and statistically significant because the *p* values for all categories are less than .001. That is, the rate difference between the NCVS and adjusted UCR, as well as the proportions between the NCVS and adjusted UCR, significantly decreased between 1973 and 2008. The regression results with the UCR rates and the adjusted UCR rates are almost identical, and the adjustment of the UCR did not make any substantial difference in the results of the regressions for the variable of rate differences over time.

Cointegration Analyses of Convergence

All three steps of cointegration analyses, adopted while testing the cointegration between the UCR and NCVS, were repeated between the adjusted UCR and NCVS. The ADF test for logged differences between the NCVS and the adjusted UCR and the ADF test for residuals of cointegration regressions between the adjusted UCR and NCVS for all crime categories were conducted, but prior to these formal tests of cointegration, rate spread between the NCVS and adjusted UCR were plotted, and a stationarity check for adjusted UCR rates were conducted.

Figure 5.7. Adjusted UCR and NCVS rates and rate difference, 1973-2008

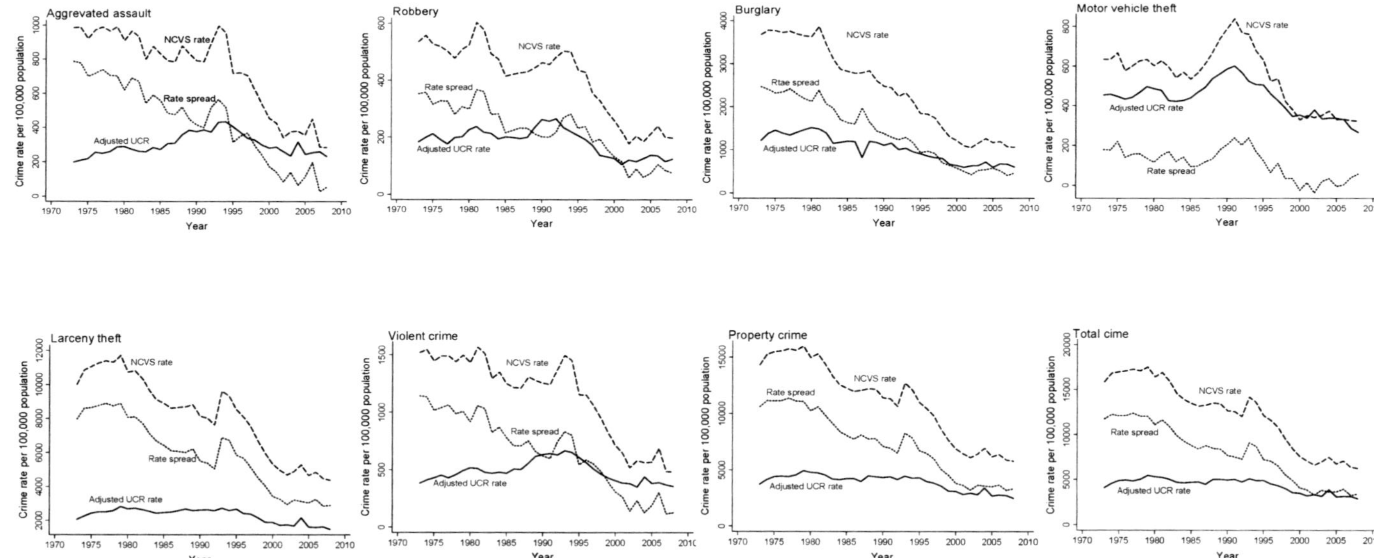

Rate spread plots:

The adjusted UCR and NCVS rates and their difference are plotted in Figure 5.7. There is no substantial change in terms of the divergence between the two series after the UCR is adjusted for rate of reporting. Because the UCR rates were flatter after the adjustment, the divergence slightly increased. The spread that is the rate difference between the adjusted UCR and NCVS is primarily influenced by the NCVS rate, and adjustment did not cause noticeable changes.

The ADF test of logged differences between adjusted UCR and NCVS rates:

The results of the ADF tests of logged differences between the adjusted UCR and NCVS rates are presented in Table 5.16. The ADF test results did not change after the UCR rates were adjusted for rate of reporting. Similar to the results of the ADF tests of logged differences between the UCR and NCVS rates presented in Table 5.6, the ADF test statistics were at less than the critical values only for aggravated assault, burglary, and the aggregated category of violent crime. In the cases of the aggravated assault category and burglary, the values of the test statistics for the model using the constant and trend were smaller than the critical values of 5% and 10%, and in case of violent crime, the value of the test statistic was smaller than the critical value of 10%. Thus, the adjustment of the UCR did not change the results, and only the logged differences of aggravated assault, burglary, and violent crime rates did not have unit roots and may be considered cointegrated according to this test.

Cointegration: Engle-Granger test:

All steps of the cointegration test were repeated with the adjusted UCR. Stationarity tests of adjusted UCR series were also conducted, and according to the test, all adjusted UCR series were nonstationary, which is required in order to conduct the Engle-Granger test of cointegration. Nonstationary series of the adjusted UCR were regressed against NCVS series, and residuals were saved. Then, the ADF tests of the saved residuals were conducted. Results are presented in Table 5.17.

Table 5.16. Augmented Dickey Fuller Test Results of Logged Differences between Adjusted UCR and NCVS, 1973-2008

Crime category	ADF test statistics	1% critical value	5% critical value	10% critical value
Aggravated assault	-0.862	-3.689	-2.975	-2.619
Model with constant	-4.615	-4.297	-3.564	-3.218
Model with constant and trend				
Robbery	-1.406	-3.689	-2.975	-2.619
Model with constant	-2.447	-4.297	-3.564	-3.218
Model with constant and trend				
Burglary	-1.217	-3.689	-2.975	-2.619
Model with constant	-4.300	-4.297	-3.564	-3.218
Model with constant and trend				
Motor vehicle theft	-1.515	-3.689	-2.975	-2.619
Model with constant	-1.762	-4.297	-3.564	-3.218
Model with constant and trend				
Larceny theft	-1.839	-3.689	-2.975	-2.619
Model with constant	-2.191	-4.297	-3.564	-3.218
Model with constant and trend				
Violent crime	-0.849	-3.689	-2.975	-2.619
Model with constant	-3.603	-4.297	-3.564	-3.218
Model with constant and trend				
Property crime	-1.518	-3.689	-2.975	-2.619
Model with constant	-2.523	-4.297	-3.564	-3.218
Model with constant and trend				
Total crime	-1.390	-3.689	-2.975	-2.619
Model with constant	-2.883	-4.297	-3.564	-3.218
Model with constant and trend	-0.862	-3.689	-2.975	-2.619

The results of the cointegration analyses through the ADF tests of residuals saved from the cointegration regression between the two series—adjusted UCR and NCVS—were almost identical to the results of the cointegration analysis with the non-adjusted UCR presented in

Table 4.10. The ADF test statistics for all categories of crime, with the exception of burglary, were more than the critical values. All of the residual series, except burglary, had unit root problems. Therefore, it can be concluded that the adjusted UCR and NCVS, similar to the UCR and NCVS, are cointegrated only for burglary.

Table 5.17. Augmented Dickey Fuller Test Results of Residuals of Cointegration Regression between Adjusted UCR and NCVS

Crime category	ADF test statistics	1% critical value	5% critical value	10% critical value
Aggravated assault	-1.785	-3.689	-2.975	-2.619
Model with constant	-1.005	-4.297	-3.564	-3.218
Model with constant and trend				
Robbery	-2.177	-3.689	-2.975	-2.619
Model with constant	-2.010	-4.297	-3.564	-3.218
Model with constant and trend				
Burglary	-4.766	-3.689	-2.975	-2.619
Model with constant	-4.700	-4.297	-3.564	-3.218
Model with constant and trend				
Motor vehicle theft	-2.231	-3.689	-2.975	-2.619
Model with constant	-1.732	-4.297	-3.564	-3.218
Model with constant and trend				
Larceny theft	-2.115	-3.689	-2.975	-2.619
Model with constant	-1.704	-4.297	-3.564	-3.218
Model with constant and trend				
Violent crime	-1.842	-3.689	-2.975	-2.619
Model with constant	-1.263	-4.297	-3.564	-3.218
Model with constant and trend				
Property crime	-2.316	-3.689	-2.975	-2.619
Model with constant	-1.942	-4.297	-3.564	-3.218
Model with constant and trend				
Total crime	-2.371	-3.689	-2.975	-2.619
Model with constant	-1.996	-4.297	-3.564	-3.218
Model with constant and trend	-1.785	-3.689	-2.975	-2.619

The results in Table 5.17 show the two series in the process of converging for robbery, motor vehicle theft, larceny theft, and property crime because the ADF test statistics for these categories are close to the critical value of 10%. The adjustment of the UCR for reporting made some differences in this regard. The ADF test statistics increased for motor vehicle theft and property crime and decreased for violent crime when the cointegration tests were conducted after adjusting the UCR for reporting.

RESULT SUMMARY AND HYPOTHESES TESTING

Research questions 1 and 2 have been addressed and the related hypotheses tested through the data analysis presented in this chapter. The following section provides brief descriptions of the results of the testing of Hypotheses 1 to 4.

H_1: The UCR and NCVS data series will have come closer to each other and moved toward convergence during the period of 1973-2008.

This hypothesis is partially supported by the data analyses. A combination of data analyses strategies were used, and the results from the different methods were not identical. Graphic analysis in which crime rates, differenced crime rates, and logged crime rates were plotted against time tended to indicate a continuous decrease of divergence between the two series. The differences and proportions between the two series have substantially decreased over time. The UCR and NCVS series move together with short-term variability after the trends were removed through differencing. The correlational analyses also partially supported the hypothesis. The correlation coefficients between the two series for the entire period were over .8 for most categories, but they decreased substantially when the trends were removed through the first differencing. However, the correlational analysis does not indicate the trend of the relationships. Split series correlation analyses, however, solves the problem to some extent, and the results of split series correlations fully support the hypothesis because the correlation coefficients for all categories improve with time and cross the threshold of .8.

The OLS regression method fully supported the hypothesis. The rate differences between the NCVS and UCR for all disaggregated and aggregated categories of crime were regressed against time. The significant and negative regression coefficients for all categories indicate that the differences between the series have decreased significantly over time. The cointegration analyses that adopted two methods supported the hypothesis partially. Only aggravated assault, burglary, and violent crime were found to be cointegrated when the ADF tests for logged crime rate differences were conducted. The more formal test of cointegration, known as the Engle-Granger test, was conducted; according to the results of this test, the UCR and NCVS series are cointegrated only for burglary, and are in the process of cointegrating for robbery, larceny theft, and violent crime.

H_2: The UCR and NCVS data series display different levels of convergence for different aggregated and disaggregated categories of crime.

Hypothesis 2 was also supported partially by the data analyses. The graphs plotting the series against time show that the relationships between the two series differ across all categories. The correlation coefficients in correctional analysis for the entire series, as well as the split series, are different for different categories. In addition, the test statistics from the ADF tests of logged differences between UCR and NCVS rates are different for different categories of crimes. Finally, the ADF test statistics from the Engle-Granger test are also different for various categories of crime.

H_3: Aggregated and disaggregated categories of violent crime should show stronger convergence than property crime categories.

This hypothesis was partially supported in the data analyses. The time-line graphs show that aggravated assault, robbery, and the aggregated violent crime are in the process of overlapping, but burglary, larceny theft, and aggregated property crime still maintain a substantial divergence. Correlational analyses did not support this hypothesis completely because the correlation coefficients of aggravated assault and violent crime for the entire period were the lowest. The split series correlation analyses, however, supported this hypothesis to some extent because the correlation coefficient of violent crime was higher than that for property crime. However, the results of cointegration analyses did not provide clear support for this hypothesis. The two series are in the process of cointegrating for robbery and violent crime, but not for aggravated assault.

H_4: Adjusted UCR rates for the reporting of crimes to police and NCVS rates for different crime categories are likely to show different levels of convergence.

This hypothesis was again partially supported in the data analyses. Although the graphic analysis shows greater divergence between the two series after the UCR rates are adjusted for rate of reporting, the results of the correlational and cointegration analyses with and without adjustment are almost identical. The results of the formal cointegration test varied slightly when the adjusted UCR rates were used in the analysis, although burglary remained the only category on which the two series were cointegrated. The two series, which were in the process of converging for robbery and violent crime, showed the process of converging for motor vehicle theft and property crime when the cointegration tests were conducted after the adjustment.

SUMMARY

In this chapter, Research Questions 1 and 2 were addressed, and the related hypotheses were tested. A combination of analytic strategies was adopted because there is no perfect strategy available to test the convergence between the two time series and other researchers have used varying strategies. A combination of graphic presentations, estimations of correlations for the entire series and split series, estimations of regression of rate differences on time, and cointegration analyses provided a better methodological strategy to explore and understand the convergence between the UCR and NCVS.

All four hypotheses related to the first two questions were not fully supported, but the value of the research is not diminished. The most important hypothesis, which addressed the convergence between the UCR and NCVS, was partially supported and provided support for the idea that the two series measure the same phenomenon and will maintain a more stable relationship in the future. The data analyses in the next chapter focus on addressing the second important question, which seeks to explain the changes documented in the relationship between the UCR and NCVS over time.

CHAPTER 6

Modeling Convergence: Investigation of Factors

The second research question addressed the factors underlying the convergence between the UCR and NCVS. The convergence analyses between the two series have shown that the divergences have decreased significantly and the series have either converged or are in the process of converging for most of the categories of crime. The second step that seeks to explain the convergence between the UCR and NCVS involves identification and estimation of time-series regression models. The first step of the modeling process includes the regression of differences between the rates of the two series against the trend variables and single-lagged value of the dependent variables (AR 1).

$$y_t - z_t = \beta_0 + \beta_1 t + \epsilon_t \quad (6.1)$$

$$y_t - z_t = \beta_0 + \beta_1 (y_{t-1} - z_{t-1}) + \epsilon_t \quad (6.2)$$

The second step of the modeling process includes regression of differences between the rates of the two series against the various predictor variables, regressions of differences between the rates of the two series against the various predictor variables and trend, and finally, the AR1 model with predictor variables.

$$y_t - z_t = \alpha_0 + \propto_1 \omega t + \epsilon_t \quad (6.3)$$

$$y_t - z_t = \alpha_0 + \alpha_1 \omega t + \alpha_2 t + \epsilon_t \quad (6.4)$$

$$y_t - z_t = \alpha_0 + \alpha_1 \omega t + \alpha_2 (y_{t-1} - z_{t-1}) + \epsilon_t \quad (6.5)$$

The model-building process in the second step of the analysis was governed by the theoretical relevance of the predictor variables, their contribution to the adjusted R^2, and the availability of longitudinal data. For every category of crime included in the study, three sets of OLS regressions were estimated. In model 1 of the first set, all predictor variables were included. In the second model, some of the variables were removed, a decision based on the theoretical importance of a variable and its contribution to the explained variance of the model. In model 3, further variables were removed and a "lean and mean" model was achieved. In the second set of models, the time trend variable was included, along with other predictor variables, and a similar process of model-building was followed. In the third sets of models, the single-lagged value of the dependent variable was included, along with other predictor variables, and a similar process of model building was followed.

ASSUMPTIONS AND DATA ISSUES

Assumptions of linearity, zero-conditional means, lack of perfect collinearity, homoscedasticity, and lack of serial correlation are important to OLS regression of time-series data. Under these assumptions, the OLS estimates with time-series data are a best linear unbiased estimator (BLUE). The assumption of a zero-conditional mean implies that the error term in any given period is uncorrelated with the explanatory variables in all the periods. Assumption of no perfect collinearity means that no independent variable is constant in a perfect linear combination with the others. Assumptions of homoscedasticity and no serial correlation are important and improve the efficiency of estimates, although the OLS estimates remain unbiased if these assumptions are not met. In addition, a homoscedasticity assumption means that the error variance is independent of all the independent variables and it is constant over time. The assumptions of autocorrelation in time-series OLS regression mean that the time series of error terms are not serially correlated. In relaxing the assumptions, the assumption of linearity and zero-conditional means were assumed, and it was decided to check the assumptions of no multicollinearity and autocorrelation.

Multicollinearity

For detecting multicollinearity, two approaches are used. One is to estimate and examine the simple correlation coefficients between explanatory variables used in the model. The second approach is to calculate the variance inflation factor (VIF). To do so, independent variables are regressed on one independent variable, and the VIFs for the coefficients are calculated. This study used both approaches to detect multicollinearity. A correlation matrix with only the relevant independent variables is presented in Table 6.1. The VIFs of the coefficients of all explanatory variables were calculated. The correlation coefficients in the correlation matrix table show high correlations among most of the explanatory variables indicating toward multicollinearity among the variables. The VIFs for almost all explanatory variables were more than 5, indicating the problem of multicollinearity in the data. Although the analysis showed a high level of multicollinearity, it was decided to do nothing and proceed with the analyses for the following reasons.

The most common and effective way to deal with the issue of multicollinearity is to drop some of the explanatory variables from the analyses, but dropping variables from the analyses may cause the potential problem of specification error. The severely limited availability of some of the time-series data and theoretical relevance of the available variables were the main concern behind the decision not to drop any explanatory variable from the analyses in the interest of more complete model specification. Exclusion of theoretically relevant variables may cause specification errors and bias the estimates while the presence of some multicollinearity only reduces the efficiency of the estimates. The issue of multicollinearity was, however, taken into account while dropping the variables during the model-buildings process.

Autocorrelation

Autocorrelation is a frequent problem in analysis with time-series data. The most common technique to check the problem of autocorrelation in

Table 6.1. Correlation Matrix between Important Explanatory Variables Used in the Models

	Household	Population	% Black	% Hispanic	% below high	Employees	% female officers	% sworn officers	Expense on police	NCVS redesign	% reporting	Fear
Household	1.00											
Population	0.99	1.00										
% Black	0.98	0.96	1.00									
% Hispanic	0.99	1.00	0.95	1.00								
% below High	-0.98	-0.96	-0.99	-0.94	1.00							
Employees	0.99	0.99	0.98	0.98	-0.97	1.00						
% female officers	0.97	0.94	0.97	0.92	-0.99	0.95	1.00					
% sworn officers	-0.97	-0.95	-0.97	-0.93	1.00	-0.96	-1.00	1.00				
Expense on police	0.96	0.99	0.92	0.99	-0.90	0.97	0.87	-0.89	1.00			
NCVS redesign	0.79	0.80	0.73	0.80	-0.76	0.77	0.77	-0.77	0.78	1.00		
% reporting*	0.83	0.86	0.88	0.85	-0.81	0.88	0.76	-0.78	0.86	0.51	1.00	
Fear	-0.74	-0.78	-0.63	-0.79	0.65	-0.74	-0.64	0.65	-0.81	-0.70	-0.55	1.00

* % of crimes reported to police as reported in the NCVS.

a time-series regression model is to run a Durbin-Watson test. The Durbin-Watson tests the null hypothesis that the residuals from an OLS with time-series data are not autocorrelated. The Durbin-Watson statistic ranges in value from 0 to 4. A value near 2 indicates non-autocorrelation while a value toward 0 indicates positive autocorrelation, and a value toward 4 indicates negative autocorrelation. Durbin-Watson tests were conducted after every regression, and d-statistics were generally between 2 and 2.5 for all regression models in each category. These results indicate a tendency toward negative and moderate autocorrelation problems in the time series of residuals.

There are two possible solutions for correcting the problems of autocorrelation in time-series regression, and both of them have positive and negative effects. The most common solution is to add a single-lagged dependent variable in the right side of an equation. The second solution, considered more effective, is differencing. A degree of freedom is lost in both of the solutions, but the second technique is very costly because it throws away long-term trends and is likely to lose more degrees of freedom. Because this study is meant to explore and explain the long-term relationship between the UCR and NCVS in terms of divergence and convergence, it was decided to use the first technique and introduce a single-lagged dependent variable in the right side of the regression equations. The decision to use the first technique was also based on the fact that the problem of autocorrelation was found to be only moderate in severity and more degrees of freedom are lost in the differencing technique, a costly loss considering that there are only 36 observation points.

MULTIVARIATE RESULTS

Table 6.2 presents the results of the regressions in which rate differences of the UCR and NCVS for the different crime categories were regressed against the trend variable of the year. The regression coefficients for all categories are statistically significant and negative, indicating that the rate differences between the two series for each category of crime have significantly decreased over time. In addition, time is a significant predictor for explaining the variance in difference of rates between the UCR and NCVS.

Table 6.2. Results of Bivariate OLS Regressions for Crime Rate Differences between the UCR and NCVS for Different Crime Categories

Crime category	Coefficient	*SE*	*t* statistics	*p* value
Aggravated assault	-22.6121	1.0842	-20.86	0.000
Robbery	-8.6067	.5988	-14.37	0.000
Burglary	-67.5904	2.3184	-29.15	0.000
Motor vehicle theft	-7.5641	.7979	-9.48	0.000
Larceny theft	-198.2202	10.5274	-18.83	0.000
Violent crime	-31.2188	1.5885	-19.65	0.000
Property crime	-273.3747	11.9517	-22.87	0.000
Total crime	-304.5936	13.1676	-23.13	0.000

Table 6.3. Results of AR1 for Different Crime Categories with differences for NCVS and UCR rates in All Categories Regressed on Their Lagged Values

Crime category	Coefficient	*SE*	*t* statistics	*p* value
Aggravated assault	.9596066	.0524	18.31	0.000
Robbery	.9497364	.0555	17.09	0.000
Burglary	.9649408	.0353	27.27	0.000
Motor vehicle theft	.9029969	.0670	13.46	0.000
Larceny theft	.9831991	.0419	23.41	0.000
Violent crime	.9625768	.0501	19.21	0.000
Property crime	.9832719	.0365	26.94	0.000
Total crime	.9838265	.0360	27.31	0.000

Table 6.3 shows the results of the AR1 models in which the rate differences between the UCR and NCVS for the different crime categories were regressed against their single-lagged values. The statistical significance of all coefficients indicate a tendency toward the autoregressive process and show that the lagged values of the rate differences between the UCR and NCVS are significant predictors of

the rate difference in a given year. That is, the significant values of the coefficients in the AR1 models indicate that the immediately previous value has a direct and significant effect on the current value.

The results of the regression models with predictors, predictors and time trend, and predictors and lagged values of the dependent variables are presented at the end of this chapter (Tables 6.4-6.27). The results of the OLS regressions of predictor variables on the aggravated assault rate difference between the NCVS and UCR are presented in Tables 6.4, 6.5, and 6.6. The coefficients for the fear of crime and total employees variables were significant in models 1 and 2 and remained significant in model 3 with increased *t* statistics. The NCVS redesign variable, which was not significant in models 1 and 2, became a significant predictor in model 3, although the coefficient value for this variable was high in models 1 and 2.

The second set of models, in which a time-trend variable was included along with other predictor variables, produces very similar results. The coefficients of the total employees, NCVS redesign of 1993, and fear of crime variables remained significant after the effects of predictor variables were controlled for in the models. In the third set of models, the year variable was removed, and the single-lagged dependent variable was included as a predictor. The results remained the same, but the coefficient values of all three significant predictors—total employees, NCVS redesign of 1993, and fear of crime—increased substantially. When controlling for other variables including the single-lagged dependent variable, a negative coefficient for the total employees variable indicates that the difference between the NCVS and UCR aggravated assault rate decreased by 181.02 for every 100,000 increase in police employed. The dichotomous variable of NCVS redesign has a coefficient value of 152.97, which means the rate difference between the NCVS and UCR aggravated assault was higher by an average of 124.58 prior to the design changes in the NCVS in 1993. The models became more efficient and the effect of significant predictors increased when autocorrelation was corrected by including a single-lagged value of the dependent variable in the models. Thus, the trend and single-lagged dependent variables are not significant predictors of the aggravated assault rate difference between the NCVS and UCR.

The results of regressions in the case of the robbery rate difference between the NCVS and UCR are almost identical to those for aggravated assault (Tables 6.7, 6.8, and 6.9). In the first set of models, in which only predictor variables were included, fear of crime remained a significant predictor in all three models, total employees was a significant predictor in models 2 and 3, and NCVS redesign of 1992 was a significant predictor only in model 3. In the second set of models, in which the time-trend variable is used along with other predictor variables, the results did not change. Similarly, in the third set of models, in which the single-lagged value of the dependent variable is used, the results remained unchanged. According to the results of model 3 in the third set, the robbery rate difference between the NCVS and UCR decreased by 57.09 with every 100,000 increase in total employees for police and increased by 9.67 with every one percent increase in fear among citizens when controlling for other variables, including the single-lagged value of the dependent variable. Finally, the robbery rate difference between the NCVS and UCR was higher by 43.76 before redesign in the NCVS in 1993. The only difference between aggravated assault and robbery is that fear of crime remained a significant predictor in all three sets of regression models for robbery. Thus, fear was a stronger predictor of variance in the robbery rate difference than it was for aggravated assault. Similar to the results for aggravated assault, the time trend and single-lagged dependent variable were not significant predictors of the robbery rate difference between the NCVS and UCR.

The regression results for burglary (Tables 6.10, 6.11, and 6.12) were different from those for aggravated assault and robbery. All education attainment variables were significant predictors in model 1 of the first set, but in models 2 and 3, they become nonsignificant. The variable of total employees was a significant predictor in all three models. In the second set of models, in which the effects of predictor variables were controlled for the trend, none of the variables were significant predictors in model 1, and only total employees was a significant predictor in models 2 and 3. In the third set of models, in which the single-lagged value of the dependent variable was included as one of the predictors, none of the predictor variables was significant except total employees, which is significant in all three models. According to the results in model 3 of the third set, the burglary rate difference between the NCVS and UCR decreased by 303.98 for every increase of 100,000 in police employment. Redesign of the NCVS in

1992 did not have effects on rate differences between the two series on burglary.

The results of regressions on the motor vehicle rate difference between the NCVS and UCR (Table 6.13, 6.14, 6.15) showed that none of the coefficients of predictor variables was significant in model 1 of the first set. The percent of sworn officers variable was significant in model 2, while the percent of less than a high school education, percent of sworn officers, and fear of crime were significant in model 3. The results did not change when the time-trend variable was included in the second set of models. In the third set of models, when a single-lagged value of the dependent variable was included, the results changed completely. The single-lagged dependent variable, which generally remained a nonsignificant predictor in all previous categories, became significant and overrides the effects of other variables, which were significant predictors in the previous two sets of regression models. A comparison of adjusted R^2 also indicates that the models were least efficient in predicting the motor vehicle theft rate difference between the NCVS and UCR.

In contrast to the results for motor vehicle theft, the models presented in three sets appeared to be most efficient in predicting the variance in rate between the NCVS and UCR for larceny theft. The results (Tables 6.16, 6.17, and 6.18) show that, in model 1 of the first set, in which only the predictor variables are used, the variables of percent Hispanic, total employees, percent of sworn officers, total expenses of police, NCVS redesign in 1993, fear of crime, and percent of larceny theft reported to police were the significant predictors. In model 2, the coefficients of all significant predictors of model 1 not only remain significant but also improve, and in model 3, the results remain unchanged. In the second set of models, the results did not change substantially when the effects of the predictors were controlled for time trend. The trend variable year, included in the second set of models, remained a significant predictor in all three models. All significant variables from the first set remained significant after the time trend variable was included in the models.

Further, the results did not change substantially when the single-lagged value of the dependent variable was included as an independent variable in the third set of models. The variables of percent Hispanic, total employees, percent of sworn officers, total expenses of police, NCVS redesign in 1993, and fear of crime remained significant predictors of the larceny theft rate difference between the NCVS and UCR. According to the results of model 3 of the third set, a one percent increase in the Hispanic population decreased the larceny theft rate difference between the NCVS and UCR by 1143.46, every 100,000 increase in police employment decreased the rate difference by 1817.79, and every single percent increase in the number of sworn officers decreased the rate difference by 445.79. The NCVS redesign of 1992 had a significant effect, and the average larceny theft rate difference between the NCVS and UCR was higher by 1771.72 before the 1992 methodological changes in the NCVS.

The regression results for the aggregated categories of violent crime, property crime, and total crime are presented in tables 6.19, 6.20, 6.21, 6.22, 6.23, 6.24, 6.25, 6.26, and 6.27. The variables of total employees, NCVS redesign of 1993, and fear of crime were the significant predictors of the violent crime rate difference between NCVS and UCR in model 3 of all three sets. The results in the case of property crime were similar to those for larceny theft, and the results for total crime were similar to those for property crime. These similarities occurred because the property crime numbers are dominated by larceny theft and the total crime numbers are dominated by property crime, thus dominated by larceny theft to some extent. The models using the aggregated categories of violent crime, property crime, and total crime did not provide any additional or interesting information in terms of the effects of predictors on rate differences between the NCVS and UCR.

RESULTS SUMMARY AND HYPOTHESES TESTING

The results for the third research question are discussed and the related hypotheses are tested through the data analysis presented in this chapter. The following section provides brief descriptions of the results of the testing of Hypotheses 5-8.

H_5: Changes in population and demographic characteristics are likely to have affected the convergence of the UCR and NCVS data series.

This hypothesis was not supported because the population, demographic characteristics, and educational attainment of people did not seem to have any significant effect on the rate differences between the NCVS and UCR. It was hypothesized that the changes in population and demographic characteristics and improvement in educational attainment were likely to have positive effects on the convergence between the two series by improving the reporting of crimes to police. The results, however, did not support the hypothesis.

H_6: Police productivity should positively affect the convergence of the UCR and NCVS data series.

The police productivity hypothesis was partially supported in the data analysis. Total police employment was perhaps the most robust predictor of the rate differences between the NCVS and UCR. Percent of sworn officers had no significant effect on the rate differences for all categories except motor vehicle theft, and percent of female sworn police officers was a nonsignificant predictor of rate difference across all aggregated and disaggregated categories of crime. The biggest limitation on testing this hypothesis arose from the unavailability of time-series data for the police productivity variables. All LEMAS variables, related to organizational and technological improvements in police, were dropped from the analyses because only a few observations were available.

H_7: Citizens' attitudes toward crime and the police should positively affect the convergence of the UCR and NCVS data series.

The data analyses provided no support for this hypothesis. According to the hypothesis, citizens' attitudes toward police and crime are likely to have positive effects on the convergence by increasing reporting of crime to the police. However, the results do not support the citizens' attitude hypothesis. The variable of fear of crime was found to be a significant predictor of the violent crime rate differences between the NCVS and UCR, but it had no effect on the rate differences between the property crime categories. The effect of fear of crime on violent crime reporting is well documented, but the positive coefficients of fear of crime in this study did not support the hypothesis that reporting of crimes and fear of crime would have a positive relationship, thus leading to a greater convergence between the two series. There are other issues involved with the citizens' attitude hypothesis. First, the variable of citizens' attitudes toward the police was dropped from the analysis because of the unavailability of time-series measures. Second, fear of crime was used as a proxy measure of citizens' attitudes toward crime because the variable of fear, drawn from the GSS data, was based on a question that asked people whether they were afraid of walking alone at night. Another problem with this variable is that many observations were missing, so the process of interpolation and extrapolation were used to complete the time series for the fear of crime variable.

H_8: Changes in measurement procedures, especially in the NCVS, should positively affect the convergence of the UCR and NCVS data series, especially after 1993.

This hypothesis was partially supported in the data analysis. The results supported one part of the hypothesis completely because the coefficient of the variable NCVS redesign of 1992 was significant in all regression models for all categories. The results, however, indicate that the increase in the number of agencies reporting to the UCR did not have significant effects on the rate differences between the UCR and NCVS.

SUMMARY

In this chapter, Research Question 3, which sought an explanation for the convergence between the UCR and NCVS, was addressed by testing a set of hypotheses. Time-series regression models with predictors were identified and estimated in order to understand the effects of different predictor variables on the rate difference of the UCR and NCVS across different categories of crime.

The results indicate that the number of police officers and the rate-affecting methodological changes to the NCVS in 1992 were the most robust predictors of the variance in rate differences between the NCVS and UCR across all disaggregated and aggregated categories of crimes and positively affected the convergence between the two series. The variables of population characteristics, educational attainment, and police employment (other than total number of employees, percentages for reporting crimes to police, and mobile phone subscriptions) were nonsignificant predictors, so did not have significant effects on the convergence between the two series. The variable of fear of crime victimization, contrary to the hypothesis, had negative effects on the convergence between the two series.

Although not all hypotheses were supported and some were supported only partially, the lack of support for some of the hypotheses does not diminish the value and findings of the research. The biggest limitation in testing these hypotheses was the unavailability of time-series data, a problem that will probably be resolved in the future.

Table 6.4: Results of OLS Regressions for Aggravated Assault

Variable	Model 1			Model 2			Model 3		
	Coefficient	*SE*	*t* statistics	Coefficient	*SE*	*t* statistics	Coefficient	*SE*	*t* statistics
Population characteristics									
Total household (in millions)	13.23	17.04	0.78						
Total population (in millions)	-42.46	30.00	-1.42						
% White	-179.69	143.84	-1.25						
% Black	-7.46	578.22	-0.01	-67.46	317.01	-0.21			
% Hispanic	34.97	142.29	0.25	-69.55	61.86	-1.12			
Educational attainment									
% below high school	169.61	131.98	1.29	-5.85	25.74	-0.23	13.24	14.58	0.91
% with high school	225.12	135.00	1.67						
% with some college	114.14	144.58	0.79						
% with 4 years college	201.46	135.52	1.49						
Police employment									
Total employees (in 100,000)	-125.93	84.60	-1.49	-186.13	79.84	-2.33*	-146.24	31.96	-4.57***
% sworn officers	13.24	29.25	0.45	-33.40	32.92	-1.01	-29.02	21.59	-1.34
% female employees	27.1	56.48	0.48	-4.86	47.37	-0.10			

Table 6.4: Results of OLS Regressions for Aggravated Assault (Continued)

Variable	Model 1			Model 2			Model 3		
	Coefficient	*SE*	*t* statistics	Coefficient	*SE*	*t* statistics	Coefficient	*SE*	*t* statistics
Total expenses on police (in millions)	0.01	0.01	1.45	0.01	0.01	1.13			
UCR Reporting agencies	0.00	0.02	-0.04	-0.01	0.01	-1.00			
NCVS redesign in 1992	135.38	78.34	1.73	113.64	67.59	1.68	124.58	45.87	2.72*
% afraid to walk at night	15.67	6.30	2.49*	10.63	6.36	1.67	10.77	3.62	2.98**
% property crime reported to police[a]	-4.00	3.66	-1.09						
Cell phone connections (in millions)	-0.23	1.64	-0.14						
Intercept	4205.56	18025.12	0.23	5332.91	3640.52	1.46	2841.33	1378.40	2.06

Note. Model 1: $df = 35$, $F = 66.10$, Adjusted $R^2 = 0.9710$; Model 2: $df = 35$, $F = 76.32$, Adjusted $R^2 = 0.9556$; Model 3: $df = 35$, $F = 169.29$, Adjusted $R^2 = 0.9601$.

* $p < 0.05$; ** $p < 0.01$; *** $p < 0.001$.

[a] % of aggravated assault reported to police as reported in the NCVS.

Table 6.5. Results of OLS Regressions with Time Trend for Aggravated Assault

Variable	Model 1			Model 2			Model 3		
	Coefficient	***SE***	***t* statistics**	**Coefficient**	***SE***	***t* statistics**	**Coefficient**	***SE***	***t* statistics**
Year	31.71	58.79	0.54	28.09	45.46	0.62	1.19	9.79	0.12
Population characteristics									
Total household (in millions)	8.62	19.39	0.44						
Total population (in millions)	-42.28	30.64	-1.38						
% White	-160.22	151.31	-1.06						
% Black	-233.27	724.02	-0.32	-149.68	347.50	-0.43			
% Hispanic	36.71	145.39	0.25	-74.34	63.11	-1.18			
Educational attainment									
% below high school	159.39	136.14	1.17	8.27	34.66	0.24	13.84	15.61	0.89
% with high school	207.40	141.77	1.46						
% with some college	93.95	152.36	0.62						
% with 4 years college	184.20	142.10	1.30						

Table 6.5. Results of OLS Regressions with Time Trend for Aggravated Assault (Continued)

Variable	Model 1			Model 2			Model 3		
	Coefficient	*SE*	*t* statistics	Coefficient	*SE*	*t* statistics	Coefficient	*SE*	*t* statistics
Police employment									
Total employees (in 100,000)	-126.60	86.43	-1.46	-182.59	81.05	-2.25*	-151.15	51.79	-2.92**
% sworn officers	17.89	31.10	0.58	-30.12	33.76	-0.89	-29.50	22.30	-1.32
% female employees	32.28	58.49	0.55	-4.11	47.99	-0.09			
Total expenses on police (in millions)	0.01	0.01	1.21	0.00	0.01	0.26			
UCR Reporting agencies	0.00	0.02	0.24	-0.01	0.01	-0.82			
NCVS redesign in 1992	151.89	85.68	1.77	121.07	69.49	1.74	124.97	46.76	2.67*
% afraid to walk at night	16.81	6.77	2.48*	10.45	6.44	1.62	10.91	3.85	2.84**
% property crime reported to police[a]	-3.54	3.83	-0.92						
Cell phone connections (in millions)	-0.68	1.87	-0.36						
Intercept	-56269.99	113635.60	-0.50	-49961.79	89568.67	-0.56	517.18	19108.97	0.03

Note. Model 1: $df = 35$, $F = 60.03$, Adjusted $R^2 = 0.9697$; Model 2: $df = 35$, $F = 67.70$, Adjusted $R^2 = 0.9545$; Model 3: $df = 35$, $F = 136.45$, Adjusted $R^2 = 0.9587$.

* $p < 0.05$; ** $p < 0.01$; *** $p < 0.001$.

[a] % of aggravated assault reported to police as reported in the NCVS.

Table 6.6. Results of OLS Regressions with Lagged Dependent Variable for Aggravated Assault

Variable	Model 1			Model 2			Model 3		
	Coefficient	*SE*	*t* statistics	Coefficient	*SE*	*t* statistics	Coefficient	*SE*	*t* statistics
Lagged dependent	-0.21	0.20	-1.06	-0.34	0.22	-1.52	-0.25	0.18	-1.39
Population characteristics									
Total household (in millions)	9.64	17.36	0.56						
Total population (in millions)	-32.21	30.01	-1.07						
% White	-143.95	141.85	-1.01						
% Black	-185.76	570.37	-0.33	-287.94	320.94	-0.90			
% Hispanic	-36.45	146.93	-0.25	-106.89	64.48	-1.66			
Educational attainment									
% below high school	92.05	136.35	0.68	-4.14	24.89	-0.17	18.35	15.13	1.21
% with high school	148.04	141.23	1.05						
% with some college	28.14	150.31	0.19						
% with 4 years college	119.82	141.73	0.85						

Table 6.6. Results of OLS Regressions with Lagged Dependent Variable for Aggravated Assault (Continued)

Variable	Model 1			Model 2			Model 3		
	Coefficient	*SE*	*t* statistics	Coefficient	*SE*	*t* statistics	Coefficient	*SE*	*t* statistics
Police employment									
Total employees (in 100,000)	-114.37	82.53	-1.39	-162.55	77.13	-2.11*	-181.02	38.77	-4.67***
% sworn officers	4.32	30.38	0.14	-40.66	32.91	-1.24	-40.54	22.67	-1.79
% female employees	35.13	55.56	0.63	1.01	46.46	0.02			
Total expenses on police (in millions)	0.01	0.01	1.53	0.01	0.01	1.34			
UCR Reporting agencies	0.01	0.02	0.53	0.00	0.01	0.04			
NCVS redesign in 1992	189.71	83.39	2.27*	178.51	73.08	2.44*	152.97	51.01	3.00**
% afraid to walk at night	21.37	7.01	3.05**	18.98	7.28	2.61*	15.11	4.50	3.36**
% property crime reported to police[a]	-3.22	3.57	-0.9						
Cell phone connections (in millions)	-0.30	1.60	-0.18						
Intercept	9835.40	18433.68	0.53	8174.75	3749.92	2.18	3757.25	1486.22	2.53

Note: Model 1: $df = 34$, $F = 62.26$, Adjusted $R^2 = 0.9716$; Model 2: $df = 34$, $F = 71.36$, Adjusted $R^2 = 0.9579$; Model 4: $df = 34$, $F = 136.49$, Adjusted $R^2 = 0.9599$.

* $p < 0.05$; ** $p < 0.01$; *** $p < 0.001$.

[a] % of aggravated assault reported to police as reported in the NCVS.

Table 6.7. Results of OLS Regressions for Robbery

Variable	Model 1			Model 2			Model 3		
	Coefficient	*SE*	*t* statistics	Coefficient	*SE*	*t* statistics	Coefficient	*SE*	*t* statistics
Population characteristics									
Total household (in millions)	11.21	6.92	1.62						
Total population (in millions)	-0.34	12.51	-0.03						
% White	32.39	56.66	0.57						
% Black	-198.17	224.17	-0.88	100.53	119.25	0.84			
% Hispanic	-4.18	57.27	-0.07	25.61	23.27	1.10			
Educational attainment									
% below high school	90.58	51.31	1.77	-10.86	9.68	-1.12	-4.12	5.91	-0.70
% with high school	90.86	52.34	1.74						
% with some college	81.79	56.11	1.46						
% with 4 years college	96.01	52.52	1.83						

Table 6.7. Results of OLS Regressions for Robbery (Continued)

Variable	Model 1			Model 2			Model 3		
	Coefficient	*SE*	*t* statistics	Coefficient	*SE*	*t* statistics	Coefficient	*SE*	*t* statistics
Police employment									
Total employees (in 100,000)	-42.72	32.28	-1.32	-100.08	30.03	-3.33**	-52.21	12.96	-4.03***
% sworn officers	7.20	11.52	0.62	-9.68	12.38	-0.78	2.66	8.75	0.30
% female employees	12.44	21.63	0.58	-20.81	17.82	-1.17			
Total expenses on police (in millions)	0.00	0.00	-0.11	0.00	0.00	-0.52			
UCR Reporting agencies	-0.01	0.01	-1.85	-0.01	0.00	-1.50			
NCVS redesign in 1992	38.63	29.00	1.33	22.98	25.42	0.90	45.76	18.60	2.46*
% afraid to walk at night	9.06	2.49	3.64**	7.36	2.39	3.08**	8.57	1.47	5.84***
% property crime reported to police[a]	-0.82	1.06	-0.77						
Cell phone connections (in millions)	-0.13	0.62	-0.21						
Intercept	-10766.07	7298.38	-1.48	707.64	1369.42	0.52	-86164.70	32652.17	-2.64

Note. Model 1: $df = 35$, $F = 68.74$, Adjusted $R^2 = 0.9721$; Model 2: $df = 35$, $F = 84.66$, Adjusted $R^2 = 0.9598$; Model 3: $df = 35$, $F = 160.88$, Adjusted $R^2 = 0.9581$.

* $p < 0.05$; ** $p < 0.01$; *** $p < 0.001$.

[a] % of robbery reported to police as reported in the NCVS.

Table 6.8. Results of OLS Regressions with Time Trend

Variable	Model 1			Model 2			Model 3		
	Coefficient	*SE*	*t* statistics	Coefficient	*SE*	*t* statistics	Coefficient	*SE*	*t* statistics
Year	-13.09	23.96	-0.55	8.92	17.14	0.52	2.99	3.93	0.76
Population characteristics									
Total household (in millions)	12.75	7.60	1.68						
Total population (in millions)	0.61	12.89	0.05						
% White	26.15	58.99	0.44						
% Black	-106.13	284.24	-0.37	74.41	131.01	0.57			
% Hispanic	-10.02	59.46	-0.17	24.08	23.80	1.01			
Educational attainment									
% below high school	95.44	53.16	1.80	-6.37	13.07	-0.49	-2.62	6.27	-0.42
% with high school	98.64	55.32	1.78						
% with some college	90.62	59.54	1.52						
% with 4 years college	103.37	55.30	1.87						

Table 6.8. Results of OLS Regressions with Time Trend (Continued)

Variable	Model 1			Model 2			Model 3		
	Coefficient	*SE*	*t* statistics	Coefficient	*SE*	*t* statistics	Coefficient	*SE*	*t* statistics
Police employment									
Total employees (in 100,000)	-41.73	33.02	-1.26	-98.96	30.56	-3.24**	-64.52	20.79	-3.10**
% sworn officers	5.63	12.11	0.47	-8.64	12.73	-0.68	1.47	8.95	0.16
% female employees	11.19	22.21	0.50	-20.57	18.09	-1.14			
Total expenses on police (in millions)	0.00	0.00	-0.01	0.00	0.00	-0.73			
UCR Reporting agencies	-0.01	0.01	-1.79	-0.01	0.00	-1.32			
NCVS redesign in 1992	34.57	30.53	1.13	25.34	26.20	0.97	46.74	18.77	2.49*
% afraid to walk at night	8.51	2.73	3.11**	7.30	2.43	3.01**	8.91	1.54	5.77***
% property crime reported to police[a]	-1.06	1.17	-0.90						
Cell phone connections (in millions)	0.10	0.76	0.13						
Intercept	13812.14	45595.85	0.30	-16855.53	33769.07	-0.50	-5698.73	7673.23	-0.74

Note. Model 1: $df = 35$, $F = 62.45$, Adjusted $R^2 = 0.9709$; Model 2: $df = 35$, $F = 74.75$, Adjusted $R^2 = 0.9586$; Model 3: $df = 35$, $F = 132.28$, Adjusted $R^2 = 0.9575$.

* $p < 0.05$; ** $p < 0.01$; *** $p < 0.001$.

[a] % of robbery reported to police as reported in the NCVS.

Table 6.9. Results of OLS Regressions with Lagged Dependent Variable for Robbery

Variable	Model 1			Model 2			Model 3		
	Coefficient	*SE*	*t* statistics	Coefficient	*SE*	*t* statistics	Coefficient	*SE*	*t* statistics
Lagged dependent	0.03	0.22	0.12	-0.01	0.17	-0.04	-0.05	0.14	-0.40
Population characteristics									
Total household (in millions)	9.11	7.37	1.24						
Total population (in millions)	1.86	14.49	0.13						
% White	38.97	70.48	0.55						
% Black	-224.81	270.82	-0.83	42.58	126.98	0.34			
% Hispanic	-21.85	65.13	-0.34	9.78	25.43	0.38			
Educational attainment									
% below high school	84.31	67.06	1.26	-12.29	9.64	-1.27	-5.18	5.56	-0.93
% with high school	89.17	70.64	1.26						
% with some college	76.59	74.04	1.03						
% with 4 years college	92.16	70.08	1.31						

Table 6.9. Results of OLS Regressions with Lagged Dependent Variable for Robbery (Continued)

Variable	Model 1			Model 2			Model 3		
	Coefficient	*SE*	*t* statistics	Coefficient	*SE*	*t* statistics	Coefficient	*SE*	*t* statistics
Police employment									
Total employees (in 100,000)	-45.01	37.70	-1.19	-92.70	31.08	-2.98**	-57.09	12.91	-4.42***
% sworn officers	8.09	11.89	0.68	-7.07	12.39	-0.57	1.92	8.20	0.23
% female employees	14.96	23.32	0.64	-15.06	18.08	-0.83			
Total expenses on police (in millions)	0.00	0.00	0.31	0.00	0.00	0.05			
UCR Reporting agencies	-0.01	0.01	-1.44	0.00	0.00	-0.97			
NCVS redesign in 1992	42.22	33.12	1.28	29.46	27.03	1.09	43.76	18.12	2.41*
% afraid to walk at night	9.61	3.63	2.65*	8.75	3.14	2.78*	9.67	1.99	4.86***
% property crime reported to police[a]	-0.73	1.10	-0.67						
Cell phone connections (in millions)	-0.21	0.65	-0.32						
Intercept	-1015.72	7576.70	-1.45	1089.70	1407.10	0.77	203.85	523.59	0.39

Note. Model 1: $df = 34$, $F = 208.45$, Adjusted $R^2 = 0.9914$; Model 2: $df = 34$, $F = 239.76$, Adjusted $R^2 = 0.9860$; Model 3: $df = 34$, $F = 299.19$, Adjusted $R^2 = 0.9859$.

* $p < 0.05$; ** $p < 0.01$; *** $p < 0.001$.

[a] % of property crime reported to police as reported in the NCVS.

Table 6.10. Results of OLS Regressions for Burglary

Variable	Model 1			Model 2			Model 3		
	Coefficient	***SE***	***t* statistics**	**Coefficient**	***SE***	***t* statistics**	**Coefficient**	***SE***	***t* statistics**
Population characteristics									
Total household (in millions)	-6.18	40.41	-0.15						
Total population (in millions)	15.80	68.12	0.23						
% White	-99.69	326.44	-0.31						
% Black	1299.09	1326.73	0.98	57.02	666.18	0.09			
% Hispanic	-243.26	315.23	-0.77	-141.64	129.99	-1.09			
Educational attainment									
% below high school	903.44	308.02	2.93**	-34.75	54.08	-0.64	21.23	33.39	0.64
% with high school	966.44	316.58	3.05**						
% with some college	974.82	346.57	2.81*						
% with 4 years college	929.86	323.37	2.88*						

Table 6.10. Results of OLS Regressions for Burglary (Continued)

Variable	Model 1			Model 2			Model 3		
	Coefficient	*SE*	*t* statistics	Coefficient	*SE*	*t* statistics	Coefficient	*SE*	*t* statistics
Police employment									
Total employees (in 100,000)	-649.59	187.50	-3.46**	-617.12	167.79	-3.68**	-333.81	73.23	-4.56***
% sworn officers	-61.17	65.81	-0.93	-69.71	69.19	-1.01	-17.42	49.47	-0.35
% female employees	-87.20	125.48	-0.69	-55.39	99.55	-0.56			
Total expenses on police (in millions)	-0.01	0.02	-0.69	0.02	0.01	1.65			
UCR Reporting agencies	-0.07	0.03	-1.97	-0.02	0.02	-0.78			
NCVS redesign in 1992	29.15	170.30	0.17	14.65	142.03	0.10	56.93	105.09	0.54
% afraid to walk at night	-17.66	14.05	-1.26	0.68	13.36	0.05	-2.51	8.29	-0.30
% property crime reported to police[a]	-12.26	10.77	-1.14						
Cell phone connections (in millions)	7.10	3.55	2.00						
Intercept	-88384.48	42205.84	-2.09	12850.42	7650.34	1.68	4561.25	3157.71	1.44

Note. Model 1: $df = 35$, $F = 113.82$, Adjusted $R^2 = 0.9831$; Model 2: $df = 35$, $F = 151.32$, Adjusted $R^2 = 0.9772$; Model 3: $df = 35$, $F = 281.88$, Adjusted $R^2 = 0.9757$.

* $p < 0.05$; ** $p < 0.01$; *** $p < 0.001$.

[a] % of burglary reported to police as reported in the NCVS.

Table 6.11. Results of OLS Regressions with Time Trend for Burglary

Variable	Model 1			Model 2			Model 3		
	Coefficient	***SE***	***t* statistics**	**Coefficient**	***SE***	***t* statistics**	**Coefficient**	***SE***	***t* statistics**
Year	-120.95	127.53	-0.95	136.70	92.15	1.48	50.92	20.33	2.50*
Population characteristics									
Total household (in millions)	11.03	44.40	0.25						
Total population (in millions)	16.49	68.33	0.24						
% White	-172.44	336.28	-0.51						
% Black	2111.49	1582.54	1.33	-343.17	704.45	-0.49			
% Hispanic	-261.71	316.76	-0.83	-164.97	127.95	-1.29			
Educational attainment									
% below high school	952.63	313.26	3.04	33.98	70.27	0.48	46.76	32.44	1.44
% with high school	1039.79	326.80	3.18						
% with some college	1062.27	359.62	2.95						
% with 4 years college	1005.06	333.88	3.01						

Table 6.11. Results of OLS Regressions with Time Trend for Burglary (Continued)

Variable	Model 1			Model 2			Model 3		
	Coefficient	*SE*	*t* statistics	Coefficient	*SE*	*t* statistics	Coefficient	*SE*	*t* statistics
Police employment									
Total employees (in 100,000)	-642.01	188.23	-3.41	-599.91	164.31	-3.65**	-543.59	107.60	-5.05***
% sworn officers	-79.44	68.76	-1.16	-53.75	68.43	-0.79	-37.71	46.34	-0.81
% female employees	-100.31	126.61	-0.79	-51.75	97.28	-0.53			
Total expenses on police (in millions)	-0.01	0.02	-0.45	0.00	0.02	-0.02			
UCR Reporting agencies	-0.09	0.04	-2.17	-0.01	0.02	-0.44			
NCVS redesign in 1992	-26.47	180.59	-0.15	50.82	140.87	0.36	73.54	97.15	0.76
% afraid to walk at night	-21.67	14.72	-1.47	-0.19	13.06	-0.01	3.29	7.99	0.41
% property crime reported to police[a]	-13.70	10.91	-1.26						
Cell phone connections (in millions)	9.06	4.11	2.20						
Intercept	141603.00	246168.60	0.58	-256262.70	181573.40	-1.41	-94601.42	39703.62	-2.38

Note. Model 1: $df = 35$, $F = 107.24$, Adjusted $R^2 = 0.9830$; Model 1: $df = 35$, $F = 144.37$, Adjusted $R^2 = 0.9783$; Model 3: $df = 35$, $F = 277.22$, Adjusted $R^2 = 0.9793$.

* $p < 0.05$; ** $p < 0.01$; *** $p < 0.001$.

[a] % of burglary reported to police as reported in the NCVS.

Table 6.12. Results of OLS Regressions with Lagged Dependent Variable for Burglary

Variable	Model 1			Model 2			Model 3		
	Coefficient	*SE*	*t* statistics	Coefficient	*SE*	*t* statistics	Coefficient	*SE*	*t* statistics
Lagged dependent	-0.03	0.26	-0.13	-0.07	0.21	-0.32	0.13	0.19	0.66
Population characteristics									
Total household (in millions)	-3.13	44.93	-0.07						
Total population (in millions)	13.08	74.46	0.18						
% White	-114.98	353.10	-0.33						
% Black	1344.25	1424.73	0.94	-141.11	752.80	-0.19			
% Hispanic	-232.84	370.32	-0.63	-191.60	153.34	-1.25			
Educational attainment									
% below high school	891.08	397.51	2.24*	-40.94	56.84	-0.72	19.15	34.65	0.55
% with high school	950.38	400.07	2.38*						
% with some college	957.63	455.14	2.10						
% with 4 years college	914.41	417.31	2.19*						

Table 6.1… …Variable for Burglary (Continued)

Variable	Model 1			Model 2			Model 3		
	Coefficient	*SE*	*t* statistics	Coefficient	*SE*	*t* statistics	Coefficient	*SE*	*t* statistics
Police employment									
Total employees (in 100,000)	-657.96	208.97	-3.15**	-621.50	185.79	-3.35**	-303.98	87.51	-3.47**
% sworn officers	-62.62	70.26	-0.89	-63.31	72.10	-0.88	-17.73	50.81	-0.35
% female employees	-89.57	134.67	-0.67	-40.41	105.19	-0.38			
Total expenses on police (in millions)	-0.01	0.02	-0.68	0.03	0.01	1.71			
UCR Reporting agencies	-0.07	0.04	-1.84	-0.01	0.03	-0.57			
NCVS redesign in 1992	23.93	186.03	0.13	27.74	148.36	0.19	71.29	110.25	0.65
% afraid to walk at night	-17.57	17.47	-1.01	6.11	16.56	0.37	-4.84	9.24	-0.52
% property crime reported to police[a]	-12.41	11.64	-1.07						
Cell phone connections (in millions)	7.29	3.87	1.88						
Intercept	-85481.74	50735.92	-1.68	14742.98	8669.61	1.70	4334.88	3261.94	1.33

Note. Model 1: $df = 34$, $F = 88.02$, Adjusted $R^2 = 0.9798$; Model 2: $df = 34$, $F = 118.96$, Adjusted $R^2 = 0.9745$; Model 3: $df = 34$, $F = 205.14$, Adjusted $R^2 = 0.9730$.

* $p < 0.05$; ** $p < 0.01$; *** $p < 0.001$.

[a] % of burglary reported to police as reported in the NCVS.

Table 6.13. Results of OLS Regressions for Motor Vehicle Theft

Variable	Model 1			Model 2			Model 3		
	Coefficient	*SE*	*t* statistics	Coefficient	*SE*	*t* statistics	Coefficient	*SE*	*t* statistics
Population characteristics									
Total household (in millions)	11.13	14.67	0.76						
Total population (in millions)	-42.41	26.40	-1.61						
% White	-105.16	128.65	-0.82						
% Black	307.40	522.15	0.59	335.73	244.81	1.37			
% Hispanic	193.86	123.44	1.57	25.61	47.77	0.54			
Educational attainment									
% below high school	126.96	117.16	1.08	15.66	19.87	0.79	24.83	11.57	2.15*
% with high school	149.08	118.46	1.26						
% with some college	114.89	128.38	0.89						
% with 4 years college	129.24	119.90	1.08						

Table 6 ... Motor Vehicle Theft (Continued)

Variable	Model 1			Model 2			Model 3		
	Coefficient	*SE*	*t* statistics	Coefficient	*SE*	*t* statistics	Coefficient	*SE*	*t* statistics
Police employment									
Total employees (in 100,000)	-60.02	73.94	-0.81	-102.18	61.66	-1.66	-0.37	25.38	-0.01
% sworn officers	-44.47	25.50	-1.74	-63.73	25.42	-2.51*	-35.81	17.15	-2.09*
% female employees	-50.81	49.18	-1.03	-43.77	36.58	-1.20			
Total expenses on police (in millions)	0.01	0.01	1.09	0.00	0.00	-0.13			
UCR Reporting agencies	0.00	0.01	0.34	-0.01	0.01	-0.68			
NCVS redesign in 1992	-16.58	64.85	-0.26	-101.49	52.19	-1.94	-46.33	36.42	-1.27
% afraid to walk at night	8.97	5.55	1.62	6.07	4.91	1.24	10.40	2.87	3.62**
% property crime reported to police[a]	-1.80	3.38	-0.53						
Cell phone connections (in millions)	-0.70	1.39	-0.51						
Intercept	3885.05	16058.73	0.24	1690.20	2811.34	0.60	1768.31	1094.44	1.62

Note. Model 1: $df = 35$, $F = 11.48$, Adjusted $R^2 = 0.8435$; Model 2: $df = 35$, $F = 16.41$, Adjusted $R^2 = 0.8149$; Model 3: $df = 35$, $F = 33.78$, Adjusted $R^2 = 0.8240$. *$p < 0.05$; **$p < 0.01$; ***$p < 0.001$.

[a] % of motor vehicle theft reported to police as reported in the NCVS.

Table 6.14. Results of OLS Regressions with Time Trend for Motor Vehicle Theft

Variable	Model 1			Model 2			Model 3		
	Coefficient	*SE*	*t* statistics	Coefficient	*SE*	*t* statistics	Coefficient	*SE*	*t* statistics
Year	69.47	48.23	1.44	33.53	34.71	0.97	9.09	7.59	1.20
Population characteristics									
Total household (in millions)	0.08	16.16	0.01						
Total population (in millions)	-41.72	25.61	-1.63						
% White	-54.23	129.68	-0.42						
% Black	-203.13	618.09	-0.33	237.58	265.37	0.90			
% Hispanic	203.46	119.90	1.70	19.89	48.20	0.41			
Educational attainment									
% below high school	108.28	114.36	0.95	32.51	26.47	1.23	29.39	12.10	2.43*
% with high school	116.69	117.07	1.00						
% with some college	78.25	127.07	0.62						
% with 4 years college	97.91	118.30	0.83						

Table 6.14. Results of OLS Regressions with Time Trend for Motor Vehicle Theft (Continued)

Variable	Model 1			Model 2			Model 3		
	Coefficient	*SE*	*t* statistics	Coefficient	*SE*	*t* statistics	Coefficient	*SE*	*t* statistics
Police employment									
Total employees (in 100,000)	-63.69	71.75	-0.89	-97.95	61.90	-1.58	-37.84	40.15	-0.94
% sworn officers	-33.07	25.96	-1.27	-59.81	25.78	-2.32*	-39.43	17.29	-2.28*
% female employees	-41.17	48.17	-0.85	-42.88	36.65	-1.17			
Total expenses on police (in millions)	0.01	0.01	0.76	-0.01	0.01	-0.82			
UCR Reporting agencies	0.02	0.02	1.07	0.00	0.01	-0.45			
NCVS redesign in 1992	10.40	65.62	0.16	-92.62	53.07	-1.75	-43.36	36.25	-1.20
% afraid to walk at night	11.39	5.64	2.02	5.85	4.92	1.19	11.44	2.98	3.84**
% property crime reported to police[a]	-1.18	3.31	-0.36						
Cell phone connections (in millions)	-1.81	1.55	-1.17						
Intercept	-129802.40	94104.63	-1.38	-64316.93	68399.61	-0.94	-15940.20	14813.78	-1.08

Note. Model 1: $df = 35$, $F = 11.67$, Adjusted $R^2 = 0.8528$; Model 2: $df = 35$, $F = 14.96$, Adjusted $R^2 = 0.8144$; Model 3: $df = 35$, $F = 28.80$, Adjusted $R^2 = 0.8265$.

* $p < 0.05$; ** $p < 0.01$; *** $p < 0.001$.

[a] % of motor vehicle theft reported to police as reported in the NCVS.

Table 6.15. Results of OLS Regressions with Lagged Dependent Variable for Motor Vehicle Theft

Variable	Model 1			Model 2			Model 3		
	Coefficient	*SE*	*t* statistics	Coefficient	*SE*	*t* statistics	Coefficient	*SE*	*t* statistics
Lagged dependent	0.37	0.27	1.36	0.57	0.22	2.60*	0.55	0.19	2.91**
Population characteristics									
Total household (in millions)	9.08	15.48	0.59						
Total population (in millions)	-27.67	29.29	-0.94						
% White	-69.12	135.60	-0.51						
% Black	326.53	541.85	0.60	174.56	232.48	0.75			
% Hispanic	135.92	137.63	0.99	10.09	46.96	0.21			
Educational attainment									
% below high school	127.92	118.95	1.08	23.10	18.29	1.26	17.55	10.44	1.68
% with high school	132.89	119.81	1.11						
% with some college	111.24	129.69	0.86						
% with 4 years college	113.77	121.45	0.94						

Table 6.15. Results of OLS Regressions with Lagged Dependent Variable for Motor Vehicle Theft (Continued)

Variable	Model 1			Model 2			Model 3		
	Coefficient	*SE*	*t* statistics	Coefficient	*SE*	*t* statistics	Coefficient	*SE*	*t* statistics
Police employment									
Total employees (in 100,000)	-45.09	75.01	-0.60	-54.02	58.00	-0.93	7.14	22.77	0.31
% sworn officers	-33.39	26.86	-1.24	-31.99	25.50	-1.25	-25.11	15.58	-1.61
% female employees	-32.06	51.80	-0.62	-0.76	36.25	-0.02			
Total expenses on police (in millions)	0.00	0.01	0.53	0.00	0.00	0.20			
UCR Reporting agencies	0.00	0.01	0.10	0.00	0.01	-0.26			
NCVS redesign in 1992	-2.13	66.44	-0.03	-50.81	50.22	-1.01	-36.96	32.56	-1.13
% afraid to walk at night	4.02	7.07	0.57	2.82	5.05	0.56	3.88	3.53	1.10
% property crime reported to police[a]	-1.35	3.58	-0.38						
Cell phone connections (in millions)	-0.32	1.44	-0.23						
Intercept	-2403.60	16790.08	-0.14	-63.13	2703.66	-0.02	1300.10	982.20	1.32

Note. Model 1: $df = 34$, $F = 10.36$, Adjusted $R^2 = 0.8396$; Model 2: $df = 34$, $F = 18.22$, Adjusted $R^2 = 0.8478$; Model 3: $df = 34$, $F = 36.09$, Adjusted $R^2 = 0.8610$.

* $p < 0.05$; ** $p < 0.01$; *** $p < 0.001$.

[a] % of motor vehicle theft reported to police as reported in the NCVS.

Table 6.16. Results of OLS Regressions for Larceny Theft

Variable	Model 1			Model 2			Model 3		
	Coefficient	***SE***	***t* statistics**	**Coefficient**	***SE***	***t* statistics**	**Coefficient**	***SE***	***t* statistics**
Population characteristics									
Total household (in millions)	96.50	87.62	1.10						
Total population (in millions)	-39.49	143.54	-0.28						
% White	-386.87	701.14	-0.55						
% Black	-128.67	2861.11	-0.04	10.16	1461.11	0.01			
% Hispanic	-1189.57	664.31	-1.79	-1005.97	285.10	-3.53**	-1236.94	234.01	-5.29***
Educational attainment									
% below high school	910.35	619.55	1.47	-59.50	118.61	-0.50	21.75	81.03	0.27
% with high school	851.37	636.35	1.34						
% with some college	881.55	687.40	1.28						
% with 4 years college	848.14	640.93	1.32						

Table 6.16. Results of OLS Regressions for Larceny Theft (Continued)

Variable	Model 1			Model 2			Model 3		
	Coefficient	*SE*	*t* statistics	Coefficient	*SE*	*t* statistics	Coefficient	*SE*	*t* statistics
Police employment									
Total employees (in 100,000)	-1344.75	388.39	-3.46**	-1741.53	368.00	-4.73***	-1992.87	254.66	-7.83***
% sworn officers	-349.87	144.63	-2.42*	-546.47	151.75	-3.60**	-430.59	114.79	-3.75**
% female employees	-156.47	274.43	-0.57	-321.85	218.35	-1.47			
Total expenses on police (in millions)	0.08	0.04	1.87	0.08	0.03	3.07**	0.12	0.02	5.59***
UCR Reporting agencies	0.05	0.07	0.75	0.10	0.05	1.89			
NCVS redesign in 1992	1724.87	341.64	5.05***	1776.11	311.52	5.70***	1847.14	240.16	7.69***
% afraid to walk at night	91.26	29.79	3.06**	77.46	29.29	2.64**	85.54	20.74	4.12***
% property crime reported to police[a]	-97.25	37.05	-2.62*						
Cell phone connections (in millions)	0.00	0.00	0.80						
Intercept	-2244.67	87318.48	-0.03	67855.45	16779.26	4.04	53737.63	8065.09	6.66

Note. Model 1: $df = 35$, $F = 239.44$, Adjusted $R^2 = 0.9919$; Model 2: $df = 35$, $F = 287.30$, Adjusted $R^2 = 0.9879$; Model 3: $df = 35$, $F = 357.51$, Adjusted $R^2 = 0.9862$.

* $p < 0.05$; ** $p < 0.01$; *** $p < 0.001$.

[a] % of larceny theft reported to police as reported in the NCVS.

Table 6.17. Results of OLS Regressions with Time Trend for Larceny Theft

Variable	Model 1			Model 2			Model 3		
	Coefficient	*SE*	*t* statistics	Coefficient	*SE*	*t* statistics	Coefficient	*SE*	*t* statistics
Year	636.53	218.80	2.91*	627.75	167.86	3.74**	480.66	100.63	4.78***
Population characteristics									
Total household (in millions)	-10.98	81.85	-0.13						
Total population (in millions)	-30.81	119.70	-0.26						
% White	68.53	605.08	0.11						
% Black	-4751.93	2866.03	-1.66	-1827.62	1283.17	-1.42			
% Hispanic	-1114.06	554.39	-2.01	-1113.09	233.06	-4.78***	-955.90	178.95	-5.34***
Educational attainment									
% below high school	721.52	520.53	1.39	256.11	127.99	2.00	412.88	75.61	5.46***
% with high school	552.25	540.35	1.02						
% with some college	532.03	585.49	0.91						
% with 4 years college	550.23	544.01	1.01						

Table 6.17. Results of OLS Regressions with Time Trend for Larceny Theft (Continued)

Variable	Model 1			Model 2			Model 3		
	Coefficient	*SE*	*t* statistics	Coefficient	*SE*	*t* statistics	Coefficient	*SE*	*t* statistics
Police employment									
Total employees (in 100,000)	-1398.23	324.29	-4.31**	-1662.47	299.29	-5.55***	-1661.77	277.50	-5.99***
% sworn officers	-238.91	126.46	-1.89	-473.18	124.66	-3.80**	-371.15	99.87	-3.72**
% female employees	-63.85	230.97	-0.28	-305.12	177.19	-1.72			
Total expenses on police (in millions)	0.06	0.04	1.65	-0.01	0.03	-0.37			
UCR Reporting agencies	0.16	0.07	2.29*	0.13	0.04	3.12**	0.14	0.04	3.30***
NCVS redesign in 1992	1985.73	298.58	6.65***	1942.18	256.60	7.57***	1951.52	214.00	9.12***
% afraid to walk at night	113.14	25.94	4.36***	73.46	23.79	3.09**	66.45	18.65	3.56**
% property crime reported to police[a]	-103.06	30.95	-3.33**						
Cell phone connections (in millions)	-7.93	7.07	-1.12						
Intercept	-1225728.00	426812.50	-2.87	-1167984.00	330741.30	-3.53	-917390.60	197724.60	-4.64

Note. Model 1: $df = 35$, $F = 326.87$, Adjusted $R^2 = 0.9944$; Model 2: $df = 35$, $F = 398.11$, Adjusted $R^2 = 0.9921$; Model 3: $df = 35$, $F = 410.77$, Adjusted $R^2 = 0.9894$.

* $p < 0.05$; ** $p < 0.01$; *** $p < 0.001$.

[a] % of larceny theft reported to police as reported in the NCVS.

Table 6.18. Results of OLS Regressions with Lagged Dependent Variable for Larceny Theft

Variable	Model 1			Model 2			Model 3		
	Coefficient	*SE*	*t* statistics	Coefficient	*SE*	*t* statistics	Coefficient	*SE*	*t* statistics
Lagged dependent	0.00	0.13	-0.04	-0.03	0.12	-0.22	0.11	0.11	1.02
Population characteristics									
Total household (in millions)	115.86	89.55	1.29						
Total population (in millions)	-78.47	148.67	-0.53						
% White	-492.42	715.60	-0.69						
% Black	189.17	2869.92	0.07	-206.25	1587.70	-0.13			
% Hispanic	-893.09	706.69	-1.26	-1083.23	324.46	-3.34***	-1143.46	275.69	-4.15***
Educational attainment									
% below high school	1107.96	640.66	1.73	-69.98	124.82	-0.56	44.47	88.02	0.51
% with high school	999.55	664.06	1.51						
% with some college	1102.60	705.69	1.56						
% with 4 years college	1033.23	662.98	1.56						

Table 6.18. Results of OLS Regressions with Lagged Dependent Variable for Larceny Theft (Continued)

Variable	Model 1			Model 2			Model 3		
	Coefficient	*SE*	*t* statistics	Coefficient	*SE*	*t* statistics	Coefficient	*SE*	*t* statistics
Police employment									
Total employees (in 100,000)	-1348.42	391.30	-3.45**	-1721.46	388.29	-4.43***	-1871.79	292.55	-6.40***
% sworn officers	-345.81	147.92	-2.34*	-534.87	158.52	-3.37**	-445.79	118.11	-3.77**
% female employees	-177.87	279.29	-0.64	-307.23	235.89	-1.30			
Total expenses on police (in millions)	0.06	0.05	1.36	0.09	0.03	2.95**	0.11	0.02	4.45***
UCR Reporting agencies	0.02	0.07	0.29	0.11	0.06	1.75			
NCVS redesign in 1992	1632.53	348.13	4.69***	1819.31	334.86	5.43***	1771.72	257.26	6.89***
% afraid to walk at night	80.77	31.45	2.57*	85.99	34.61	2.48**	71.90	25.13	2.86**
% property crime reported to police[a]	-111.76	38.50	-2.90*						
Cell phone connections (in millions)	3.39	7.53	0.45						
Intercept	-8073.93	87429.85	-0.09	69519.81	17630.03	3.94***	52850.41	8512.68	6.21***

Note. Model 1: $df = 34$, $F = 217.97$, Adjusted $R^2 = 0.9918$; Model 2: $df = 34$, $F = 234.01$, Adjusted $R^2 = 0.9869$; Model 3: $df = 34$, $F = 272.50$, Adjusted $R^2 = 0.9863$.

* $p < 0.05$; ** $p < 0.01$; *** $p < 0.001$.

[a] % of larceny theft reported to police as reported in the NCVS.

Table 6.19. Results of OLS Regressions for Violent Crime

Variable	Model 1			Model 2			Model 3		
	Coefficient	*SE*	*t* statistics	Coefficient	*SE*	*t* statistics	Coefficient	*SE*	*t* statistics
Population characteristics									
Total household (in millions)	21.08	20.83	1.01						
Total population (in millions)	-36.02	35.78	-1.01						
% White	-130.25	168.81	-0.77						
% Black	-207.00	666.37	-0.31	33.07	393.98	0.08			
% Hispanic	4.75	162.43	0.03	-43.94	76.87	-0.57			
Educational attainment									
% below high school	266.23	152.44	1.75	-16.71	31.98	-0.52	9.12	18.13	0.50
% with high school	324.98	156.92	2.07						
% with some college	203.95	167.63	1.22						
% with 4 years college	303.77	156.88	1.94						

Table 6.19. Results of OLS Regressions for Violent Crime (Continued)

Variable	Model 1			Model 2			Model 3		
	Coefficient	*SE*	*t* statistics	Coefficient	*SE*	*t* statistics	Coefficient	*SE*	*t* statistics
Police employment									
Total employees (in 100,000)	-168.60	97.09	-1.74	-286.21	99.23	-2.88**	-198.44	39.75	-4.99***
% sworn officers	24.02	34.52	0.70	-43.08	40.92	-1.05	-26.36	26.85	-0.98
% female employees	41.98	64.40	0.65	-25.67	58.88	-0.44			
Total expenses on police (in millions)	0.01	0.01	1.18	0.01	0.01	0.75			
UCR Reporting agencies	-0.01	0.02	-0.70	-0.02	0.01	-1.26			
NCVS redesign in 1992	180.81	86.09	2.10*	136.63	84.00	1.63	170.35	57.05	2.99**
% afraid to walk at night	24.06	7.41	3.25**	17.99	7.90	2.28*	19.35	4.50	4.30***
% property crime reported to police[a]	-6.40	5.69	-1.13						
Cell phone connections (in millions)	-0.23	1.83	-0.12						
Intercept	-10042.48	21701.19	-0.46	6040.55	4524.38	1.34	2961.46	1714.12	1.73

Note. Model 1: $df = 35$, $F = 96.10$, Adjusted $R^2 = 0.9800$; Model 2: $df = 35$, $F = 95.66$, Adjusted $R^2 = 0.9643$; Model 3: $df = 35$, $F = 212.04$, Adjusted $R^2 = 0.9679$.

* $p < 0.05$; ** $p < 0.01$; *** $p < 0.001$.

[a] % of violent crime reported to police as reported in the NCVS.

Table 6.20. Results of OLS Regressions with Time Trend for Violent Crime

Variable	Model 1			Model 2			Model 3		
	Coefficient	*SE*	*t* statistics	Coefficient	*SE*	*t* statistics	Coefficient	*SE*	*t* statistics
Year	9.95	73.42	0.14	37.01	56.44	0.66	4.18	12.15	0.34
Population characteristics									
Total household (in millions)	20.02	22.86	0.88						
Total population (in millions)	-36.55	37.07	-0.99						
% White	-125.89	176.86	-0.71						
% Black	-278.33	865.10	-0.32	-75.27	431.44	-0.17			
% Hispanic	7.04	168.18	0.04	-50.26	78.36	-0.64			
Educational attainment									
% below high school	262.47	159.47	1.65	1.89	43.03	0.04	11.21	19.38	0.58
% with high school	318.30	169.02	1.88						
% with some college	196.62	180.97	1.09						
% with 4 years college	297.55	168.03	1.77						

Table 6.20. Results of OLS Regressions with Time Trend for Violent Crime (Continued)

Variable	Model 1			Model 2			Model 3		
	Coefficient	*SE*	*t* statistics	Coefficient	*SE*	*t* statistics	Coefficient	*SE*	*t* statistics
Police employment									
Total employees (in 100,000)	-168.44	100.03	-1.68	-281.55	100.63	-2.80*	-215.67	64.28	-3.35**
% sworn officers	25.08	36.41	0.69	-38.76	41.91	-0.92	-28.02	27.68	-1.01
% female employees	43.63	67.45	0.65	-24.68	59.58	-0.41			
Total expenses on police (in millions)	0.01	0.01	1.05	0.00	0.01	-0.01			
UCR Reporting agencies	-0.01	0.02	-0.50	-0.02	0.01	-1.06			
NCVS redesign in 1992	185.99	96.59	1.93	146.42	86.27	1.70	171.71	58.04	2.96**
% afraid to walk at night	24.50	8.27	2.96**	17.75	8.00	2.22*	19.82	4.77	4.15***
% property crime reported to police[a]	-6.03	6.45	-0.93						
Cell phone connections (in millions)	-0.37	2.16	-0.17						
Intercept	-28665.95	139258.00	-0.21	-66817.28	111204.80	-0.60	-5181.57	23720.76	-0.22

Note. Model 1: $df = 35$, $F = 85.79$, Adjusted $R^2 = 0.9787$; Model 2: $df = 35$, $F = 85.02$, Adjusted $R^2 = 0.9635$; Model 3: $df = 35$, $F = 171.53$, Adjusted $R^2 = 0.9669$.

* $p < 0.05$; ** $p < 0.01$; *** $p < 0.001$.

[a] % of violent crime reported to police as reported in the NCVS.

Table 6.21. Results of OLS Regressions with Lagged Dependent Variable for Violent Crime

Variable	Model 1			Model 2			Model 3		
	Coefficient	*SE*	*t* statistics	Coefficient	*SE*	*t* statistics	Coefficient	*SE*	*t* statistics
Lagged dependent	-0.28	0.20	-1.42	-0.38	0.21	-1.83	-0.22	0.13	-1.62
Population characteristics									
Total household (in millions)	21.02	20.57	1.02						
Total population (in millions)	-19.87	34.07	-0.58						
% White	-49.50	160.76	-0.31						
% Black	-628.59	649.27	-0.97	-317.96	390.00	-0.82			
% Hispanic	-102.68	160.04	-0.64	-89.74	77.70	-1.15			
Educational attainment									
% below high school	106.05	164.59	0.64	-15.44	29.85	-0.52	18.49	14.81	1.25
% with high school	153.05	176.37	0.87						
% with some college	21.21	184.52	0.11						
% with 4 years college	130.63	174.45	0.75						

Table 6.21. Results of OLS Regressions with Lagged Dependent Variable for Violent Crime (Continued)

Variable	Model 1			Model 2			Model 3		
	Coefficient	*SE*	*t* statistics	Coefficient	*SE*	*t* statistics	Coefficient	*SE*	*t* statistics
Police employment									
Total employees (in 100,000)	-125.76	94.43	-1.33	-237.82	93.59	-2.54*	-183.53	37.56	-4.89***
% sworn officers	6.84	34.87	0.20	-49.82	39.07	-1.28	-40.48	22.06	-1.84
% female employees	61.96	60.48	1.02	-17.52	55.88	-0.31			
Total expenses on police (in millions)	0.01	0.01	1.26	0.01	0.01	0.90			
UCR Reporting agencies	0.00	0.02	-0.01	0.00	0.01	-0.09			
NCVS redesign in 1992	271.64	93.08	2.92*	233.13	88.74	2.63*	156.38	50.01	3.13**
% afraid to walk at night	35.57	9.08	3.92**	32.38	9.45	3.43**	16.84	4.91	3.43**
% property crime reported to police[a]	-3.22	5.53	-0.58						
Cell phone connections (in millions)	-0.46	1.71	-0.27						
Intercept	2288.10	21899.69	0.10	10112.33	4509.94	2.24*	3727.63	1432.38	2.60*

Note. Model 1: $df = 34$, $F = 98.92$, Adjusted $R^2 = 0.9821$; Model 2: $df = 34$, $F = 95.48$, Adjusted $R^2 = 0.9683$; Model 3: $df = 34$, $F = 139.73$, Adjusted $R^2 = 0.9608$.

* $p < 0.05$; ** $p < 0.01$; *** $p < 0.001$.

[a] % of violent crime reported to police as reported in the NCVS

Table 6.22. Results of OLS Regressions for Property Crime

Variable	Model 1			Model 2			Model 3		
	Coefficient	*SE*	*t* statistics	Coefficient	*SE*	*t* statistics	Coefficient	*SE*	*t* statistics
Population characteristics									
Total household (in millions)	89.35	118.00	0.76						
Total population (in millions)	-72.59	193.16	-0.38						
% White	-640.11	933.40	-0.69						
% Black	1866.71	3776.55	0.49	124.51	2026.99	0.06**			
% Hispanic	-1091.49	891.95	-1.22	-1282.39	366.71	-3.50	-1358.08	308.87	-4.40***
Educational attainment									
% below high school	2203.69	861.06	2.56*	-133.53	157.04	-0.85	48.23	106.95	0.45
% with high school	2251.67	891.36	2.53*						
% with some college	2250.46	962.76	2.34*						
% with 4 years college	2180.08	897.85	2.43*						

Table 6.22. Results of OLS Regressions for Property Crime (Continued)

Variable	Model 1			Model 2			Model 3		
	Coefficient	*SE*	*t* statistics	Coefficient	*SE*	*t* statistics	Coefficient	*SE*	*t* statistics
Police employment									
Total employees (in 100,000)	-2172.49	531.25	-4.09**	-2696.12	460.45	-5.86***	-2538.91	336.14	-7.55***
% sworn officers	-469.94	190.63	-2.47*	-682.03	212.41	-3.21**	-510.13	151.51	-3.37**
% female employees	-330.96	361.71	-0.91	-395.14	304.60	-1.30			
Total expenses on police (in millions)	0.08	0.06	1.38	0.13	0.03	3.88**	0.13	0.03	4.91***
UCR Reporting agencies	-0.02	0.10	-0.19						
NCVS redesign in 1992	1479.71	479.25	3.09**	1656.52	434.89	3.81**	1868.98	317.00	5.90***
% afraid to walk at night	81.78	40.05	2.04	87.37	40.89	2.14*	100.18	27.38	3.66**
% property crime reported to police[a]	-133.29	51.73	-2.58*						
Cell phone connections (in millions)	7.73	10.02	0.77						
Intercept	-109497.00	120222.80	-0.91	89692.38	22369.49	4.01***	64066.85	10645.32	6.02***

Note. Model 1: $df = 35$, $F = 239.97$, Adjusted $R^2 = 0.9919$; Model 2: $df = 35$, $F = 300.84$, Adjusted $R^2 = 0.9872$; Model 3: $df = 35$, $F = 379.55$, Adjusted $R^2 = 0.9870$.

* $p < 0.05$; * $p < 0.01$; ***$p < 0.001$.

[a] % of property crime reported to police as reported in the NCVS.

Table 6.23. Results of OLS Regressions with Time Trend for Property Crime

Variable	Model 1			Model 2			Model 3		
	Coefficient	*SE*	*t* statistics	Coefficient	*SE*	*t* statistics	Coefficient	*SE*	*t* statistics
Year	614.24	333.55	1.84	692.59	252.24	2.75*	453.85	242.11	1.87
Population characteristics									
Total household (in millions)									
Total population (in millions)									
% White									
% Black	-2536.76	4268.67	-0.59	-2054.38	1978.06	-1.04			
% Hispanic	-1007.50	836.40	-1.20	-1487.73	336.22	-4.42***	-1371.19	295.96	-4.63***
Educational attainment									
% below high school	2030.53	811.69	2.50*	184.83	182.07	1.02	316.46	175.98	1.80
% with high school	1970.92	848.40	2.32*						
% with some college	1920.13	919.12	2.09						
% with 4 years college	1900.39	854.28	2.22*						

Table 6.23. Results of OLS Regressions with Time Trend for Property Crime (Continued)

Variable	Model 1			Model 2			Model 3		
	Coefficient	*SE*	*t* statistics	Coefficient	*SE*	*t* statistics	Coefficient	*SE*	*t* statistics
Police employment									
Total employees (in 100,000)	-2228.89	498.36	-4.47***	-2736.73	411.85	-6.64***	-2741.64	339.67	-8.07***
% sworn officers	-365.83	187.23	-1.95	-602.33	192.08	-3.14**	-487.27	145.65	-3.35**
% female employees	-247.42	341.70	-0.72	-362.63	272.53	-1.33			
Total expenses on police (in millions)	0.06	0.05	1.06	0.03	0.05	0.67	0.06	0.05	1.35
UCR Reporting agencies	0.08	0.11	0.79						
NCVS redesign in 1992	1720.43	467.39	3.68**	1821.96	393.39	4.63***	1839.58	304.07	6.05***
% afraid to walk at night	102.52	39.16	2.62*	84.68	36.56	2.32*	80.55	28.24	2.85**
% property crime reported to police[a]	-138.15	48.51	-2.85*						
Cell phone connections (in millions)	-2.07	10.79	-0.19						
Intercept	-1290030.00	650874.50	-1.98	-1269841.00	495545.20	-2.56*	-841749.50	483319.60	-1.74

Note. Model 1: $df = 35$, $F = 259.50$, Adjusted $R^2 = 0.9929$; Model 2: $df = 35$, $F = 339.60$, Adjusted $R^2 = 0.9898$; Model 3: $df = 35$, $F = 362.36$, Adjusted $R^2 = 0.9880$.

* $p < 0.05$; ** $p < 0.01$; *** $p < 0.001$.

[a] % of property crime reported to police as reported in the NCVS

Table 6.24. Results of OLS Regressions with Lagged Dependent Variable for Property Crime

Variable	Model 1			Model 2			Model 3		
	Coefficient	*SE*	*t* statistics	Coefficient	*SE*	*t* statistics	Coefficient	*SE*	*t* statistics
Lagged dependent	-0.03	0.14	-0.21	0.04	0.13	0.28	0.08	0.13	0.60
Population characteristics									
Total household (in millions)	115.12	122.85	0.94						
Total population (in millions)	-114.69	203.34	-0.56						
% White	-762.40	967.68	-0.79						
% Black	2352.50	3868.79	0.61	-138.65	2214.38	-0.06			
% Hispanic	-756.28	978.20	-0.77	-1333.57	454.70	-2.93**	-1345.39	368.99	-3.65**
Educational attainment									
% below high school	2426.31	927.33	2.62*	-131.05	173.50	-0.76	50.61	116.41	0.43
% with high school	2405.84	964.67	2.49*						
% with some college	2505.09	1022.98	2.45*						
% with 4 years college	2384.21	965.12	2.47*						

Table 6.24. Results of OLS Regressions with Lagged Dependent Variable for Property Crime (Continued)

Variable	Model 1			Model 2			Model 3		
	Coefficient	*SE*	*t* statistics	Coefficient	*SE*	*t* statistics	Coefficient	*SE*	*t* statistics
Police employment									
Total employees (in 100,000)	-2211.89	549.98	-4.02**	-2631.67	523.86	-5.02***	-2462.18	407.04	-6.05***
% sworn officers	-478.38	197.95	-2.42*	-668.77	222.04	-3.01**	-523.18	156.67	-3.34**
% female employees	-377.47	373.48	-1.01	-352.95	327.98	-1.08			
Total expenses on police (in millions)	0.05	0.06	0.89	0.13	0.04	3.23**	0.13	0.03	4.07***
UCR Reporting agencies	-0.05	0.10	-0.52						
NCVS redesign in 1992	1333.42	503.62	2.65*	1664.67	456.71	3.64**	1808.83	335.98	5.38***
% afraid to walk at night	71.72	44.62	1.61	87.59	49.13	1.78	89.68	35.17	2.55*
% property crime reported to police[a]	-150.11	54.63	-2.75*						
Cell phone connections (in millions)	9.33	10.41	0.90						
Intercept	-115566.60	123017.00	-0.94	90451.78	24625.91	3.67**	64205.50	11428.29	5.62***

Note. Model 1: $df = 34$, $F = 208.45$, Adjusted $R^2 = 0.9914$; Model 2: $df = 34$, $F = 239.76$, Adjusted $R^2 = 0.9860$; Model 3: $df = 34$, $F = 299.19$, Adjusted $R^2 = 0.9859$.

* $p < 0.05$; ** $p < 0.01$; *** $p < 0.001$.

[a] % of property crime reported to police as reported in the NCVS.

Table 6.25. Results of OLS Regressions for Total Crime

Variable	Model 1			Model 2			Model 3		
	Coefficient	*SE*	*t* statistics	Coefficient	*SE*	*t* statistics	Coefficient	*SE*	*t* statistics
Population characteristics									
Total household (in millions)	96.85	126.77	0.76						
Total population (in millions)	-118.72	204.38	-0.58						
% White	-801.74	986.28	-0.81						
% Black	1749.69	3976.31	0.44	223.87	2211.19	0.10			
% Hispanic	-1003.17	944.79	-1.06	-1288.14	400.04	-3.22**	-1377.30	336.13	-4.10***
Educational attainment									
% below high school	2533.15	915.48	2.77*	-137.16	171.31	-0.80	54.88	116.39	0.47
% with high school	2692.61	954.80	2.82*						
% with some college	2537.44	1025.18	2.48*						
% with 4 years college	2585.97	958.98	2.70*						

Table 6.25. Results of OLS Regressions for Total Crime (Continued)

Variable	Model 1			Model 2			Model 3		
	Coefficient	*SE*	*t* statistics	Coefficient	*SE*	*t* statistics	Coefficient	*SE*	*t* statistics
Police employment									
Total employees (in 100,000)	-2368.33	564.92	-4.19**	-2926.311	502.2889	-5.83***	-2745.90	365.81	-7.51***
% sworn officers	-416.98	205.00	-2.03	-724.6005	231.7141	-3.13**	-537.60	164.89	-3.26**
% female employees	-283.34	381.90	-0.74	-426.9672	332.2781	-1.28			
Total expenses on police (in millions)	0.09	0.06	1.54	0.1260463	0.035259	3.57**	0.1363988	0.029822	4.57***
UCR Reporting agencies	-0.03	0.10	-0.33						
NCVS redesign in 1992	1620.80	511.18	3.17**	1800.946	474.4136	3.80**	2038.461	344.9802	5.91***
% afraid to walk at night	109.44	42.51	2.57*	104.6026	44.60335	2.35*	119.532	29.79796	4.01***
% property crime reported to police[a]	-150.55	56.44	-2.67*						
Cell phone connections (in millions)	7.39	10.63	0.69						
Intercept	-126182.00	128056.70	-0.99	93995.69	24402.24	3.85**	67331.2	11584.96	5.81***

Note. Model 1: $df = 35$, $F = 264.47$, Adjusted $R2 = 0.9927$; Model 2: $df = 35$, $F = 313.53$, Adjusted $R2 = 0.9877$; Model 3: $df = 35$, $F = 397.50$, Adjusted $R2 = 0.9875$.

* $p < 0.05$; ** $p < 0.01$; *** $p < 0.001$.

a % of total crime reported to police as reported in the NCVS.

Table 6.26. Results of OLS Regressions with Time Trend for Total Crime

Variable	Model 1			Model 2			Model 3		
	Coefficient	*SE*	*t* statistics	Coefficient	*SE*	*t* statistics	Coefficient	*SE*	*t* statistics
Year	598.37	359.03	1.67	743.15	276.51	2.69*	492.65	263.57	1.87
Population characteristics									
Total household (in millions)	2.00	133.37	0.01						
Total population (in millions)	-115.38	194.47	-0.59						
% White	-405.60	968.07	-0.42						
% Black	-2451.68	4546.35	-0.54	-2114.07	2168.36	-0.97			
% Hispanic	-916.22	900.47	-1.02	-1508.47	368.57	-4.09***	-1391.54	322.19	-4.32***
Educational attainment									
% below high school	2344.71	878.38	2.67*	204.43	199.58	1.02	346.03	191.58	1.81
% with high school	2393.14	926.09	2.58*						
% with some college	2186.02	997.98	2.19*						
% with 4 years college	2287.19	929.91	2.46*						

Table 6.26. Results of OLS Regressions with Time Trend for Total Crime (Continued)

Variable	Model 1			Model 2			Model 3		
	Coefficient	*SE*	*t* statistics	Coefficient	*SE*	*t* statistics	Coefficient	*SE*	*t* statistics
Police employment									
Total employees (in 100,000)	-2417.02	538.31	-4.49***	-2969.88	451.48	-6.58***	-2965.96	369.77	-8.02***
% sworn officers	-320.46	203.47	-1.57	-639.08	210.56	-3.04**	-512.78	158.56	-3.23**
% female employees	-209.81	366.04	-0.57	-392.09	298.75	-1.31			
Total expenses on police (in millions)	0.07	0.06	1.21	0.02	0.05	0.48	0.06	0.05	1.15
UCR Reporting agencies	0.07	0.11	0.58						
NCVS redesign in 1992	1866.93	508.31	3.67**	1978.46	431.23	4.59***	2006.55	331.01	6.06***
% afraid to walk at night	129.14	42.14	3.06**	101.72	40.08	2.54*	98.22	30.75	3.19**
% property crime reported to police[a]	-150.29	53.71	-2.80*						
Cell phone connections (in millions)	-2.10	11.61	-0.18						
Intercept	-1272373.00	698447.10	-1.82	-1364781.00	543219.00	-2.51*	-915920.90	526155.60	-1.74

Note. Model 1: $df = 35$, $F = 276.90$, Adjusted $R^2 = 0.9934$; Model 2: $df = 35$, $F = 350.44$, Adjusted $R^2 = 0.9901$; Model 3: $df = 35$, $F = 379.22$, Adjusted $R^2 = 0.9886$.

* $p < 0.05$; ** $p < 0.01$; *** $p < 0.001$.

[a] % of total crime reported to police as reported in the NCVS

Table 6.27. Results of OLS Regressions with Lagged Dependent Variable for Total Crime

Variable	Model 1			Model 2			Model 3		
	Coefficient	*SE*	*t* statistics	Coefficient	*SE*	*t* statistics	Coefficient	*SE*	*t* statistics
Lagged dependent	-0.07	0.15	-0.51	-0.01	0.14	-0.10	0.03	0.13	0.24
Population characteristics									
Total household (in millions)	121.05	133.93	0.90						
Total population (in millions)	-135.87	219.76	-0.62						
% White	-829.60	1046.17	-0.79						
% Black	2056.12	4153.88	0.49	-296.44	2404.69	-0.12			
% Hispanic	-827.54	1055.71	-0.78	-1462.03	491.66	-2.97**	-1459.44	396.91	-3.68**
Educational attainment									
% below high school	2595.00	1005.57	2.58*	-165.60	187.14	-0.88	36.88	125.31	0.29
% with high school	2679.22	1055.07	2.54*						
% with some college	2635.87	1109.03	2.38*						
% with 4 years college	2625.88	1051.43	2.50*						

Table 6.27. Results of OLS Regressions with Lagged Dependent Variable for Total Crime (Continued)

Variable	Model 1			Model 2			Model 3		
	Coefficient	*SE*	*t* statistics	Coefficient	*SE*	*t* statistics	Coefficient	*SE*	*t* statistics
Police employment									
Total employees (in 100,000)	-2426.69	591.95	-4.10**	-2942.33	562.61	-5.23***	-2769.64	438.42	-6.32***
% sworn officers	-438.58	216.60	-2.02	-705.70	241.31	-2.92**	-548.77	170.00	-3.23**
% female employees	-336.52	400.25	-0.84	-381.04	355.95	-1.07			
Total expenses on police (in millions)	0.07	0.07	1.03	0.14	0.04	3.26**	0.14	0.04	4.09***
UCR Reporting agencies	-0.05	0.11	-0.48						
NCVS redesign in 1992	1519.37	545.08	2.79	1850.30	498.43	3.71**	1985.26	369.07	5.38***
% afraid to walk at night	109.53	49.22	2.23*	118.14	54.14	2.18	117.27	38.89	3.02**
% property crime reported to police[a]	-163.79	60.33	-2.72*						
Cell phone connections (in millions)	9.14	11.21	0.82						
Intercept	-125338.10	133278.70	-0.94	99213.89	26931.09	3.68**	69015.64	12452.02	5.54***

Note. Model 1: $df = 35$, $F = 221.57$, Adjusted $R^2 = 0.9920$; Model 2: $df = 35$, $F = 251.85$, Adjusted $R^2 = 0.9866$; Model 3: $df = 35$, $F = 312.96$, Adjusted $R^2 = 0.9866$.

* $p < 0.05$; **$p < 0.01$; ***$p < 0.001$.

[a] % of total crime reported to police as reported in the NCVS.

CHAPTER 7

Discussion and Conclusions

The present research study sought to explore and explain the convergence between the UCR and NCVS data series and had two primary objectives. The first objective was to understand the dynamic relationship between the nation's two crime data series and to determine whether the two crime data series have converged as predicted (Blumstein et al., 1992). The second objective was to identify factors responsible for bringing the two measures close to convergence. An overview of the UCR and NCVS indicated that the discrepancies in the two data series decreased after 1973, and several factors have been responsible for bringing them closer together. The intent of this study was to provide important research, policy, and methodological contributions that would be relevant in future policy decisions made for improving measures of crime and victimization and guiding future research from a methodological point of view. This chapter is organized into six sections: (1) a brief summary of the study; (2) discussion of the findings; (3) policy and methodological implications (4) limitations; (5) future research directions; and (6) major conclusions.

BACKGROUND AND SUMMARY OF THE STUDY

The first report of the NCS in 1973 reported more than twice the number of crimes as the UCR (Skogan, 1974) and fueled discussion about the comparative validity of the two crime measures. Some researchers argued in favor of the UCR (Skogan, 1974), some opined in favor of the NCS (Decker, 1977; O'Brien et al., 1980), and some argued in favor of according considerable validity to both measures (Booth et al., 1977; Cohen & Land, 1984; Cohen & Lichbach, 1982).

As the discussion later changed direction, researchers began explaining the divergence and convergence between the two data series and started the debate over convergence definition and methodology. Several studies reported convergence between the two series (Biderman et al., 1991; Blumstein et al., 1991; Catalano, 2006; O'Brien, 1990, 1996) and argued that both measure the same fundamental phenomenon and that divergence between them is caused by differences in the methods of measurement. A few researchers reported a substantial lack of convergence and argued that both measure fundamentally different phenomena (Menard, 1987; Menard & Covey, 1988).

The UCR and NCVS are important data series, and their validity has serious potential implications for research in the field and in the formulation of public policies directed toward crime reduction. The divergence between the UCR and NCVS is obvious because they use different data-collection methods while measuring overlapping, but nonidentical, set of offenses in overlapping but nonidentical populations (Rand & Rennison, 2002). However, the initial divergence in the two measures was too great to be attributed to differences in the methods estimation alone. A potential convergence between the two data series along with a certain degree of divergence is perhaps desirable from a triangulation viewpoint. The convergence between the two data series provides convergent validity to both \ measures of crime. Therefore, testing and explaining the convergence are important from the perspective of policy implications. In view of the constantly changing relationship between the two data series, the great temporal and crime-specific variability in their relationship, the conflicting results of convergence studies, and a lack of consensus on methodology for testing the convergence, the current research becomes an important contribution to the research literature in criminal justice and criminology.

The data for the research reported here were drawn from different sources beyond the UCR and NCVS, and a combination of strategies was used for testing a set of research hypotheses in order to address the research questions that seek to explore and explain the convergence between the UCR and NCVS.

DISCUSSION OF FINDINGS

The empirical findings of the research were presented in Chapters 5 and 6. Prior to the data analyses, descriptions of dependent variables and some of the important predictor variables were provided in Chapter 4. The findings, therefore, were presented in three chapters that included descriptive and inferential or associational analyses of the data. In this section, a brief account of descriptive analyses is presented, followed by discussion of the findings of inferential and associational analyses as related to the findings reported by the relevant literature on the subject.

The descriptive statistics of the dependent variables give valuable information about the trend of UCR and NCVS rates and their dynamic relationship over the past 36 years. Crime rates in both data series have shown substantial changes over time in the past. The change of rates, however, has been different for the UCR and NCVS across the categories of crime. This variation indicates a potential convergence between the two series, with differing degrees of convergence for different crime categories. The UCR crime rates for robbery, burglary, and motor vehicle theft decreased, but the rates increased for aggravated assault and larceny theft during the period of 1973 to 2008. The aggravated assault rate showed a 38% increase while burglary and motor vehicle theft showed 40% and 30% decreases, respectively. NCVS rates, on the other hand, showed a substantial decrease across all categories of crime between 1973 and 2008. The NCVS aggravated assault and burglary rates showed more than a 70% decrease, followed by robbery at over 60% decrease. Motor vehicle theft showed the least decrease (49%), and larceny theft decreased 56%.

The UCR and NCVS crime rates showed substantial variability between 1973 and 2008, variation which is reflected in the standard deviations from their means and the differences between maximum and minimum rates provided in the descriptive statistics table in Chapter 4. The percent change between the maximum and minimum UCR rates during the period was 55% for aggravated assault, 57% for burglary, about 50% for robbery and motor vehicle theft, and 36% for larceny theft. However, the NCVS has shown even greater variability in rates. The percent change between the maximum and minimum NCVS rates during the period was about 70% for aggravated assault, robbery and burglary, and about 60% for motor vehicle theft and larceny.

Two inferences can be drawn from the above description of the trends in the UCR and NCVS rates over the past 36 years. First, the higher percentages of decrease in the NCVS rates are indicative of potential convergence between the two data series. Second, the higher percentages of decrease reported for the violent crime categories are indicative of a differential level of convergence for different crime categories and the likelihood of a higher level of convergence for the violent crime categories.

One important phenomenon can be noticed in the two data series in the beginning of the 1990s in terms of their rates. The UCR rates were continuously increasing after 1973, and reached an all-time high in 1991. The increase in the UCR rates may be attributed to several factors, such as the effects of baby boomers, the crack epidemic, and the demise of blue-collar-job-intensive industries (Blumstein, 2008) as well as increased police productivity (O'Brien, 1996). The NCVS rates maintained stability and showed a moderate increase during this same period. The anomaly of the rate change between the two series was responsible for their convergence before the 1990s.

After the turning point in 1991, the UCR crime rates started decreasing. Several factors, such as the high rate of incarceration, the end of the crack epidemic, the economy and job market, and legalization of abortion were thought to be responsible for the decrease in the UCR rates (Blumstein, 2008). The turning point for the NCVS came in 1993, which coincided with the rate-affecting changes in methodology, and after 1993 the NCVS crime rates also started decreasing. The rates of change in both series were again not identical. The NCVS showed substantially higher percentages of change in rates than the UCR for all categories of crime. This differential rate of change is responsible for the convergence documented after 1993.

Population and demographic variables used in the time-series regression models for explaining the factors responsible for the convergence have two distinctive features. First, the percent increase in the household numbers (77%) during the period from 1973 to 2008 was higher than the percent increase in the residential population (50%). Second, the percent increase in the Hispanic population (200%) during the period was higher than the percent increase in the White (9%) and Black (13%) populations. In addition, educational attainment of Americans changed significantly between 1973 and 2008. The percent of the population with high school educations decreased moderately while the percent of the population with some college increased moderately; however the population with less than a high school education decreased substantially, and the population with 4 years of college showed substantial increase.

The total number of law enforcement employees and the police-to-population ratio (number of police officers for every 1,000 population) increased substantially from 1973 to 2008. Total law enforcement recorded 150% growth, and the police-to-population ratio rose to 3.4 in 2008 from 1.9 in 1973. The percentage of sworn officers who were female was 11% in 1973 but 27% in 2008, showing over 150% growth. The percent of police department employees who were civilians increased while the percent who were sworn officers decreased. Total expenses for police grew 14 times during that period, and per capita spending on police rose from $36 in 1973 to $354 in 2008.

The NCVS data show that the percentages of reporting to police increased for all categories of crime during that period. The reported crimes that showed maximum increase was aggravated assault and larceny theft, which were the most divergent categories in 1973. The crime showing the least increase was burglary. Therefore, the variables of aggravated assault and larceny theft reporting showed maximum variability whereas the burglary-reporting variable shows minimum variability.

Four hypotheses related to Research Question 1 and 2, which addressed whether the two series were converging, were tested, and the results reported in Chapter 5 provide partial support for the hypotheses. The hypotheses were tested through a combined strategy that included graphic, correlational, bivariate regression, and cointegration analyses. Graphic analyses showed that the two series, which were divergent in 1973, had come close to each other in 2008. The series overlapped somewhat in cases of aggravated assault and motor vehicle theft, but the trends of rate differences for different categories were different. The aggregated categories of violent crimes showed a smaller divergence in 2008 than the aggregated categories of property crime.

The results from the correlational analyses provided partial support for the first hypothesis concerning convergence, full support for the second hypothesis concerning a differential level of convergence for different categories of crime, and no support for the third hypothesis concerning a greater level of convergence for violent crime. The correlation coefficients between detrended crime rates did not cross the threshold of .8 for any category of crime. This result conflicts with the results reported by the earlier studies (Blumstein et al., 1991; O'Brien, 1990), which found nearly perfect correlations between the two series after detrending. O'Brien, responding to the results of Menard and Covey (1988), strongly recommended detrending the series through differencing before estimating correlations and argued that the lack of convergence reported by Menard and Covey was due to their not having detrended the time series. O'Brien argued that once the series are detrended by either controlling for the time trend or differencing, they would converge. The findings of this study did not support the findings and arguments of O'Brien (1990) and Blumstein et al. (1991). Those studies had used time-series data with approximately 15 observations and showed a very clear trend of increasing UCR and NCVS stability. Once they removed the trend, the series correlated perfectly, so they concluded in favor of convergence and the methodology of estimating correlations after detrending the series. The opposite results in this study indicated that detrending of the series does not always produce significant correlations, and correlational analyses for testing convergence are not free of the limitations.

The correlational coefficient between the series for the entire period may not help in testing the convergence between the two series. A correlation between two time series indicates the strength and the direction of association rather than convergence. Series with greater discrepancies at the beginning, such as aggravated assault, will show a lack of correlation even though they have overlapped recently. Conversely, series that have maintained stability in terms of discrepancies over time, such as burglary, will show stronger correlation. The solution to this problem is to examine the trend of the correlation rather than the size of the correlation for the entire period. The trend of the correlation between the two series was examined in this study through split series correlations, and the results provided complete support for all the hypotheses of convergence.

The third strategy for testing convergence in rate differences between the NCVS and UCR involved regressing the data over time and produced results supporting the overall hypothesis related to convergence. Regression coefficients for all categories of crime included in the study were negative and significant, indicating that the rate differences between the NCVS and UCR have significantly decreased over time and the two series have converged. The final strategy was using cointegration analysis between the two series. The two series were found to be converging in the aggravated assault, burglary, and violent crime categories when ADF tests of logged differences between the NCVS and UCR rates were conducted, controlling for trend. This test, although not a completely preferred test of convergence, provided partial support to the hypotheses related to convergence.

Finally, a more formal and acceptable test of convergence, known as the Engle-Granger test, was conducted, and the results of this analysis again provided partial support for the convergence hypotheses. According to the cointegration test, the UCR and NCVS were cointegrated only for burglary, but were in the process of converging for robbery, larceny theft, and violent crime. The cointegration test results were different from the results reported by McDowell and Loftin (2007), who reported cointegration between the two series for all categories except for robbery. The difference in results reported may be attributed to the difference in methods used for testing cointegration. The cointegration results reported in this study are substantiated by the graphic analyses which clearly show that burglary is the only category in which both series are moving together without major deviation.

The hypothesis-testing results of the cointegration tests were different from the results of the graphic and correlational analyses. The difference can be understood in view of the differences in definitions of *convergence*. In the graphic analyses, the UCR and NCVS were found to be converging across categories, thus reducing their discrepancies significantly. In correlational analysis, the increasing trend in correlation coefficients supported the hypotheses related to convergence. Cointegration analysis, however, tests for long-term equilibrium, and two longitudinal data series are said to be cointegrated when they move together in the long run. Therefore, cointegration analysis also has limitations in helping to understand the convergence, especially when a time series with a limited number of observations is used.

The analyses presented in Chapter 6 tested four remaining hypotheses concerning the convergence or reduced discrepancies between the two data series. Two robust predictors—increase in total number of employees in police and methodological changes in NCVS in 1993—significantly predicted the change in the rate differences between the UCR and NCVS for most of the categories of crime included in the study. This conclusion is based on the results of time-series regression models with lagged dependent variables, analysis in which effects of other independent variables and the problem of autocorrelations were controlled for by adding a single-lagged dependent variable in the right side of the equation.

The increase in the number of police employees has the greatest effect on the rate differences between the UCR and NCVS for aggravated assault, robbery, larceny theft, violent crime, and property crime; it has significant effects on burglary; and the nonsignificant effects on motor vehicle theft. This finding is also supported by the percentage of reporting crime to police as reported by respondents in the victimization survey. The increased number of total employees in police departments is likely to increase police productivity in terms of discovery, notification, and reporting of crime (Levitt, 1998). The finding partially supports the police productivity hypothesis.

Police productivity has increased over time because of organizational and technological development, further development in police professionalization, changed demography of police employees, and changes in police response to certain social issues such as domestic violence and hate crimes (Catalano, 2006; Langan & Farrington, 1988; O'Brien, 1999). The increased police productivity has helped in convergence between the UCR and NCVS by increasing the rates of the UCR (Catalano, 2006; O'Brien, 1999), especially for violent crimes such aggravated assault (Catalano, 2006). The problem in testing the police productivity hypothesis was the limitation of the time-series data, which caused most of the police productivity variables from the LEMAS data to be dropped from the analyses.

The 1992 rate-affecting changes in NCVS methodology were another factor that predicted the changes in rate differences between the UCR and NCVS during the period from 1973 to 2008. This finding supports earlier findings in the literature (Catalano, 2006, 2007). The effects of redesign in 1992 of the NCVS were significant for the rate changes between the UCR and NCVS for larceny theft, property crime, aggravated assault, and violent crime but nonsignificant for burglary and motor vehicle theft. These findings can be explained by considering the comparative changes in the rates of both series over the last 36 years. First, the NCVS larceny theft rate showed more than a

56% decrease, and the UCR larceny theft rate showed a 6% increase between 1973 and 2008, so the difference between the two series significantly decreased. Similarly, the NCVS aggravated assault rate showed a 71% decrease, and the UCR aggravated assault rate showed a 38% increase, so the rate difference between the two series decreased significantly.

In the case of burglary, although the NCVS rate showed a high level of decrease, the UCR rate also decreased substantially, so the rate difference remained high. Similarly, in the case of motor vehicle theft, the NCVS rate showed a 49% decrease, but the UCR rate showed a 31% decrease as well, so the rate difference remained almost unchanged. Two inferences can be drawn from the findings and the above discussion. First, the effects of the 1992 redesign changes on the convergence between the two series were largest for aggravated assault, larceny theft, and property crime; moderate for robbery and violent crime; and nonsignificant for burglary and motor vehicle theft. Second, the effects of the NCVS redesign of 1992 on the convergence should be considered in terms of the rate changes in the UCR.

The analyses did not show significant effects for the variables of population, demographic characteristics, educational attainment, percent of female employees in police, percent of civilians and sworn police officers, increase in reporting agencies to the UCR program, and mobile phone subscription on the rate differences between the NCVS and UCR.

The results of the convergence tests show evidence in support of convergence between the UCR and NCVS and provide convergent validity to both of the measures. One of the objectives of the national crime victimization survey was to provide independent calibration for the UCR. The discrepancy reported by the first NCS report raised serious questions about the validity of the UCR, and most of the studies concluded that the NCS was a more valid measure of crime than the UCR. The rate trends of the two series over the past 36 years, however, indicate that both series had problems of validity in terms of their ability to measure what they purported to measure. The total crime rate, as calculated in this study, has decreased by 11% for the UCR and 60% for the NCVS. The two series are converging primarily because of the substantial decrease in the NCVS. If the NCVS were a more valid measure of crime, as declared by several studies in its early years, then the rate decrease of the NCVS should not have been as sharp as it has been over the past 36 years. The significant effects of the 1992 NCVS redesign on the convergence across the categories of crime provide powerful support to the argument that the victimization survey was not free from measurement problems at its outset and the initial discrepancies did not reflect the dark figure of crime in the UCR; instead, they primarily reflected the differences in the measurement approaches adopted.

IMPLICATIONS

The purpose of research is to provide theoretical and practical implications and directions for future research addressing a noteworthy problem. The findings reported in this study, the use made of archival crime data, and the methods of analysis adopted for exploring and explaining the convergence between the UCR and NCVS have research, public policy, and methodological implications.

The present study has important general research implications for criminological studies that use the UCR and NCVS data for addressing theory and policy questions. As already noted, the convergence between the two series for most of the categories of crime provides evidence in favor of convergence validity for both data series. Questioning the validity of the UCR on the basis of the discrepancies reported by the NCVS is problematic because the rate change in the NCVS over the past 36 years has been several times higher than the rate change in the UCR. However, researchers can use either of the data series, and the selection should be based on the types of research questions and crime categories of interest. Nevertheless, this study offers two principal caveats in this regard. First, crime data from the UCR and NCVS can be used, but the findings based on the data from one series should be reviewed by using related data from the other series. Second, the UCR and NCVS data can be used alternatively for the highly converged crime categories of burglary, robbery, and motor vehicle theft, but due caution is called for concerning the data for larceny theft and aggravated assault. A detailed discussion on policy and methodological implications is provided in the following section.

Policy Implications

Some important public policy implications emerge from the results and the limitations of this study. The most important finding of this study is that the UCR and NCVS crime data series have shown a strong tendency toward convergence over the past years across almost all categories of crime, thus boosting their validity. In this study, two limitations on studying the convergence of the UCR and NCVS data emerged. First, the NCVS does not estimate geographic or city-level variations in criminal victimization. Second, the UCR data provide only summary statistics. Major cities reported disproportionately higher levels of crime, and law enforcement is extremely decentralized in this country. The study of convergence between the UCR and NCVS data series does not provide geographic, city-based or state-based information on the relationship between the official crime statistics and survey-based victimization estimates. This limitation may have consequences for local law enforcement policy making concerning improving professionalization in police in terms of their crime reporting and recording practices. The following policy implications are suggested.

- The first policy implication is that most law enforcement agencies have achieved a greater level of consistency in terms of recording and reporting crimes to the UCR because of numerous organizational and technological changes. Organizational and policy focus on improving the recording and reporting of crime data should cause such improvement to continue.
- The second policy implication is to have a state- and city-based victimization survey along with the national victimization survey. The NCVS is undergoing cost-cutting measures, and the survey is facing tough challenges to survive in its present form (Groves & Cork, 2008; Rand, 2007). In view of the financial difficulties and challenges faced by the national survey, the recommendation for city- and state-based components in the victimization survey seems to be unrealistic. In 2008, the NCVS interviewed 77,852 respondents from 42,093 households. However, the sample size of the national survey can be reduced to an acceptable limit without compromising sampling error, and some of the financial resources

could be directed to the state- and city-level surveys. The states and large police departments could be motivated to have voluntary participation in the survey to make use of local resources and minimize the cost to the federal government.

- The NCVS data provide information on types, time, and location of crimes; victim-offender relations; characteristics of offenders; type of property lost and weapon used; reporting of crime to police; and many other aspects of victimization, but the information in the UCR is limited to summary estimates of Part I crimes. This difference inhibits researchers from using crime incident, victim, and offender-related variables to study the convergence between the two crime data series. Although the establishment of NIBRS will mitigate this limitation in the future, the development of NIBRS is extremely slow because of its ambitious objective to collect incident-based information on 46 offenses in 22 categories. It is, therefore, recommended that the NIBRS be developed in two phases. In the first phase, incident-based reporting for all Part I offenses could be achieved. Once phase one is achieved, the second phase could begin focusing on developing the incident-based reporting for all other offenses.

Methodological Implications

This study is important from the aspect of providing methodological implications for testing and explaining the convergence between the UCR and NCVS data series. The following methodological implications are indicated for testing and explaining convergence between the UCR and NCVS.

- Convergence as identical rates, identical rates after the adjustments, correlated rates, and long-term equilibrium are four different definitions of convergence that have been used in the literature (McDowell & Loftin, 2007). Because both series measure crime differently, convergence as identical rates with or without adjustment is not possible. Therefore, two definitions remain: convergence as correlated rates and convergence as long-term equilibrium.
- The strategy of testing convergence as correlated rates is problematic. A correlation between two time series indicates the

strength and the direction of association rather than convergence. Series with greater discrepancies at the beginning, such as aggravated assault, will show a lack of correlation even if they have overlapped recently. Conversely, series that have maintained stability in terms of discrepancies over time, such as burglary, will show stronger correlation. The solution to this problem is to examine the trend of correlation rather than the correlation for the entire period. The trend of the correlation between the two series has been examined in this study through split series correlations, and the results provided complete support for all the hypotheses of convergence. Therefore, it is recommended that correlational analysis of convergence be used for cross-sectional data only. In case of two time series, the trend of correlation should be analyzed through split-series correlation in which series may be split from the middle and several series should be created with half of the observations with a gradual increase over the years.

- In case of correlational analysis of convergence between two series, detrending is not recommended because the correlations between the detrended series are largely meaningless (Menard, 1990), and more importantly detrending series will not provide greater correlations as reported and claimed by O'Brien (1990) and Blumstein et al. (1991). The findings in this study indicated that the correlations between the two series for every category were significantly low when the series were detrended through the first differencing. Therefore, it is recommended that non-detrended series be used for estimating correlations and understanding the direction and strength of association between two longitudinal data series.
- Convergence as long-term equilibrium appears to be the most appropriate definition of convergence to be used for testing the convergence between the UCR and NCVS. The two data series measure the same social phenomenon called crime. Efforts have been made to improve the validity of measurement of each. In this case, the two data series measure total crime committed. The two data series, however, use entirely different approaches to measurement. Thus, the differences between the two data series are obvious, but they should move together on the differences, and the power of the invisible number of total crimes would keep them

together if they are measuring the same phenomenon. This is exactly captured by the definition of *cointegration*, a concept in econometrics for testing long-term equilibrium between two time series. According to cointegration theory, two variables will be cointegrated if they have a long-term or equilibrium relationship (Gujarati, 2004). The theory behind cointegration is that if two or more series are influenced by a similar factor they are pulled and kept together by that factor, and any observed divergence is temporary. The series can diverge for a period, but they eventually come back together. The only problem in using this method is that the UCR and NCVS series have fewer numbers of observations than are required for a formal time-series analysis.

- In time-series regression models, all variables have to be stationary in order to avoid meaningless and spurious relationships. A nonstationary time-series variable will not be independent, and the use of the variable in a model will lead to inefficient or even biased estimation of coefficients. The ideal way to manage this particular problem is to transform the nonstationary time series into stationary time series by differencing. Differencing, however, is very costly to robustness because it throws away long-term trends and reduces statistical degrees of freedom. The second way to deal with the problem of nonstationarity and autocorrelation is to add a single-lagged dependent variable in the right side of an equation, a measure which was taken in the present study. The study is about understanding long-term trend of the relationship between the UCR and NCVS, but the two series have a limited number of observations. Therefore, it is recommended that a single-lagged dependent variable in the right side of the equation be used rather than the method of differencing.

LIMITATIONS

The results of the study have provided valuable contributions to the literature and suggested several policy and methodological implications. The importance of the results should be understood while acknowledging the limitations of the study. Acknowledging limitations applies caveats to the results and opens avenues for future research. In this section, some of the methodological and result-based limitations are presented, followed by recommendations for future research in this area.

The most important limitation lies in the fact that the UCR and NCVS data series have only a limited number of observations. This study used the UCR and NCVS data from 1973 to 2008 for testing and explaining their degree of convergence. The minimum requirement of observations for time-series analysis is about 50, but only 36 observations were available, placing severe methodological limitations on the analysis performed. Previous researchers studying the convergence between the UCR and NCVS data series by using time-series data reported different, sometimes conflicting results. The inconsistency in the results may be emanating from the fact that all of them have used different numbers of time series observations. O'Brien (1990) and Blumstein et al. (1991) found that the correlations between the two series cross the threshold of .8 for all categories of crime once the series are detrended. The current study, however, reported opposite results. The limitation of observations also affects the results of time-series models in terms of the effects of predictor variables on the rate differences between the UCR and NCVS. The series were not made stationary because of the extremely limited number of observations, which may also have had some adverse consequences for the estimated coefficients.

The second most important limitation was the lack of availability of time-series data for most of the predictor variables thought to be responsible factors in affecting the relationship between the two data series. All LEMAS variables that are components of police productivity ultimately had to be dropped from the analyses because of the extremely limited number of observations available. Some of the variables, such as fear of crime victimization and mobile phone connections, were used, but the processes of linear interpolation and extrapolation had to be used to replace missing observations. Although the effects of relevant predictor variables were controlled by adding the single-lagged value of a dependent variable in the right side of the equation, the effects of these variables on convergence between the UCR and NCVS cannot be known with certainty.

Another limitation of the study is that the findings and policy implications may not be relevant to the local dynamics of the relationship between the total number of victimization and official crime rates. More importantly, the results do not reveal the effects of local policy making and development in police in terms of increased professionalization and productivity on the relationship between the UCR and NCVS.

Finally, the data analyses in this study were unable to investigate the effects of factors related to offenses, offenders, and victims. Several factors related to offenses, offenders, victims, and police response in terms of investigation could provide valuable insight in understanding the reporting, notification, and recording of crime. The NCVS data have information on these aspects of crime, but the UCR contains only summary data. The NIBRS will resolve these limitations in the future, but it will be several years before the time-series incident-based data are available.

FUTURE RESEARCH DIRECTIONS

Virtually all serious research, while addressing a question and filling a gap in the literature, leaves many issues unresolved and raises several more questions as it is carried out. This research is no exception. The avenues for future research on the subject of convergence between the UCR and NCVS data series are presented in this section.

The collection of official crime statistics and victimization data is a continuous process, and involves dynamism in terms of what the two crime measurements are measuring and how they are measuring it. This fact provides the opportunity and responsibility for continuous investigation into the changing relationship between the UCR and NCVS. The investigation results would be more meaningful with a greater number of observations in the future.

One important avenue for future research on the subject is to study the relationship between the official crime statistics and estimated survey-based victimization at the state and city level. Such research could only be possible if there were a city and state-based surveys of crime victimization. The availability of geographically classified victimization data would provide opportunities for studying the effects of state and local institutional mechanisms on the convergence between the UCR and NCVS data series.

The official crime statistics are in good part a function of the crime reporting and recording practices of the police. People reporting crime to the police and police practices in terms of defining and recording crime are the main factors that determine UCR rates. There are temporal- and crime-based variations in reporting crime to the police. In addition, there is evidence that suggests that police have recorded more aggravated assaults, and many instances of simple assault have been upgraded to aggravated assault because of police practices (Rosenfeld, 2007). The UCR rates were adjusted for the percentages of crime reported to the police, and separate tests on the convergence were conducted, but they were not adjusted for the police practices of defining and recording crime. This is another avenue for future research on the subject of convergence between the UCR and NCVS. It would be interesting to understand how the series converge and diverge after the UCR rates are adjusted for people reporting crime and the police practices of defining and recording crime.

CONCLUSIONS

The discrepancy between the nation's two most important crime data sources—the UCR and the NCVS—raised several questions regarding their divergence and comparative validity. The series, however, rapidly began decreasing their divergence and have come near convergence in recent years. The issue of comparative validity remains alive, but the focus of research, generally due to the availability of time-series data and substantially reduced divergence, began focusing on the issue of convergence between the two data series, another way to examine the divergence and answer the questions of comparative validity. This study delved into the subject of convergence and sought to test and explain the convergence between the two data series. The two objectives of the study included testing and explaining the convergence between the two data series by using different methods and appropriate definitions of convergence and providing explanations of the convergence by identifying and understanding the different factors that played roles in reducing the rate differences between the two crime data series.

The findings of the analyses reported here provide partial support for the overall hypothesis that the two data series have converged. Different methods of the convergence tests produced different results that are indicative of the importance of definition and methods of testing convergence between the UCR and NCVS. The findings, however, do indicate a process of convergence between the two crime data series for nearly all categories. The most important questions are what is meant by convergence between the UCR and NCVS, and whether their continued discrepancy should be reduced to zero. Perfect convergence where the rate differences between the two series become zero is neither possible nor desirable. If it were to happen, then the victimization survey would perhaps lose its relevance. Rand and Rennison (2002), while explaining the divergence between the UCR and NCVS, observed the following: "They use different data collection methods and measure an overlapping—but not identical—set of offenses against an overlapping—but not identical—population" (p. 48). If convergent validity is one of the tools available for understanding the validity of a measure, then the findings in this study indicate that both data series are valid measures of crime.

The process of convergence between the UCR and NCVS data series is affected by decrease in the proportion or rate differences between the UCR and NCVS, and this decrease can be achieved either by increasing UCR rates or decreasing NCVS rates, or both. The convergence in the 1980s, as reported by the researcher, was influenced by a substantial increase in UCR rates, and the convergence in post-1992 was primarily influenced by the substantial decrease in NCVS rates. The rate of increase in the UCR in the 1980s was, to some extent, affected by the increased police productivity characterized by the organizational and technological development in police forces that improved crime reporting and the recording practices of police. The substantial decrease in NCVS rates in the post-1992 period has been explained by the changes in methods of measurement. This study provided support for these reasons by showing significant effects on the convergence of the UCR and NCVS by the increase in number of employees by police departments and the methodological changes of 1992 in the NCVS.

Although the study is not free of limitations, it provides important policy implications that would help in understanding the relationship between the official crime statistics and the victimizations reports. The methodological implications provided in this study will help guide future research on convergence, which is needed to answer many remaining questions. The results in the study should, however, be accepted and generalized with caution because of the study's acknowledged limitations in data availability and breath of factors taken into proper consideration.

APPENDIX A

Comparison between the UCR and NCVS in Research

Purpose of the study	Crime categories	Data: scope, nature, and year	Calculation of rates and adjustments	Analytical tools
Wesley G. Skogan, 1974				
Studying the validity of official crime statistics by comparing the UCR with the NCVS	• Robbery because it covers a large domain, is considered a violent and property offense, and is highly correlated with other Part I offenses • Motor vehicle theft because it is the most accurately measured crime	• Scope of the study was limited to 10 cities • Cross-sectional data • UCR 1970 • Survey of 10 cities in 1970 by National League of Cities and the United States Conference of Mayors Secretariat	Rates per 10,000 population with no adjustment in the numerator and denominator	• Pearson correlation • Regression

Results and conclusions:

- Pearson correlation between robbery and auto theft rates of the survey and the official statistics were .39 and .94 respectively.
- At the second level of the analysis, correlation coefficients were calculated using several demographic and socioeconomic independent variables and crime rates of the survey and the official statistics.
- At the third level of the analysis, the study used some police variables, such as professionalism, public opinion, and community relations, to determine their correlations with the crime rates of the survey and the official statistics.
- Finally, crime rate variables were regressed on several important variables, such as the police-public ratio, expenditure, and rate of unemployment.

Purpose of the study	Crime categories	Data: scope, nature, and year	Calculation of rates and adjustments	Analytical tools
• The variables—demographic and socioeconomic—included in the analysis wer conceptualized as causes of crime and criminogenic in nature. The police organizational variables were perceived as the factors affecting the discovering, classifying, and reporting capacity of police. • The results of the analyses show moderate correlations between the two measures, distribution of crime in different cities were almost identical in both of the measures, and correlates and regression coefficients of different categories were similar in both of the measures. • The official crime statistics were found to be moderately correlated with the survey victimization. • Independent variables were correlated with the two series in a similar fashion, and errors appeared to be randomly distributed; thus, measurement error in the official statistics did not lead to a false conclusion. • The conclusion of the study was that the **official statistics are more valid** than the victimization survey data and can be used as valid measures of crime, especially for geographical comparison of crime data.				
lan Booth, David R. Johnson, Harvey M. Choldin, 1977				
To determine whether the UCR or NCVS is a more valid measure of crime	• Robbery • Burglary • Motor vehicle theft	• 26 cities in the U.S. • Cross-sectional data • 26 cities victimization survey data of 1974 • UCR 1972, 1973, 1974 • Census *County and City Data Book*, 1973	Personal and commercial robbery and burglary incidents added and divided by the population of 12 and above age and multiplied by 100,000	• Correlation • Multiple regression

Purpose of the study	Crime categories	Data: scope, nature, and year	Calculation of rates and adjustments	Analytical tools

Results and conclusions

- Multiple regression was used to assess the effect of each independent variable (population density, percent household crowded, percent unemployed, percent Black, percent families female headed, percent youth, percent household heads residentially mobile, percent city budget for police and fire) on the two crime indices.
- The correlation coefficients between the UCR and NCS robbery, burglary, and auto theft were .62, 60, and .70.
- The study **did not find similar correlation**s between an independent variable and a measure of crime. In case of one independent variable, two crime measures showed opposite correlations.
- The study regressed the crime rates of both series on different explanatory variables that supported the conclusion that the two series are independent.
- Rate change of robbery in the UCR was significantly explained by the variables of population density, household crowding, and Black percentage, whereas population density remains the only significant predictor in the NCS.
- In case of NCS rate of burglary, percent unemployed and household mobility were found significant, and in case of the UCR, the percent unemployed and household mobility were found significant and the percent of youth variable showed negative significance.
- In case of the UCR, only family stability showed significant effect on auto theft, whereas family stability, household crowding, and percent Black variables were found significant in case of the NCS.
- The analyses of the effects of eight different factors on the incidence of robbery, burglary, and auto theft showed that quite different conclusions would be reached, depending on whether the measure of crime was the UCR index or was based on the victimization surveys.
- The study did not conclude in favor of one of the two series and concluded that the validity of measure depends on the crime being measured.

Purpose of the study	Crime categories	Data: scope, nature, and year	Calculation of rates and adjustments	Analytical tools
Stock H. Decker, 1977				
To compare the UCR and NCS, and assess their validity and compatibility	• Rape • Aggravated assault • Robbery • Burglary • Larceny • Automobile theft	• 26 cities in the US • Cross-sectional data • 26 cities victimization survey data of 1974 • UCR 1973, 1974	No adjustments for the calculation of rates were used	• Difference-of-means tests • Correlational analysis
Results and conclusions: • Except motor vehicle theft, the study reported significant differences of means for all offenses between the UCR and NCS. • Except aggravated assault, UCR and NCS rates of all offenses were found to be significantly correlated. • The author concluded that the results of the study cast **considerable doubts on the accuracy of official crime statistics**.				
Robert M. O'Brien, David Shichor, David L. Decker, 1980				
The study measured the validity of the two data series by estimating the correlations between the two measures for six different crimes	• Robbery • Burglary • Rape • Aggravated assault • Personal larceny • Motor vehicle theft	• 26 cities in the US • Cross-sectional data • 26 cities victimization survey data of 1973 and 1974 • UCR data for 1973	The NCS rates for burglary and robbery were calculated by combining commercial and household rates.	Correlational analysis

Purpose of the study	Crime categories	Data: scope, nature, and year	Calculation of rates and adjustments	Analytical tools
(convergent validity) and estimating correlations with other correlates (nomological validity).		and 1974 • The U.S. Census Bureau, 1973		
Results and conclusions: • The study reported significant correlations between the NCS and UCR rates of motor vehicle theft, burglary, and robbery. • Motor vehicle theft especially reported 81% common variability (.81). • In nomological analysis, where correlations between different correlates of crime and crime rates of the NCS and UCR were estimated, NCS rates were more significantly correlated with the correlates than UCR rates. • The authors provided their verdict in favor of the NCS and stated that the **NCS measure is a more valid measure of crime than the UCR**, and if researchers have a choice, they should use the NCS instead of the UCR.				
Larry J. Cohen and Mark I. Lichbach, 1982				
The purpose of the study was to explore the comparability of the two data series and to understand how the two measures are equivalent, comparable, and	• Auto theft • Burglary • Larceny • Robbery • Rape • Assault	• 39 US. cities for all six categories and 10 additional cities for auto theft and robbery • Cross-sectional data • National Crime Survey's City Survey	• Because the surveys of cities were conducted in 2 years, the study takes the mean of the same 2-year data of the UCR for	Regression analysis

Purpose of the study	Crime categories	Data: scope, nature, and year	Calculation of rates and adjustments	Analytical tools
divergent.		Report 1976a, 1976b, and 1976c • UCR, 1971-75	achieving temporal consistency. • Adjustments were made in the denominator (population), and rate was calculated per 100,000 populations.	

Results and conclusions:

- Convergence approach, which attempts to measure how much two series converge, was wrong because the two measures, despite attempting to measure the same sociological phenomenon called *crime*, are inherently different and exploring the validity of the two data series on the basis of the convergence is not appropriate. The authors also argue that determining or exploring the degree of convergence between the two measures does not have any significant use for policy makers and researchers.
- In the analysis, first, NCS six crime numbers were regressed on UCR crimes and population; then, NCS crime rates were regressed on UCR crime rates.
- Variance in the NCS was best explained by UCR data for auto theft category, and the effect of population variable remained non-significant.
- Measures of assault by the two measures are neither equal nor comparable but different.
- The study concluded that there was **considerable correspondence between the two measures**. However, there are

Purpose of the study	Crime categories	Data: scope, nature, and year	Calculation of rates and adjustments	Analytical tools
certain differences that require explanations.				
Lawrence E. Cohen and Kenneth C. Land, 1984				
Estimating and explaining the discrepancies between the NCS and UCR by controlling city level structural variables	• Rape • Robbery • Aggravated Assault • Burglary • Larceny theft • Vehicle theft	• The scope was limited to 26 cities in the U.S. • The NCS survey of the 26 cities, 13 in 1972 and 13 in 1973 • Cross-sectional data • UCR 1972, 1973 • Lagged structural variables from 1970 census were used because they do not change quickly.	• The adjustment in the denominator to calculate the rates was done as the study used a population spanning 12 years for the calculation of rates for the NCS and UCR both. • Per 100,000 population rates were computed	• First UCR rates and then ratios of UCR rates to NCS rates were regressed on NCS rates for all six offenses while controlling for several demographic, structural, city level, and organizational variables.

Results and conclusions:

- Total variance explained by the model is higher than the variance explained by zero-order correlation, supporting the point that regression analysis is a better option than the correlation that does not control the effects of covariates.
- The important finding of the study is that the discrepancy between the two data series reported by the correlational studies is largely because of the fact that zero-order correlation does not control for the effects of city-level structural

Purpose of the study	Crime categories	Data: scope, nature, and year	Calculation of rates and adjustments	Analytical tools

- variables. When the structural variables are controlled for in the regression model, the discrepancy between the UCR and NCS decreased because each city is different and crime as a social phenomenon is affected by unique city-level variables that have to be controlled for in order to understand the discrepancy between the two data series that measure the same phenomenon.
- The study showed **greater comparability between the two series** on four of the six crime categories, excepting aggravated assault and larceny theft.

Walter R. Gove, Michael Hughes, and Michael Geerken, 1985

Purpose of the study	Crime categories	Data: scope, nature, and year	Calculation of rates and adjustments	Analytical tools
The purpose of the study was to reevaluate the validity of the official crime statistics while comparing them with the NCS data	• Motor theft • Robbery • Burglary • Larceny • Aggravated Assault • Rape			Correlational analyses

Results and conclusions:

- Correlations between UCR and NCS crime rates depend on several factors such as the population as denominator as well as measurement of crime. For example, Nelsons' use of population denominator that included fleeting population was likely to yield higher correlation for robbery and auto theft and lower for burglary. Similarly, exclusion of commercial larceny thefts from NCS larceny theft rate would affect the correlation.
- The examination of the validity of the official crime statistics is based on estimating correlational coefficients between

Purpose of the study	Crime categories	Data: scope, nature, and year	Calculation of rates and adjustments	Analytical tools
the true crime rates and the official crime rates. However, the true crime rate is not known, therefore causing the importance of proxy measures for the true crime rate. Authors estimated the true crime rate by considering the errors in the victimization survey. First, the correlational coefficients between the true crime rates and the victimization rates were estimated as t1; then, t1 was multiplied by the correlational coefficients of the UCR and NCS in order to arrive at the value of t2, the correlational coefficients between the true crime rates and UCR rates. • **UCR is a fairly valid measure of true crime**, but it should be remembered that the UCR reports relatively serious crime, which passes through the filters of citizens and police.				
Scott Menard, 1987 Comparing the validity of the UCR, victimization, and self-reporting delinquency of measuring crime using time series data and trend analysis.	• Homicide • Forcible rape • Robbery • Aggravated assault • Burglary • Larceny • Motor vehicle theft • Several other small and victimless crime categories	• National • Time-series data • UCR 1973-82 • NCVS 1973-82 • U.S. Census Bureau	• Rates were calculated by dividing total number of crimes by total population. • The use of the total population was justified because population under 12 years of age experience less than 1% victimization but make up more than	• Trend analysis • Correlation • Bivariate regression

Purpose of the study	Crime categories	Data: scope, nature, and year	Calculation of rates and adjustments	Analytical tools
			20% of the total population.	
Results and conclusions: • The NCS trend has remained almost static, but the UCR trend has changed significantly. The discrepancy between the two data series arises from the fact that the NCS is based on household surveys and includes crimeS against households, whereas the UCR is based on population and includes household as well as commercial victimization. Second, the UCR reports only crime known to police, whereas the NCS reports all victimization. Generally, serious crimes and crimes committed by nonstrangers are more reported to police and known to police. Among property crimes, robbery and burglary with forced entry are most likely to be reported to and by police. • The trend analysis of the data in the study was conducted by presenting rates for different crimes for the period between 1973 and 1981 for official, victimization, and self-reporting crime data. • The study found different short-term trends of crimes in the victimization and self-reporting data than in the official crime data. • The study concluded the rates of actual crime are stable, but reporting and arresting by police are increasing.				
Scott Menard and Herbert C. Covey, 1988				
The purpose of the study was to understand the convergence between the UCR and NCS through temporal and spatial comparison		• 26 cities of the US as well as national • Cross-sectional and time-series data • 26 LEAA city survey 1975a, 1975b, and		• Correlation • Regression • Significance test of means differences

Purpose of the study	Crime categories	Data: scope, nature, and year	Calculation of rates and adjustments	Analytical tools
of crime rates. The study also evaluated the findings of Grover et al. (1985), who concluded that the UCR data are more valid measure of crime than the NCS data.		1976 • NCS 1973-82 • UCR 1973-82 • U.S. Census Bureau		

Results and conclusions:

- The argument of Grove et al. (1985) that offenses not reported to police are generally trivial and nonserious is problematic because a large number of serious offenses such as robbery are not reported to police by citizens.
- Research comparing the two series or attempting to explain convergence have generally compared six Part I crime rates of the UCR and NCS using cross-sectional data of 26 cities. The statistical analyses used in such research include significance tests of difference of means, zero-order correlation, and regression analyses.
- Apart from comparing the rates of the UCR and NCVS crime rates, studies estimated correlations between the rates and independent variables or regressed one crime rate over the other while controlling the effects of covariates.
- Some studies also did trend analysis and compared UCR rates with NCS rates using time-series data. The trend analyses showed a gradual increase in UCR crime rates and almost nonsignificant change in NCS rates.
- The study uses the 26-city survey data for temporal comparison because NCS did not have geographically classified data.
- A perfect correspondence between the two measures would result in a correlation of one, an unstandardized regression coefficient of one, and an intercept of zero.

Purpose of the study	Crime categories	Data: scope, nature, and year	Calculation of rates and adjustments	Analytical tools
• In the geographic comparison of crime rates, only motor vehicle theft and restricted aggravated assault rates (with injury) were found to be significantly correlated. • Correlations between UCR and NCS rates fell within the range of previous studies except burglary, probably because the rate for burglary in this study was computed per capita rather than per household. • Second, the study tested the significance of difference between UCR and NCS means of crime rates for the period between 1973 and 1982 and reported significant difference except aggravated assault with injury. • **The study did not find convergence or comparability between the two data series** except in some cases where a restrictive definition of NCS crime has been used. Any restriction that reduces the number in the NCS reduces the discrepancy. • The study also suggested that different measures should be used for different purposes. For the purpose of stranger-perpetrated crimes, the UCR is a better choice, and for nonstranger-perpetrated crimes, the NCVS is a better choice.				
Robert M. O'Brien, 1990				
To show the effects of detrending the data on the convergence between the UCR and the survey	• Total rate • Rape • Aggravated assault • Robbery • Burglary • Larceny • Motor vehicle theft	• National • NCS data 1973-86 • UCR data 1973-86	Rates of overall crime and different crimes were used as calculated by the UCR and the NCS programs and no adjustment was done	• Detrending of the data before making comparison • Zero-order correlation • Partial correlations between UCR and NCS rates

Purpose of the study	Crime categories	Data: scope, nature, and year	Calculation of rates and adjustments	Analytical tools
				(controlling for year) • Detrending and correlation between the first differences for UCR and NCS rates

Results and conclusions:

- The convergence between the UCR and NCS varies with crime type, scope, and analytical tools. Motor vehicle theft showed convergence (O Brien et al., 1980; Menard & Covey, 1988) but other categories did not. Furthermore, geographic comparison showed convergence but temporal did not (Menard & Covey, 1988). Different analytical tools, such as zero-order correlation and regression analyses, also showed different levels of convergence.
- Usually series analyses comparing national crime data did not report convergence (Menard, 1987; Menard & Covey, 1988), prompting comparison of the detrended data of time series rather than raw crime rates. Therefore, it was decided to detrend the data before making comparisons.
- Examining the correlations between UCR and NCS rates after detrending is the only method for comparing the two series.
- In order to control the effect of independent variables, it is important to use lagged crime rates as an independent variable or use first differencing.
- Although the correlation between UCR and NCS rates are near zero, a close look at the variance indicates a pattern of high correlation between them, and if the trend were controlled, then both series would be perfectly correlated.
- The study reported a partial correlation of .994 after controlling for year and a correlation of .998 after first differencing.

Purpose of the study	Crime categories	Data: scope, nature, and year	Calculation of rates and adjustments	Analytical tools
• The zero-order correlations for all crimes rates showed no convergence. However, after the detrending, all crime categories showed statistically significant partial correlation, except robbery with injury and larceny with contact, which reported significance at .06 level.				
Alfred Blumstein, Jacqueline Cohen, and Richard Rosenfeld, 1991				
To examine the convergence between the two series over time in terms of crime trends and fluctuation of crime trends and to assess the influence of changes in reporting to police on the convergence	• Robbery • Burglary • The purpose of choosing these offenses is that they are serious violent and property offenses with less ambiguity	• National • UCR 1973-87 • NCS 1973-87 • U.S. Census Bureau	• UCR rates per 100,000 were calculated by using the total population. • The NCS robbery and burglary rates were calculated by dividing by the total population and using multiplier of 100,000. • Although the rates for commercial robbery and burglary are significant, they	• Detrending • Multivariate regression

Purpose of the study	Crime categories	Data: scope, nature, and year	Calculation of rates and adjustments	Analytical tools
			remain constant and not including them will not make a substantial change in the association of the series that is the focus of the study.	

Results and conclusions:

- Several studies examining the time-series data reported a lack of convergence between the series, and a common reason given for the lack of convergence is that the UCR has been changing while the victimization survey has remained unchanged.
- Previous studies have generally used trends in the analysis. Ignoring the deviation or misunderstanding the meaning of trend deviation has serious consequences in understanding the convergence.
- Menard and Covey (1988) and O' Brien (1990) focused on trend and deviation (detrended data) respectively, whereas the current study intended to assess the relative roles of trend and deviance both.
- The study reported a strong consistency between UCR and NCS robbery and burglary rates and concluded that both of the series measure the same phenomenon called crime.
- However, the correspondence between the two series is not shown when trends are compared. When the two series are compared by looking at the year-to-year deviation from trends, a strong correspondence is found.

Albert, D. Biderman and James P. Lynch, 1991

The main purpose of the	Total crime and victimization	• NCS & UCR, 1973-	Adjustment in	

Purpose of the study	Crime categories	Data: scope, nature, and year	Calculation of rates and adjustments	Analytical tools
study was to understand how the two series diverge.		1986 • National	denominator and numerator	

Results and conclusions:

- The purpose of the book was to explore the causes of the divergence between the two series and argue in favor of comparability.
- The study showed how the nonuniformities and different use of denominator and nominator in calculating rates make the both series look different.
- The central argument of the study was that both of the series measure the same social phenomenon differently; they are complimentary to each other.
- The study argued that the two series measure the overlapping sets of criminal events with different measurement procedures. Following are the main reasons for divergence of rates between the UCR and NCS.
    1. Comparison of sample and non-sample statistics cause the discrepancy.
    2. Both series use different denominators in calculating rates. The UCR uses total residential population while the NCS uses population above 12 years.
    3. The NCS uses household number as the denominator for calculating victimization against households. Since the size of households is decreasing, the growth percent of households would be higher than the population growth, and therefore, the property crime rate in the NCS is likely to show less positive change than the violent crime rate.
    4. Use of inter-census population data by the UCR is another reason for divergence.
    5. The NCS excludes the population living in ocean vessels, in institutions, and members of the Armed Forces

Purpose of the study	Crime categories	Data: scope, nature, and year	Calculation of rates and adjustments	Analytical tools

living in barracks. The UCR includes all these excluded habitations, although crimes committed in these environments are not recorded in the UCR.

6. The UCR does not include the traveling population, foreigners, legal and illegal immigrants, although these people can be victims of crime.
7. The UCR reports only crime reported to police whereas the NCS reports all victimizations, including crimes reported to police. This is probably the biggest reason for the discrepancy between the two series. Crimes reported to police are also affected by several factors. Age of victims, seriousness of crime, and to some extent race are important factors affecting reporting of crime to police.
8. Changed racial composition and age of the population are important factors that should be considered when explaining the divergence between the two series.
9. The NCS does not include crimes committed in commercial establishments, en important source of discrepancy between the two series. Large percentages of robbery, burglary, motor vehicle theft, and simple theft occur at commercial premises.
10. Unfounding crime in the UCR also makes a difference. Almost 4% of crimes are unfounded but are included in the NCS.
11. Series victimization (earlier 4 and now 6) is reported as only one crime in the NCS, another important reason for the discrepancy.
12. Hotel and hierarchy rules of the UCR are also factors that affect the numerator of crimes in the UCR and help broaden the discrepancy between the two series.

- After all possible adjustments concerned with the procedural anomalies and definitional incongruities between the UCR and NCS are done, the divergence between the two series decreased, although it remained significantly high.
- The study, assessing convergence after adjustments with rates, concluded that the trends for the two series between 1973

Purpose of the study	Crime categories	Data: scope, nature, and year	Calculation of rates and adjustments	Analytical tools
and 1986 converged rather than diverged. • The study also concluded that the discrepancy between the UCR rates and NCS estimates of police reported victimization, after the adjustments, showed either overestimation by the NCS or undercounting by the UCR. • The study argued that focusing on complementarity rather than on comparability will enable researchers to exploit the potential use of the data and strongly recommended considering the two series as complimentary and using them for different research questions in order to solve the problems of crimes.				
Robert M. O'Brien, 1996				
To explore the difference of change in the UCR and NCVS and explain the reasons for dramatic changes in the crime rates of the UCR between 1973 and 1992	• Rape • Robbery • Aggravated assault	• National • UCR 1973-1992 • NCS 1973-1992	Rates were used as calculated by the UCR and NCVS.	• Detrending using first differencing and by controlling for time • Dickey-Fuller test for stationarity • Test of linearity • Durbin Watson test of autocorrelation
Results and conclusions: • From the outset until the early 1990s, the victimization data remained stable, but UCR crime rates grew substantially. If both of the series measure the same underlying phenomenon, then there should have been identical changes in both, but				

Purpose of the study	Crime categories	Data: scope, nature, and year	Calculation of rates and adjustments	Analytical tools

the anomaly of change between the UCR and NCVS demands the investigation and explanation.

- Detrending through controlling for time produced expected results as UCR rates showed an increasing trend and victimization rates showed either a flat or a decreasing trend. This resulted in a negative correlation between the two series.
- A failure to detrend data may result in spurious correlations, so all time-series data are detrended before the analyses so as to meet the assumption of stationarity.
- Correlations after detrending by controlling for time changed dramatically as correlations for most of the crimes became positive and significant.
- Correlations after the detrending through the first differencing method were weaker but positive and stronger than the correlation with non-detrended data.
- Meeting stationarity is the most important assumption of time-series analysis. The DF test is used to test the stationarity of data. The study used two sets of the DF test after the first differencing.
- Because first differencing is the acceptable method recommended by statisticians, the correlations calculated after the detrending through controlling for time is problematic. Apart from this, the correlations after detrending by controlling for time also have the problem of autocorrelation.
- Increase in UCR crime rates is not because of increase in crime but because of increase in police productivity. The increase in police productivity is caused by several factors:
    1. Justice Department's initiative and focus on overall improvement of paperwork, reporting, and recordkeeping
    2. Computerization of police departments and record keeping or data management systems
    3. Reporting requirements for dealing with the discretion
    4. Mobile computers and video cameras
    5. Increase in number of police officer per 100,000 people (183 to 225 from 1973 to 1992)

Purpose of the study	Crime categories	Data: scope, nature, and year	Calculation of rates and adjustments	Analytical tools

6. Increase in number of civilian experts to manage record keeping and computers, thus freeing police officers
7. Increase in the state level UCR programs

- For example, a sharp increase in rape is not because of increase in problems but several factors affecting reporting and recording are responsible. Efforts of organizations and media have increased the awareness and consciousness. A larger number of women acting as police dispatchers, police officers, and special units are playing roles in discovering, reporting, and recording rape and sexual assault.
- The second reason is the change in methodology of the victimization survey that has affected the convergence between the two series. The methodology changes that may be responsible for affecting the victimization rate were use of telephone-based interviews and a shrinking response rate.
- The study plotted the detrended rates of homicide and other violent crimes together. It was hypothesized that, if both of them move together, then the changes in the UCR are because of the change in crime. It was found that the homicide rate remained stable while violent crime rate changed upwardly. Thus, the change in the overall UCR rate is influenced by the reporting practices of police, which can affect reporting of all crimes other than homicide.
- The correlations between the two series were also positive and significant. A DF test showed that the detrending should be done by first differencing in order to meet the assumption of stationarity, and Durbin Watson statistics after the first differencing did not show the problem of autocorrelation.
- Because the two time series do not trend together, some other variable is playing role. That is police productivity, which has limitations in affecting homicide in comparison with other forms of violent crimes.
- The study, while answering several important questions about the convergence and trends of both of the series, concluded the following:
    1. Although the UCR and NCVS trend differently and show a great degree of discrepancy, detrending of the series

<table>
<tr><th>Purpose of the study</th><th>Crime categories</th><th>Data: scope, nature, and year</th><th>Calculation of rates and adjustments</th><th>Analytical tools</th></tr>
<tr><td colspan="5">prior to the analyses revealed greater correlations.
2. The two series, at least for more than 15 years after the beginning of the victimization survey, trended differently. The NCVS remained almost stable while the UCR kept increasing. The study provided evidence through analysis that it happened because of police productivity, which was influenced by the efforts of the Justice Department, and changes in technology.
3. Thus, the continuous increase in UCR crime rates between 1973 and 1992 was not because of increase in crime problems but because of increase in police productivity.</td></tr>
<tr><td colspan="5">Catalano, 2006</td></tr>
<tr><td>To explain the convergence between the UCR and NCVS</td><td>• Violent crime
• Homicide
• Aggravated assault
• Robbery</td><td>• National data between 1973 and 2002
• UCR
• NCVS
• Census
• LEMAS
• Sourcebook of Criminal Justice Statistics
• GSS</td><td>Raw data with no calculation of rates or adjustment</td><td>Univariate and multivariate time-series analysis (autoregressive models)</td></tr>
<tr><td colspan="5">Results and conclusions:
• The study hypothesized that the convergence between the two series may have happened because of three factors: change in police practices, change in demography, and change in social attitude.</td></tr>
</table>

Purpose of the study	Crime categories	Data: scope, nature, and year	Calculation of rates and adjustments	Analytical tools
• Other than the three external factors, methodological changes in the UCR and NCVS are responsible for bringing the series closer.				
• Changes in demographics were dropped due to lack of variability and changes in UCR methodology variable were dropped because it was not measurable.				
• The study reported two major findings. First, the convergence between the UCR and NCVS on the aggravated assault category is due to positive changes in police recording of aggravated assault offenses, especially related to domestic violence cases. Second, the convergence for the rape category is also related to the changes in public reporting and police recording practices rather than just methodological changes in the NCVS.				

APPENDIX B

List of Variables Explored and Used in the Study

DEPENDENT VARIABLES

UCRTOTAL	**UCR Total Annual Crime** This variable includes total annual violent and property crime reported to the program. The violent crime category, for the purpose of this study, includes aggravated assault, robbery, and simple assault.
UCRVIO	**UCR Total Annual Violent Crime** Total number of aggravated assaults and robberies reported to the program.
UCRPROP	**UCR Total Annual Property Crime** Total number of burglary, motor vehicle theft, and larceny theft incidents annually reported to the program.
UCRAGAS	**UCR Total Annual Aggravated Assault** Total number of aggravated assault incidents annually reported to the program.
UCRROBB	**UCR Total Annual Robbery** Total number of robbery incidents annually reported to the program.
UCRBURG	**UCR Total Annual Burglary** Total number of burglary incidents annually reported to the program.
UCRMOT	**UCR Total Annual Motor Vehicle Theft**

	Total number of motor vehicle thefts annually reported to the program.
UCRLARC	**UCR Total Annual Larceny Theft** Total number of larceny thefts annually reported to the program.
NCVSTOTAL	**NCVS Total Annual Crime** This variable includes total annual violent and property crime reported to the victimization survey. The violent crime category, for the purpose of this study, includes aggravated assault and robbery.
NCVSVIO	**NCVS Total Annual Violent Crime** Total number of aggravated assault and robbery incidents annually reported to the survey.
NCVSPROP	**NCVS Total Annual Property Crime** Total number of burglary, motor vehicle theft, and larceny theft incidents annually reported to the survey.
NCVSAGAS	**NCVS Total Annual Aggravated Assault** Total number of aggravated assaults annually reported to the survey.
NCVSROBB	**NCVS Total Annual Robbery** Total number of robberies annually reported to the survey.
NCVSBURG	**NCVS Total Annual Burglary** Total number of burglaries annually reported to the survey.
NCVSMOT	**NCVS Total Annual Motor Vehicle Theft** Total number of motor vehicle thefts annually reported to the survey.
NCVSLARC	**NCVS Total Annual Larceny Theft** Total number of larceny thefts, including total thefts and personal thefts, annually reported to the survey.
REPTOTAL	**Total Crime Reported to Police in the NCS/NCVS** This variable includes total annual violent and property crimes reported to police by NCS/NCVS respondents. The violent crime category for the purpose of this study includes aggravated assault and robbery.

REPVIO	**Total Violent Crime Reported to Police in the NCS/NCVS** Total violent crime includes the total number of aggravated assaults and robberies annually reported to police by NCS/NCVS respondents.
REPPROP	**Total Property Crime Reported to Police in the NCS/NCVS** Total number of burglary, motor vehicle theft, and larceny theft incidents annually reported to police by NCS/NCVS respondents.
REPAGAS	**Total Aggravated Assault Reported to Police in the NCS/NCVS** Total number of aggravated assaults annually reported to police by NCS/NCVS respondents.
REPROBB	**Total Robbery Reported to Police in the NCS/NCVS** Total number of robberies, both committed and attempted, annually reported to police by NCS/NCVS respondents.
REPBURG	**Total Burglary Reported to Police in the NCS/NCVS** Total number of burglaries annually reported to police by NCS/NCVS respondents.
REPMOT	**Total Motor Vehicle Theft Reported to Police in the NCS/NCVS** Total number of motor vehicle thefts annually reported to police by NCS/NCVS respondents.
REPLARC	**Total Larceny Theft Reported to Police in the NCS/NCVS** Total number of larceny thefts, including total theft and personal theft, annually reported to police by NCS/NCVS respondents
UCRIMRATE	**UCR Annual Crime Rate** The total UCR crime rate is computed through the following formula: total number of crimes/total U.S. residential population x 100,000. The total crime index includes the aggregated value of violent and property crimes as defined in the study and reported

annually to the program. Other aggregated crime rate variables—violent crime and property crime—and disaggregated crime rate variables—aggravated assault, robbery, burglary, motor vehicle theft, and larceny theft—are calculated using the same formula.

UVIORATE **UCR Annual Violent Crime Rate**

UPROPRATE **UCR Annual Property Crime Rate**

UAGASRATE **UCR Annual Aggravated Assault Rate**

UROBBRATE **UCR Annual Robbery Rate**

UBURGRATE **UCR Annual Burglary Rate**

UMOTRATE **UCR Annual Motor Vehicle Theft Rate**

ULARCRATE **UCR Annual Larceny Theft Rate**

NTOTRATE **NCS/NCVS Annual Crime Rate**

All NCVS aggregated and disaggregated crime rate variables are computed using the same formula used for calculating the UCR crime rates.

NVIORATE **NCS/NCVS Annual Violent Crime Rate**

NPROPRATE **NCS/NCVS Annual Property Crime Rate**

NAGASRATE **NCS/NCVS Annual Aggravated Assault Rate**

NROBBRATE **NCS/NCVS Annual Robbery Rate**

NBURGRATE **NCS/NCVS Annual Burglary Rate**

NMOTRATE **NCS/NCVS Annual Motor Vehicle Theft Rate**

NLARCRATE **NCS/NCVS Annual Larceny Theft Rate**

RTOTRATE **Rate of Crimes Reported to Police in the NCS/NCVS**

Rate of crimes reported to police in the NCS/NCVS is computed using the following formula: total number of crimes reported to police/total U.S. residential population x 100,000.

RVIORATE **Rate of Violent Crime Reported to Police in the NCS/NCVS**

RPROPRATE **Rate of Property Crime Reported to Police in the NCS/NCVS**

RAGASRATE **Rate of Aggravated Assault Reported to Police in the NCS/NCVS**

RROBBRATE **Rate of Robbery Reported to Police in the NCS/NCVS**

RBURGRATE **Rate of Burglary Reported to Police in the NCS/NCVS**

RMOTRATE	**Rate of Motor Vehicle Theft Reported to Police in the NCS/NCVS**
RLARCRATE	**Rate of Larceny Theft Reported to Police in the NCS/NCVS**

EXPLANATORY VARIABLES

Demographic Variables

POPTOTAL	**Total Population** Total residential population is used in the study.
POPWHITE	**Total White Population**
PERWHITE	**White Percentage of the Total Population**
POPBLACK	**Total Black Population**
PERBLAK	**Black Percentage of the Total Population**
POPHISP	**Total Hispanic Population**
PERHISP	**Hispanic Percentage of the Total Population**
POPOTHERS	**Total Other Population**
POPMALE	**Total Male Population**
PERMALE	**Male Percentage of the Total Population**
POPFEMALE	**Total Female Population**
PERFEMALE	**Female Percentage of the Total Population**
HOUSHOLD	**Total Number of Households**
PBHIGH	**Percent of Population with Less Than a High School Education**
PHIGH	**Percent of Population with a High School Education**
PSCOLL	**Percent of Population with Some College**
PCOLL	**Percent of Population with 4 Years of College**
PBPOVERTY	**Population Living Below the Poverty Line**
PPBPOVERTY	**Percent of Population Living Below the Poverty Line**

Police Organizational and Operational Variables

POLEXPENSE	**Total Expenses of Police**
EPCAPITA	**Expense of Police Per Capita**
POPRATIO	**Police Officers per 1000 Population**

TOTEMP **Total Law Enforcement Employment**

TOTSWORN **Total Sworn Police Officers**

PTOTSWORN **% Total Sworn Police Officers**

Total employees in police departments include sworn officers and civilians. The percent of sworn officers and civilians is important organizational determinants, which affects the crime reporting and recording

PMSWORN **Percent of Male Sworn Police Officers**

PFESWORN **Percent of Female Sworn Police Officers**

TOTCIVIL **Total Civilians in Police Departments**

PTOTCIVIL **Percent of Civilians in Police Departments**

PMCIVIL **Percent of Male Civilians in Police Departments**

PFECIVIL **Percent of Female Civilians in Police Departments**

PERPATROL **Percent of Patrol Officers in the Total Sworn Officers**

The patrol is known as the backbone of police and majority offenses reporting and arrests are done by patrol officers. A greater proportion of patrol officers is likely to increase total reporting of crimes.

PERBLACK **Percent of Black Police Officers**

PERHISP **Percent of Hispanic Police Officers**

COMMPO **Total Community Police Officers**

PERCOMM **Percent of Community Police Officers among Total Sworn Officers**

NSUBSTN **Neighborhood Substation Fixed and Mobile**

Neighborhood substations—fixed and mobile—are likely to increase discovery and reporting of crimes.

COMMUNIT **Community Policing Unit**

A dichotomous variable will be computed using the ordinal variable of community policing unit in the LEMAS data set.

DVIOUNIT **Domestic Violence Unit**

Police officers use maximum discretion in domestic violence cases and, for several reasons, avoid making arrests. The presence of a domestic violence unit may increase the reporting of domestic violence cases, thus increasing the total reporting.

REPUNIT **Research and Planning Unit**

	Research and planning units involve research-based findings related to some of the issues and help the leadership in formulating more effective policies. They also play roles in mobilizing resources from different outside funding agencies so are likely to increase the effectiveness of policing and reporting and recording of crimes.
COLDEGREE	**College Degree Required at the Entry Level** Although, there is no evidence that such education makes a better police office, it is hypothesized that the increased number of college-educated police officers increases the reporting of crime because college educated officers are likely to be more comfortable in reporting.
TRAINHOURS	**Total Hours of Training** This variable is measured by adding the total hours of mandated academy and field training. Performance during the training is one of the factors used in predicting a good police officer.
EMERPHONE	**Emergency Telephone System of 911**
NONEMER	**Non-emergency Telephone System** Non-emergency phones, such as 311, are likely to reduce the load on the 911 system and increase the efficiency of 911, resulting in increase of reporting.
SPPERCEP	**Surveyed Public Perception**
SPSATIS	**Surveyed Public Satisfaction**
POLCARS	**Number of Marked Cars**
VIDEOCAME	**Number of Video Cameras**
VIDEOCAR	**Number of Cars with Video Cameras** The mounted video camera on the patrol car is important in two ways. First, it controls the discretion and behavior of an officer and minimizes the possibility of complaints against an officer. Second, it maximizes the reporting of incidents. Because this study is concerned about the reporting of offenses and incidents, it is important to learn whether video cameras on patrol cars have made any difference in reporting of crimes.

MOBCOMPU **Number of Vehicle-Mounted Computers**

IREPTRANS **Incident Reports Transmitted Through Computers**

CRBOARD **Civilian Complaint Review Board**

ICRBOARD **Civilian Review Board Independence**

COMPSTAT **Number of Agencies Doing COMPSTAT**

Social Attitude Variables

Some variables reflecting social attitudes toward crime, police, and other related issues were drawn from the GSS.

FEAR **Fear of Walking Alone at Night**

Fear variable in the GSS is measured by asking respondents the following question: "Is there any area right around here—that is, within a mile—where you would be afraid to walk alone at night?" Observations on the fear variable are available from 1973-2008, but many observations are missing in between. For completing the series for the entire period of the study (1973-2008), linear interpolation and extrapolation were used.

FEARHOME **Fear in Home at Night**

ACQCOPS **Number of Police Officers Acquainted with**

TRTCOPS **Trusted People who are Police Officers**

Other Variables

REDESIGN **NCVS Redesign of 1992**

CELLPHONE **Cell Phone Connection**

REPAGENCIES **Number of Law Enforcement Agencies Reporting to the UCR**

APPENDIX C

Stationarity Check and Transformation

CHECKING FOR STATIONARITY

One of the classic assumptions for cross-sectional data is the independent and identically distributed sample. If this least square assumption were violated, then the parameter estimate would be biased. Assumption of stationarity in time-series data is akin to the assumption of identical and independent distribution of cross-sectional data. A violation of the stationarity assumption may produce several problems, such as bias and inefficiency in the forecast and spurious relationships in time-series regression models. In other words, if time series is nonstationary, its behavior may not be generalized for other time periods and remain important for the period under consideration (Gujarati, 2004). Therefore, the first step in the process of time-series analysis is to perform the test of stationarity to see whether the data are nonstationary. The UCR and NCVS have stochastic trends, and ensuring the stationary stochastic process in both of the series is essential before model identification and specification. A time series is said to be nonstationary if the mean and variance change over time. In other words, a stochastic process is stationary if its mean and variance are constant over time. A nonstationary time series is known as random walk, which can be with or without drift. When only the mean changes over time and the model does not have a constant term, a series is known as pure random walk, and when variance also changes and a constant term is added in the model, the series is known as random walk with drift.

$Y_t = \rho Y_{t-1} + e_t$ Pure Random Walk (1)

$Y_t = \propto + \rho Y_{t-1} + e_t$ Random Walk with drift (2)

Stationarity of a time series is often tested through a unit root test, but the literature also suggests using graphical analysis and a correlogram test (Gujarati, 2004). The first step is to plot the time series to get an initial idea of the nature of the series. A line graph gives rough but valuable information about stationarity and nonstationarity of the data. The second step is to check the stationarity of a series is to obtain a correlogram by plotting an autocorrelation function (ACF) against different lags in a series. A high autocorrelation coefficient for the first lag, which diminishes as the number of lags increase, is an indication that the series is nonstationary.

The most popular test of stationarity is the test of unit root (Gujarati, 2004). In this test, a series is tested for unit root, and if the null hypothesis of unit root is rejected, then the series is said to be stationary. Conversely, if a series has a unit root, then it is nonstationary. A unit root test for testing a series with nonstationarity and stationarity uses the following model

$$Y_t = \alpha + \rho Y_{t-1} + e_t \tag{3}$$

In its simplest illustration, if Y_t is regressed on its lagged value of Y_{t-1} and the coefficient of Y_{t-1} is exactly 1, then the series has a unit root. That is, the value of Y does not change substantially, and change in the series over time occurs because of a "white noise" error. If $\propto = 0$ and $\rho = 1$, then the series is nonstationary and follows a random walk without drift, and if $\propto \neq 0$ and $\rho = 1$, then the series is nonstationary and follows a random walk with drift. In other words, the means and variances of the series undergo substantial changes over time. The null hypothesis for testing a unit root in a series states that Y_t has a unit root.

H_0: $\rho = 1$

An acceptable practice is to test the null hypothesis using the following model rather than the model in Equation 3.

$$\Delta Y_t = \alpha + \delta Y_{t-1} + e_t \tag{4}$$

To run the unit root test, the difference of Y_t is regressed on Y_{t-1} and the slope coefficient δ is estimated. If the slope coefficient δ is zero, then the null hypothesis of a unit root is rejected, and the series is declared nonstationary. However, if δ is negative, then the series is said to be stationary (Gujarati, 2004). The slope coefficient of zero in model 4 would be equal to the slope coefficient of 1 in model 4.3. In the following, the null hypothesis is tested with model 3.

$H_0: \delta = 0$

The null hypothesis, $H_0: \delta = 0$, means there is a unit root and the series is nonstationary. The alternative hypothesis is that $\delta < 0$; that is, the time series is stationary. In other words, if the null hypothesis of $\delta = 0$ is rejected, then the series is stationary, and if the null hypothesis is not rejected, then the series is nonstationary. Under the null hypothesis of zero coefficient in model 4, where the first difference of Y_t is regressed on Y_{t-1}, the coefficient follows *tau* distribution rather than the usual *t* distribution. The critical values of **τ** (*tau*) distribution are calculated by Dickey-Fuller, which is popularly known as the Dickey-Fuller test of unit root. In the Dickey-Fuller test, the absolute value of **τ** is calculated and compared with the critical values of **τ** provided by Dickey-Fuller or McKinnon, and if the absolute value of **τ** exceeds the critical value at an acceptable significance level, the null hypothesis of $\delta = 0$ is rejected, and the conclusion is that the series is stationary. If the absolute value of **τ** does not exceed the critical value at an acceptable significance level, the null hypothesis of $\delta = 0$ is not rejected, and it is concluded that the series has a unit root and is nonstationary.

MAKING A TIME-SERIES STATIONARY

For detrending a time series or making it stationary, two processes are often used. A series is made trend stationary when a time or trend variable is used in the right side of the regression equation to avoid the problem of a spurious relationship because of the stationarity problem. The second method of making a series stationary is differencing, and a series made stationary though differencing is known as difference-stationary. Studies explaining the convergence between UCR and

NCVS have used trend-stationary processed (Blumstein et al., 1991; Catalano, 2006, 2007; O'Brien, 1996) and difference-stationary processes (O'Brien, 1996). Although a differencing process is recommended over a trend-stationary process, studies (Catalano, 2006, 2007) have used trend or time variables in the right side of the equation rather than differencing to avoid losing data points from the UCR and NCVS series, which have fewer observations than required for time series modeling.

The trend-stationary process is challenged by econometricians, who have recommended not using a trend-stationary process for a series that has a stochastic trend. A trend-stationary process can be used only if the trend variable is deterministic (Gujarati, 2004). Most series, including UCR and NCVS, have stochastic trends; therefore, using a trend-stationary process to make them stationary results in inaccuracy.

References

Addington, L. A. (2005). Disentangling the effects of bounding and mobility on reports of criminal victimization. *Journal of Quantitative Criminology, 21*(3), 321-343.

Addington, L. A. (2007). Using NIBRS to study methodological sources of divergence between UCR and NCVS. In J. P. Lynch & L. A. Addington (Eds.), *Understanding crime statistics: Revisiting the divergence of NCVS and UCR* (pp. 225-250). New York, NY: Cambridge University Press.

Addington, L. A. (2008). Assessing the extent of nonresponse Bias on NIBRS estimates of violent crime. *Journal of Contemporary Criminal Justice, 24*(1), 32.

Anderson, Elijah (1999). *Code of the street: Decency, violence and the moral life of the inner city*. New York: W.W. Norton.

Austin, R. L. (1993). Recent trends in official male and female crime rates: The convergence controversy. *Journal of Criminal Justice, 21*(5), 447-466

Barnett-Ryan, C. (2007). Introduction to the uniform crime reporting program. In J. P. Lynch & L. A. Addington (Eds.), *Understanding crime statistics: Revisiting the divergence of NCVS and UCR* (pp. 225-250). New York, NY: Cambridge University Press.

Baum, C. F. (2001). Stata: The language of choice for time series analysis? *Stata Journal, 1*(1), 1-16

Baumer, E. P. (2008). An empirical assessment of the contemporary crime trends puzzle: A modest step toward a more comprehensive research agenda. In A. S. Goldberger & R. Rosenfeld (Eds.), *Understanding crime trends: Workshop report* (pp. 127-176). Washington, DC: National Academic Press.

Baumer, E. P., & Lauritsen, J. L. (2010). Reporting crime to the police, 1973–2005: A multivariate analysis of long-term trends in the National Crime Survey (NCS) and National Crime Victimization Survey (NCVS). *Criminology, 48*(1), 131-185.

Bernard, A. B. & Durlauf, S. N. (1995). Convergence in International Output. *Journal of Applied Econometrics, 10,* (2), 97-108.

Biderman, A. D. (1967a). *Report on a pilot study in the District of Columbia on victimization and attitudes toward law enforcement.* Washington, DC: U. S. Government Printing Office.

Biderman, A. D. (1967b). Surveys of population samples for estimating crime incidence. *The Annals of the American Academy of Political and Social Science, 374*(1), 16-33.

Biderman, A. D., & Cantor, D. (1984). *A longitudinal analysis of bounding, respondent conditioning, and mobility as sources of panel bias in the National Crime Survey.* Washington, DC: U. S. Government Printing Office.

Biderman, A. D., Cantor, D., Lynch, J. P., & Martin, E. (1985). F*inal report of the National Crime Survey redesign: Bureau of Social Science Research.* Washington, DC: U. S. Government Printing Office

Biderman, A. D., Lynch, J. P., & Peterson, J. L. (1991). *Understanding crime incidence statistics: Why UCR diverges from the NCS.* New York, NY: Springer Verlag.

Biderman, A. D., & Reiss, A. J. (1967). On exploring the "dark figure" of crime. *The Annals of the American Academy of Political and Social Science, 374*(1), 1.

Black, D. J. (1970). Production of crime rates. *American Sociological Review, 35*, 733-748.

Blumstein, A. (2000). Disaggregating the violence trends. In A. Blumstein & J. Wallman (Eds.), *The crime drop in America* (pp. 13-44). New York, NY: Cambridge University Press.

Blumstein, A., Cohen, J., & Rosenfeld, R. (1991). Trend and deviation in crime rates: A comparison of UCR and NCS data for burglary and robbery. *Criminology, 29*(2), 237-263.

Blumstein, A., Cohen, J., & Rosenfeld, R. (1992). The UCR-NCS relationship revisited: A reply to Menard. *Criminology, 30*(1), 115-124.

Blumstein, A. & Rosenfeld, R. (2008). Factors contributing to U.S. crime trends. In A. S. Goldberger & R. Rosenfeld (Eds.), *Understanding crime trends: Workshop report* (pp. 13–44). Washington, DC: The National Academic Press.

Blumstein, A., & Wallman, J. (2000). The recent rise and fall of American violence. In A. Blumstein & J. Wallman (Eds.), *The crime drop in America* (pp. 1–12). New York, NY: Cambridge University Press.

Booth, A., Johnson, D. R., & Choldin, H. M. (1977). Correlates of city crime rates: Victimization surveys versus official statistics. *Social Problems, 25*(2), 187-197.

Box, G., & Jenkins, G. M. (2008). *Time series analysis: Forecasting and control* (4th ed.). Hoboken, NJ: Wiley.

Britt, C. L. (1994). Crime and unemployment among youths in the United States, 1958-1990: A time series analysis. *American Journal of Economics and Sociology, 53*(1), 99-109.

Bureau of Justice Statistics. (2001). *Criminal victimization in the United States—Statistical tables* (NCJ-184938). Washington, DC: Author. Retrieved from http://www.ojp.usdoj .gov/bjs/abstract/cvusst.htm.

Cantor, D., & Lynch, J. P. (2005). Exploring the effects of changes in design on the analytical uses of the NCVS data. *Journal of Quantitative Criminology, 21*(3), 293-319.

Catalano, S. M. (2006). *The measurement of crime: Victim reporting and police recording*. New York, NY: LFB Scholarly Publishing.

Catalano, S. M. (2007). Methodological change in the NCVS and the effect on convergence. In J. P. Lynch & L. A. Addington (Eds.), *Understanding crime statistics: Revisiting the divergence of the NCVS and the UCR* (pp. 125-155). New York, NY: Cambridge University Press.

Chamlin, M. B. (1988). Crime and arrests: An autoregressive integrated moving average (ARIMA) approach. *Journal of Quantitative Criminology, 4*(3), 247-258.

Cohen, L. E., Felson, M., & Land, K. C. (1980). Property crime rates in the United States: A macrodynamic analysis, 1947-1977; with *ex ante* forecasts for the mid-1980s. *American Journal of Sociology, 86*(1), 90-118.

Cohen, L. E., & Land, K. C. (1984). Discrepancies between crime reports and crime surveys—Urban and structural determinants. *Criminology, 22*(4), 499-530.

Cohen L. J. & Lichbach, M. I. (1982). Alternative measures of Crime: A statistical evaluation. *The Sociological Quarterly, 23*(2), 253-266.

Decker, S. H. (1977). Official crime rates and victim survey: an empirical comparison. *Journal of Criminal Justice*, 5, 47-54.

Decker, S. H. (1982). Comparing victimization and official estimates of crime: A re-examination of the validity of police statistics. *American Journal of Police, 2*, 193.

Dugan, L. (2002). *Domestic violence policy: Exploring impacts on informing police, arresting the offender, and deterring domestic violence. A final report to the National Institution of Justice for Grant #97WTVX0004* (Report No. 196854). Retrieved from http://www.ncjrs.gov/pdffiles1/nij/grants/196854.pdf.

Dugan, L. (2003). Domestic violence legislation: Exploring its impact on the likelihood of domestic violence, police involvement, and arrest. *Criminology & Public Policy, 2*(2), 283-312.

Dugan, L., Nagin, D. S., & Rosenfeld, R. (2003). Exposure reduction or retaliation? The effects of domestic violence resources on intimate-partner homicide. *Law & Society Review, 37*(1), 169-198.

Eck, J. E., & Riccio, L. J. (1979). Relationship between reported crime rates and victimization survey results: An empirical and analytical study. *Journal of Criminal Justice, 7*, 293-308.

Federal Bureau of Investigation. (2004). *Uniform crime reporting handbook.* Washington, DC: Author.

Federal Bureau of Investigation. (2009). *Crime in the United States, 2008*. Washington, DC: Author.

Felson, R. B., Messner, S. F., Hoskin, A. W., & Deane, G. (2002), Reasons for reporting and not reporting domestic violence to the police. *Criminology, 40*(3), 617-648.

Fox, J. (1991). *Regression diagnostics*. Thousand Oaks, CA: Sage.

Goudriaan, H., Wittebrood, K., & Nieuwbeerta. P. (2006). Neighborhood characteristics and reporting crime: Effects of social cohesion, confidence in police effectiveness and socio-economic disadvantage. *British Journal of Criminology, 46,* 719-742

Gove, W. R., Hughes, M., & Geerken, M. (1985). Are uniform crime reports a valid indicator of the index crimes? An affirmative answer with minor qualifications. *Criminology, 23*(3), 451-502.

Gottfredson, M. R., and Gottfredson, D. M. (1988). *Decision making in criminal justice* (2nd ed.). New York, NY: Plenum Press.

Groves, R. M. (2006). Nonresponse rates and nonresponse bias in household surveys. *Public Opinion Quarterly, 70*(5), 646-675.

Grove, R. M. & Cork, D. L. (Eds.). (2008). *Surveying victims: options for conducting the National Crime Victimization Survey*. Washington, DC: National Academies Press.

Gujarati, D. N. (2004). *Basic econometric* (4th ed.). New York, NY: McGraw-Hill/Irwin.

Heimer, K., & Lauritsen, J. L. (2008). Gender and violence in the United States: Trends in offending and victimization. In A. S. Goldberger & R. Rosenfeld (Eds.), *Understanding crime trends: Workshop report* (pp. 45-80). Washington, DC: National Academic Press.

Hubble, D. L. (1995). *NCVS: New questionnaire and procedures development and phase-in methodology.* Washington, DC: U.S. Bureau of the Census.

Kindermann, C., Lynch, J., & Cantor, D. (1997). *Effects of the redesign on victimization estimates*. Washington, DC: U.S. Department of Justice Statistics.

Land, K. C. (2007). Understanding crime statistics: Revisiting the divergence of the NCVS and UCR. *Contemporary Sociology: A Journal of Reviews, 36*(5), 481-483.

Langan, P. A., & Farrington, D. P. (1998). *Crime and justice in the United States and in England and Wales, 1981-96* (NCJ No. 169284). Washington, DC: U. S. Government Printing Office.

Lauritsen, J. L., Schaum, R. J. (2005). *Crime and victimization in the three largest metropolitan areas, 1980-98* (NCJ No. 208075). Washington, DC: U. S. Government Printing Office.

Lauritsen, J. L., & Heimer, K. (2008). The Gender Gap in Violent Victimization, 1973–2004. *Journal of Quantitative Criminology, 24*(2), 125-147.

Lauritsen, J. L., Heimer, K., & Lynch, J. P. (2009). Trends in the Gender Gap in Violent Offending: New Evidence from the National Crime Victimization Survey. *Criminology, 47*(2), 361-399.

Lehnen, R. G., & Skogan, W. G. (1981). *The National Crime Survey: Working papers, Vol. 1. Current and historical perspectives*. Washington, DC: U. S. Government Printing Office.

Lehnen, R. G., & Skogan, W. G. (1983). *National Crime Survey: Working papers, Vol. 2. Methodological studies*. Washington, DC: Government Printing Office.

Levitt, S. D. (1996). The effect of prison population size on crime rates: Evidence from prison overcrowding litigation. *The Quarterly Journal of Economics, 111*, 319-351.

Levitt, S. D. (1998). The relationship between crime reporting and police: Implications for the use of uniform crime teports. *Journal of Quantitative Criminology, 14*(1), 61-81.

Lynch, J. P., & Jarvis, J. P. (2008). Missing data and imputation in the uniform crime reports and the effects on national estimates. *Journal of Contemporary Criminal Justice, 24*(1), 69.

Lynch, J. P. (2011). A Strategic Vision for the Bureau of Justice Statistics. The Criminologist, 36(3): 1-6.

Maguire, E. R. (2002). Multiwave establishment surveys of police organizations. *Justice Research and Policy, 4*(1), 39-60.

Maguire, E. R., Snipes, J. B., Uchida, C. D., & Townsend, M. (1998). Counting cops: estimating the number of police departments and police officers in the USA. *Policing: An International Journal of Police Strategies and Management, 21*(1), 97-120.

Maltz, M. D. (2007). Missing UCR data and divergence of the NCVS and UCR trends. In J. P. Lynch & L. A. Addington (Eds.), *Understanding crime statistics: Revisiting the divergence of the NCVS and the UCR* (pp. 269-291). New York, NY: Cambridge University Press.

Marvell, T. B., & Moody, C. (1996). Specification problems, police levels, and crime rates. *Criminology, 34*(4), 609-646.

Maxfield, M. G. (1999). The national incident-based reporting system: Research and policy applications. *Journal of Quantitative Criminology, 15*(2), 119-149.

McCleary, R., Hay, R. A., Meidinger, E. E., & McDowall, D. (1980). *Applied time series analysis for the social sciences*. Beverly Hills, CA: Sage.

McDowall, D., & Loftin, C. (1992). Comparing the UCR and NCS over time. *Criminology, 30*(1), 125-132.

McDowall, D., & Loftin, C. (2007). What is convergence, and what do we know about it? In J. P. Lynch & L. A. Addington (Eds.), *Understanding crime statistics: Revisiting the divergence of the NCVS and the UCR* (pp. 93-124). New York, NY: Cambridge University Press.

Menard, S. (1987). Short-term trends in crime and delinquency: A comparison of UCR (Uniform Crime Reports), NCS (National Crime Survey), and self-report data. *Justice Quarterly, 4*(3), 455-474.

Menard, S. (1991). Encouraging news for criminologists (in the year 2050)? A comment on O'Brien (1990). *Journal of Criminal Justice, 19*(6), 563-567.

Menard, S. (1992). Residual gains, reliability, and the UCR-NCS relationship: A comment on Blumstein, Cohen, and Rosenfeld (1991). *Criminology, 30*(1), 105-114.

Menard, S., & Covey, H. C. (1988). UCR and NCS: Comparisons over space and time. *Journal of Criminal Justice, 16*(5), 371-384.

Mullins, R. (2008). *Can you find me now? Cell phones hard for 911to trace.* Retrieved from http://www2.tbo.com/content/2008/dec/28/280011/na-can-you-find-me-now/news-breaking/

Nelson, J. F. (1980). Multiple victimization in American cities: A statistical analysis of rare events. *American Journal of Sociology, 85*, 870-891.

O'Brien, R. M. (1985). *Crime and victimization data.* Beverly Hills, CA: Sage.

O'Brien, R. M. (1990). Comparing detrended UCR and NCS crime rates over time: 1973-1986. *Journal of Criminal Justice, 18*(3), 229-238.

O'Brien, R. M. (1991). Detrended UCR and NCS crime rates: Their utility and meaning. *Journal of Criminal Justice, 19*(6), 569-574.

O'Brien, R. M. (1996). Police productivity and crime rates: 1973-1992. *Criminology*, 34(2), 183-207.

O'Brien, R. M. (1999). Measuring the convergence/divergence of "serious crime" arrest rates for males and females: 1960–1995. *Journal of Quantitative Criminology, 15*(1), 97-114.

O'Brien, R. M. (2001). Theory, operationalization, identification, and the interpretation of different differences in time series models. *Journal of Quantitative Criminology, 17*(4), 359-375.

O'Brien, R. M. (2003). UCR violent crime rates, 1958–2000: Recorded and offender-generated trends. *Social Science Research, 32*, 499-518.

O'Brien, R. M., Shichor, D., & Decker, D. L. (1980). An empirical comparison of the validity of UCR and NCS crime rates. *Sociological Quarterly, 21*, 391-401.

Ostrom, C. W. (1990). *Time series analysis: Regression techniques*: Newbury Park, CA: Sage.

Oxley, L. & Greasley, D. (1995) A time series perspective on convergence: Australia, UK and USA since 1870. *The Economic Record, 71*, 259-270.

Penick, B., & Owens, M. (1976). *Surveying crime.* Washington, DC: National Academy Press.

Planty, M. (2007). Series victimization and divergence. In J. P. Lynch & L. A. Addington (Eds.), *Understanding crime statistics: Revisiting the divergence of the NCVS and the UCR* (pp.125-156). New York, NY: Cambridge University Press.

Planty, M., & Strom, K. J. (2007). Understanding the role of repeat victims in the production of annual US victimization rates. *Journal of Quantitative Criminology, 23*(3), 179-200.

President's Commission on Law Enforcement and the Administration of Justice. (1967). *Task Force report: Crime and its impact: An assessment.* Washington, DC: Author.

President's Commission on Law Enforcement and the Administration of Justice. (1967). *The challenge of crime in a free society.* Washington, DC: Author.

Rand, M. (2006). The national crime victimization survey: 34 years of measuring crime in the United States. *Statistical Journal of the United Nations Economic Commission for Europe*, 23(4), 289-301.

Rand, M (2007). The National Crime Victimization Survey at 34: Looking back and looking ahead. In M. Hough & M. Maxfield (Eds.), *Surveying crime in the 21st Century* (pp. 145-164). Monsey, NY: Criminal Justice Press.

Rand, M. R., Lynch, J. P., & Cantor, D. (1997). *Criminal victimization, 1973-95. Bureau of Justice Statistics Special Report: National Crime Victimization Survey.* Washington, DC: U. S. Government Printing Office.

Rand, M. R., & Rennison, C. M. (2002). True crime stories? Accounting for differences in our national crime indicators. *Chance, 15*(1), 47-51.

Rand, M. R., & Rennison, C. M. (2005). Bigger is not necessarily better: An analysis of violence against women estimates from the National Crime Victimization Survey and the National Violence Against Women Survey. *Journal of Quantitative Criminology, 21*(3), 267-291.

Rennison, C. M. (2001a). *Criminal victimization 2000: Changes 1999-2000 with trends 1993-2000.* Washington, DC: U. S. Government Printing Office.

Rennison, C. M. (2001b). *Violent victimization and race, 1993-98*. Washington, DC: U.S. Department of Justice, Office of Justice Programs.

Rennison, C. (2007). *Victim and household characteristics: Reporting violence to the police. Illinois Crime Victimization Survey 2002 data analysis.* Retrieved from http://www.icjia.state.il.us/public/pdf/ResearchReports/Illinois%20Crime%20Victimization%20Survey%202002%20Data%20Analysis.pdf.

Rennison, C. M., & Rand, M. R. (2007). Introduction to the National Crime Victimization Survey. In J. P. Lynch & L. A. Addington (Eds.), *Understanding crime statistics: Revisiting the divergence of the NCVS and the UCR* (pp. 55-92). New York, NY: Cambridge University Press.

Rosenfeld, R. (2007). Explaining the divergence between UCR and NCVS aggravated assault trends. In J. P. Lynch & L. A. Addington (Eds.), *Understanding crime statistics: Revisiting the divergence of the NCVS and the UCR* (pp. 251-268). New York, NY: Cambridge University Press.

Rosenfeld, R. & Fornango, R. (2007). The impact of economic conditions on robbery and property crime: The role of consumer sentiment. *Criminology, 45*(4), 735-769

Rosenfeld, R., Lynch, J. P., & Addington, L. A. (2007). Introduction. In J. P. Lynch & L. A. Addington (Eds.), *Understanding crime statistics: Revisiting the divergence of the NCVS and the UCR* (pp. 3-16). New York, NY: Cambridge University Press.

Sellin, T. (1962). Crime and delinquency in the United States: an over-all view. *Annals of the American Academy of Political and Social Science, 339*, 11-23

Sellin, T., & Wolfgang, M. E. (1964). *The measurement of delinquency*: New York, NY: Wiley.

Sherman, L. W., Schmidt, J. D., & Rogan, D. P. (1992). *Policing domestic violence: Experiments and dilemmas*. New York, NY: Free Press

Skogan, W. G. (1974). The validity of official crime statistics: An empirical investigation. *Social Science Quarterly, 55*(2), 25-38.

Skogan, W. G. (1975). Measurement problems in official and survey crime rates. *Journal of Criminal Justice, 3*(1), 17–31.

Skogan, W. G. (1977). Dimensions of the dark figure of unreported crime. *Crime & Delinquency, 23*(1), 41-50.

Skogan, W. G. (1984). Reporting crimes to the police: The status of world research. *Journal of Research in Crime and Delinquency, 21*(2), 113-137.

Steffensmeier, D., Zhong, H., Ackerman, J., Schwartz, J., & Agha, S. (2006). Gender gap trends for violent crimes, 1980 to 2003: A UCR-NCVS comparison. *Feminist Criminology, 1*(1), 72.

Stock, J. H., & Watson, M. W. (2003). *Introduction to econometrics*. Boston, MA: Addison Wesley.

U.S. Census Bureau (2003). *National Crime Victimization Survey: Interviewing Manual for Field Representatives*. NCVS550. Washington, DC: U.S. Census Bureau.

U.S. Census Bureau. (2009). *Survey abstracts*. Retrieved from http://www.census.gov/ aboutus/surveyabstracts.pdf.

U.S. Department of Commerce & Bureau of the Census. (1968). *Report on nation needs for criminal justice statistics*. Washington, DC: U. S. Government Printing Office.

U.S. Department of Justice. (2004). *The nation's two crime measures* (NCJ No. 122705). Washington, DC: U. S. Government Printing Office.

U.S. Department of Justice, Bureau of Justice Statistics. (1974). *Criminal victimization in the United States, 1973* (No. SD-NCP-N-4). Washington, DC: U. S. Government Printing Office.

U.S. Department of Justice, Bureau of Justice Statistics. (1994). *Technical background on the redesigned National Crime Victimization Survey* (NCJ No. 151172). Washington, DC: U. S. Government Printing Office.

U.S. Department of Justice, Bureau of Justice Statistics. (2007). *Criminal victimization, 2006* (NCJ No. 219413). Washington, DC: U. S. Government Printing Office.

U.S. Department of Justice, Bureau of Justice Statistics. (2008). *Criminal victimization, 2007* (NCJ No. 224390). Washington, DC: U. S. Government Printing Office.

U.S. Department of Justice, Bureau of Justice Statistics. (2009). *Criminal victimization, 2008* (NCJ No. 227777). Washington, DC: U. S. Government Printing Office.

Wolfgang, M. E. (1963). Uniform Crime Reports: A Critical Appraisal. *University of Pennsylvania Law Review, 111*(6), 708-738.

Index

CPSIA information can be obtained at www.ICGtesting.com
Printed in the USA
LVOW07*2229171114

414215LV00005B/11/P